Music as Multimodal Discourse

Bloomsbury Advances in Semiotics

Semiotics has complemented linguistics by expanding its scope beyond the phoneme and the sentence to include texts and discourse, and their rhetorical, performative, and ideological functions. It has brought into focus the multimodality of human communication. *Advances in Semiotics* publishes original works in the field demonstrating robust scholarship, intellectual creativity, and clarity of exposition. These works apply semiotic approaches to linguistics and non-verbal productions, social institutions and discourses, embodied cognition and communication, and the new virtual realities that have been ushered in by the Internet. It also is inclusive of publications in relevant domains such as socio-semiotics, evolutionary semiotics, game theory, cultural and literary studies, human-computer interactions, and the challenging new dimensions of human networking afforded by social websites.

Series Editor: Paul Bouissac is Professor Emeritus at the University of Toronto (Victoria College), Canada. He is a world renowned figure in semiotics and a pioneer of circus studies. He runs the SemiotiX Bulletin [www.semioticon. com/semiotix] which has a global readership.

Titles in the Series:

Music as Multimodal Discourse

Semiotics, Power and Protest

Edited by Lyndon C. S. Way and Simon McKerrell
Bloomsbury Advances in Semiotics

BLOOMSBURY ACADEMIC
LONDON • NEW YORK • OXFORD • NEW DELHI • SYDNEY

BLOOMSBURY ACADEMIC
Bloomsbury Publishing Plc
50 Bedford Square, London, WC1B 3DP, UK
1385 Broadway, New York, NY 10018, USA

BLOOMSBURY, BLOOMSBURY ACADEMIC and the Diana logo
are trademarks of Bloomsbury Publishing Plc

First published in Great Britain 2017
Paperback edition first published 2018

A catalogue record for this book is available from the British Library.

Library of Congress Cataloging-in-Publication Data
Names: Way, Lyndon C. S. | McKerrell, Simon.
Title: Music as multimodal discourse: semiotics, power and protest /
edited by Lyndon C. S. Way and Simon McKerrell.
Description: New York: Bloomsbury Academic, 2016. |
Series: Bloomsbury advances in semiotics; 10 |
Includes bibliographical references and index.
Identifiers: LCCN 2016038832| ISBN 9781474264426 (hb) |
ISBN 9781474264440 (epdf)
Subjects: LCSH: Music–Political aspects. |
Music–Social aspects. | Music–Semiotics.
Classification: LCC ML3916.M8738 2016 | DDC 781.1–dc23
LC record available at https://lccn.loc.gov/2016038832

ISBN: HB: 978-1-4742-6442-6
PB: 978-1-3500-7986-1
ePDF: 978-1-4742-6444-0
ePub: 978-1-4742-6443-3

Series: Bloomsbury Advances is Semiotics

Typeset by Newgen Knowledge Works (P) Ltd., Chennai, India

To find out more about our authors and books visit
www.bloomsbury.com and sign up for our newsletters.

This book is dedicated to all those everyday composers, musicians, lyricists, fans and listeners who instinctively know how powerful music can be in communicating social change.

Contents

List of Figures

List of Tables

List of Contributors

Rusty Barrett is Associate Professor in the Linguistics Department at the University of Kentucky. His research focuses on highland Mayan languages, language revitalization, and language, gender, and sexuality. His book *From Drag Queens to Leathermen: Language, Gender, and Gay Male Subcultures* is forthcoming.

Eoin Devereux is Assistant Dean of Research in the Faculty of Arts, Humanities and Social Sciences at the University of Limerick, Ireland, and is Adjunct Professor of Contemporary Culture at the University of Jyvasklya, Finland. Eoin's books include *Understanding the Media* (3rd edition, 2014) and *Media Studies: Key Issues and Debates* (2007).

Aileen Dillane is an ethnomusicologist and Lecturer in Music in the Irish World Academy of Music and Dance at the University of Limerick with particular interests in the folk, vernacular and popular musics of Ireland, the United Kingdom, the United States and Australia. She is co-editor of *David Bowie: Critical Perspectives* (2015) and *Morrissey: Fandom, Representations, Identities* (2011).

Göran Eriksson is Professor of Media and Communication Studies, Örebro University, Sweden. He writes in the areas of politics and media, and is also involved in projects concerned with television history and reality TV. His research is published in journals such as *Text & Talk, Journalism, Critical Discourse Studies, International Journal of Press/Politics and Media* and *Culture and Society*.

Laura Filardo-Llamas lectures in English at the University of Valladolid, Spain. Her main research areas is discourse analysis and conflict resolution, applied particularly to ethno-nationalist conflicts and domestic violence. She has also done research on the relation that can be established between music and society. Some of her publications can be found in *Ethnopolitics, Peace and Conflict Studies, Critical Approaches to Discourse Analysis Across Disciplines (CADAAD) Journal* and *Critical Discourse Studies*. She has recently co-edited the volume *Space, Time and Evaluation in Ideological Discourse*, which is based on a special issue of *Critical Discourse Studies*.

Theo van Leeuwen is Emeritus Professor at the University of Technology, Sydney, and Professor of Language and Communication at the University of Southern

Denmark. He has published widely on critical discourse analysis, multimodality, social semiotics and visual semiotics. His books include *Reading Images: The Grammar of Visual Design* (with Gunther Kress); *Introducing Social Semiotics*; *Speech, Music, Sound*; *The Language of Colour* and *Discourse and Practice*. He is a founding editor of the journal *Visual Communication*.

David Machin works in the department of Media and Communication, Örebro University, Sweden. His interests lie in Multimodality, Critical Discourse Studies and Visual Design. His books include The *Language of War Monuments* (2013) and *Visual Journalism* (2015). He has also published extensively on music and discourse, for example, in the book *Analysing Popular Music* (2010). His current research is in the multimodal communication of administration in institutions. He is also co-editor of the journals *Social Semiotics* and *Journal of Language and Politics*.

Simon McKerrell is a Senior Lecturer and Head of Music at The International Centre for Music Studies, Newcastle University, United Kingdom. He is interested in how music communicates meaning in everyday life, particularly how this is constructed as discourse. He is the author of *Focus: Scottish Traditional Music* (2015) and co-editor of *The International Journal of Traditional Arts*. He is also an expert performer of Highland-, Border- and Uilleann-pipes having toured, taught and performed throughout the world.

Matthew Ord is a folk musician and doctoral student at Newcastle University. His research combines a historical approach with techniques from multimodal discourse analysis and conceptual metaphor theory to consider the impact of recording technologies on the social semiotics of recorded folk song. His other research interests include the history of film and radio documentary, and the place of music in contemporary political discourse.

Martin J. Power is Lecturer in the Department of Sociology at the University of Limerick, Ireland. He has previously co-edited books on Morrissey (2011) and David Bowie (2015).

John E. Richardson is Reader in Critical Discourse Studies in the Department of Social Sciences at Loughborough University. His research interests include structured Social Inequalities, British Fascism, Critical Discourse Studies and Argumentation. His recent books include *Analysing Fascist Discourse* (co-edited with Wodak, 2013), *Advances in Critical Discourse Studies* (co-edited with Krzyżanowski, Machin, Wodak, 2014) and *Cultures of Post-War British Fascism* (co-edited with Copsey, 2015). He is currently writing a book analysing the multimedia discourses of British fascism. He is the editor of the international journal *Critical Discourse Studies*.

Lyndon C. S. Way is an associate professor at Izmir University of Economics in Izmir, Turkey. His main field of interest is Multimodal Critical Discourse Studies where he analyses and publishes regularly on both subversive discourses in music and political manipulation in news.

Johnny Wingstedt is Assistant Professor and Head of Sound and Music Production at Dalarna University, Falun, Sweden. His main field of study is multimodality and social semiotics. Publications include *Narrative Music, Visuals and Meaning in Film* (2010) and he is co-editor of Swedish anthology *På tal om musikproduktion* (Talking about music production) (2012, with Gunnar Ternhag).

Preface

This book arose out of a panel entitled 'Music and Discourse' at the *Critical Approaches to Discourse Analysis Across Disciplines* (CADAAD) 2014 conference in Budapest. Lyndon Way organized the panel, while most of the other contributors in this book presented at the conference. The papers and panel as a whole were well received by a large, curious audience. It was this response combined with our own enthusiasm for examining the communicative power of music, which has led to this edited volume. At the conference, we were part of a diverse group of scholars with backgrounds in ethnomusicology, linguistics, media studies, and discourse analysis studying music and presenting on music as multimodal discourse. This resulting edited collection presents both those people who presented at the CADAAD conference, but also one or two others who also study music as multimodal discourse. We concluded that the momentum from this meeting of like-minded scholars could contribute to taking forward the understanding of music as multimodal discourse, which is the principal focus of this book.

To achieve this we wish to reflect two key aspects of our discussions in this volume. First, the study of music has been conducted from many, plural, often contested disciplinary perspectives. The scholarship examining music as but one mode of communication alongside other modes such as text, still images, moving images, colour, gesture and so on is however relatively recent. We believe this approach to music has great potential for both the rehabilitation of music studies into the more vital strands of socio-political analysis, and also offers a well-defined method, drawing on Critical Discourse Studies and Social Semiotics, which can help us answer questions about how music meaning is part of broader socio-cultural and political discourses exposing how it has real power and agency in the social world. This volume is therefore multidisciplinary, and at times, an interdisciplinary project, and this reflects the various approaches to analysis we witnessed of each other at the conference. Principally, analytical and conceptual territory from Social Semiotics, Critical Discourse Analysis (CDA), Multimodal Critical Discourse Studies (MCDS), ethnomusicology, popular music studies and linguistics, inform multimodal analysis and we hope will reach back into music-based disciplines. Consequently, it is therefore our firm belief that this interdisciplinarity is lacking in much musically focused analysis where 'music' has been the object of study and that approaching music as multimodal discourse with an interdisciplinary predisposition is one of the key means by which our analyses can allow us to move beyond the subject-object stumbling blocks of much music-focused analysis. This is, of course, rooted in a belief that the object of study is people's discourses of power and agency in everyday life, and that music is vitally important in constructing them. By analysing music as multimodal discourse, we are able to expose in great detail exactly how it is that music can articulate discourses not only of power, exploitation, abuse and hate, but also resistance, subversion, belonging, community and hope. We hope that this book provides a step forward in understanding people and society with an ear to the sonic.

Second, we also believe our book is a significant contribution to the study of discourse. Though discourse analysis has its roots in the study of written language and most published work examines news reports and political and public textual discourses, we take the view that discourse is almost always multimodal. This is not unique, as discourse analysis has taken a multimodal turn of late. What is more rare is the integrated analysis of musical communication, whether through music videos, performances or sound recordings, being seen as articulating discourses through the modes and the relations between the modes of musical sounds, text and images.

We hope that our book achieves its aim of contributing to the momentum we have experienced since the CADAAD conference and hope that it offers the reader some novel insights into this new and exciting interdisciplinary field of enquiry.

Chapter summaries

In this volume, Simon McKerrell and Lyndon C. S. Way examine the scholarly positioning of a project that considers music as multimodal discourse. They offer an epistemological framework for the multimodal analysis of music that engages with ideas from CDA, ethnomusicology and popular music studies, multimodality, MCDS and linguistics. This first chapter engages with the question of why multimodal discourses are so powerful in our lives, and how we might better understand them as communicative events.

Theo van Leeuwen critically analyses how sound and music are used to convey corporate identities and values through audiovisual logos. Investigating the audiovisual logos of a range of IT corporations, the chapter argues that they use 'heroic' motifs with a long history, first in classical music, then in advertising and news theme music, but refurbish them with new, chime-like timbres and electronic whooshes. Thus ascending melodies position the corporations as expansive and dynamic; electronic drones, evoking outer space, position them as global; and metallic, tinkling timbres suggest technological perfection, yet also imbue the themes with new age cool, with a human touch added by traditional instrumentation. This creates continuity with the brass and drums fanfares of nationalistic power, and change through the mix of technical perfection, pristine nature and individual lifestyle freedom that can also be seen, for instance, in advertisements where sleek cars drive through empty landscapes, or satellite-like windows float in an ethereal world of blue hazes and white butterflies.

The musical analysis is benchmarked against the normative discourses that inform this form of communication, as expressed, especially, in the websites and statements of the designers and companies who produce this form of communication, and in the rebranding rationales that inform the creation of specific audiovisual logos. Finally, the chapter shows how ringtones provide very similar melodic motifs and timbres (with titles like 'iphone', 'google', 'apple' and so on) for personal use, thus bringing connections between corporate and personal identities and values into our everyday sonic experience.

Johnny Wingstedt considers van Leeuwen's (2005: 106) position that 'discourses consist of a version of social practice plus ideas about it and attitudes to it' and discusses and exemplifies how such ideas and attitudes are expressed by combining the modes of music, voice and speech in the advertising jingle. In examining discursive aspects of the jingle, different semiotic resources and choices must be taken into consideration compared with looking at speech alone. To illustrate this, three jingles are analysed taking Halliday's (1978) metafunctions of communication, the textual, ideational and interpersonal functions, as a starting point.

On a textual/structural level, musical resources such as metre, period, melody and harmony provide structural frameworks for targeted language components to achieve *salience*. One example is how cyclical patterns make repetition of key words (*overlexicalization*) possible to an extent not available in speech alone. On the ideational/content level, resources such as instrumentation, tempo and rhythm contribute metaphorically descriptive qualities of participants and actions, akin to what van Leeuwen (2008) calls *eligibility conditions*. Instrumentation, voice character, genre and style inform aspects of gender, location, cultural setting and so on. An important feature for building brand identity is 'recognizability', which in music is often achieved through melody. The jingle can thus be seen as an entity, signifying/denoting a product. This can be described as a kind of *nominalization*. As Machin and Mayr (2012) point out, 'nominalisations can themselves become stable entities that will enter common usage'.

Interpersonally, melodic pitch and direction (musical 'prosody') regulate aspects of attitude and energy. Metrical and tonal regularities or irregularities engage and activate the listener by creating or breaking expectations. In this, music performs what van Leeuwen (1999) describes as *sound acts*. Instrumentation, how music 'dress up' (or down), and musical genres carry cultural or subcultural associations to attitudes, values and ideologies. Advantage is also taken of music's aptness for expressing emotions and narratives (Wingstedt, 2008, 2010). A complex interplay of semiotic resources, including expression styles and production techniques, combine to establish a sense of personal address and *modality* (aspects of 'truth'), including how music can convey discourses on social status and authenticity (Machin, 2010).

John E. Richardson's chapter is founded on an interest in the ways that music represents and constructs antagonistic political identities. However, the vast majority of work examining identity and politics in musicology, and in popular music studies in particular, presumes and sometimes explicitly argues that music is personally and socially therapeutic – that since music enacts social identities it is a force for good, particularly in relation to marginalized groups. This chapter will bring together two areas of critical examination: the sociological analysis of fascist music; and the concept of recontextualization developed in discourse analytic literature. Recontextualization is a specific intertextual relationship, wherein the contents of one text reappear in another text. Following Reisigl and Wodak (2001, 2009), if a textual element is taken from a specific context we argue it is decontextualized; when this same element is inserted into a new context, we argue it is recontextualized. Meanings are formed in use; and so, through this process of 'textual borrowing', (partly) new meanings are produced. Whilst this idea has been discussed in classical musicology (e.g. the appropriation of Hellenism in German romantic music) and popular music studies (e.g. sampling, remixing, mash-up), the examination tends towards the descriptive rather than close analytic detail. This chapter will examine three ways in which recontextualization occurs in fascist song and music – through appropriation; through interpolation; and through ideological realignment – and will explore the functions that this, and the performance of song and music more generally, serves to fascist cultural projects.

Lyndon Way critically examines subversive articulations in popular music commodities. Protest songs not only enable musicians to express social concerns in the public domain, they also shape musicians' personal narratives of authenticity about themselves, their fans and others. This chapter analyses how authenticity and subversion are articulated in protest music videos. After Turkey's 2013 June protests, a number of Turkish and international musicians have used semiotic resources from the protests in official videos. One of these is analysed here to reveal how musicians use protest to express authenticity, opposition to authority and subversion. Visuals, lyrics and musical sounds are analysed using MCDS to lyrics (van Leeuwen, 1995, 1996), visuals (Kress and van Leeuwen, 1996; Machin, 2007) and sounds (van Leeuwen, 1999; Machin, 2010). The chapter demonstrates how a full range of semiotic resources are used to articulate popular politics, despite being presented as serious and authentic. This case study extends the theorization of authenticity and subversion in music and considers music's likely place in political debates about politics and democracy.

Laura Filardo-Llamas's chapter follows new trends in Critical Discourse Studies which focus on understanding how meaning can be made in multimodal communication, and how this can be related to given social practices (van Leeuwen, 2012; Machin, 2013). In this chapter, Laura analyses a set of Spanish songs produced in Spain between 2004 and 2008 with the aim of fighting against domestic violence. She hypothesizes that institutional discourse opposing domestic violence is recontextualized in these songs. The fact that songs (and the videos used with them) are made up of different semiotic resources – including text, music, and image – help in spreading the message in a way that cannot be done by institutional language (cf. Machin, 2013).

To prove this, a cognitive approach to discourse studies is followed. Two linguistic approaches are considered in the analysis: (1) the textual construction of a discourse world, following Werth's (1999) Text-World-Theory, and (2) the association of those discourse worlds to ideological beliefs, which are identified by placing those mental representations on three axes: time, space and modality. The virtual and cognitive space determined by those axes is the discourse space (Chilton, 2004, 2005), and the location of entities within that discourse space explains how those are (ideologically) related to the speaker.

The meaning potential of this text-determined discourse space is widened because it is integrated with two other modes of communication: music and images. The analysis also incorporates tools aimed at uncovering the meaning potential of the images used in the videos (Kress and van Leeuwen, 1996) and the one of music (Machin, 2010; van Leeuwen, 2012). It is argued that the combination of meanings stemming from these three semiotic resources results in a new blended mental space (Mark and Turner, 2002) where institutional discourse about domestic violence is recontextualized. It is also argued that this combination of semiotic resources becomes more communicatively effective, thus making it easier for people to understand – and believe – the message. In this way, these anti-domestic-violence songs become an important element in the wider context of the socio-political practice in which they are embedded.

David Machin and Göran Eriksson observe that a number of scholars have begun to show how working-class people's behaviours and lifestyles are increasingly being devalued in the media (Lyle, 2008; Lockyer, 2010; Bennett, 2013; Eriksson, 2015). Represented as part of a flawed and problematic culture, the working classes often appear as repulsive, silly or excessive and as a consequence are ridiculed or humiliated. Programme participants are often presented as insular and as lacking cultural and social resources necessary for a more proper (middle-class) life. This has been linked to wider political and ideological shifts which represent the poor and unemployed as a moral underclass (Levitas, 2005). Rather than these people being viewed as part of wider structural inequalities where government policy and economic systems have responsibility, it is their negative characteristics and flawed characters that are foregrounded as part of legitimizing a neoliberal ideological climate where the individual is increasingly responsible for their own welfare.

This chapter is interested in the way that reality TV plays a role in this deligitimization of the working class. Specifically it seeks to contribute to the literature in the subject by showing the important role of music and sound in the way that characters, settings and narratives are set up and evaluated, often playing a central role in the kinds of evaluations that are taking place.

The chapter carries out a multimodal CDA of a docu-soap titled *Böda Camping*, aired on Swedish television since 2010. The programme follows the activities at a busy campsite in Sweden during the summer. It focuses on the campers' daily life at the campground, demonstrating the routines, (implicit) rules and norms guiding this life. This particular programme is part of a trend of reality TV appearing in the late 2000s in Sweden (cf. Eriksson, 2015) that are characterized by the use of representational strategies that ridicule working-class participants' behaviours, ideas and lifestyles (Eriksson, 2015).

In fact this discourse is something much more recent in Sweden which has for many decades celebrated a culture of 'Folkhemmet' which emphasis the absolute centrality of social equality, social welfare and social interdependence. This discourse is part of a process of the legitimization of shift away from welfare and equality, and it is no coincidence that this is taking place now in Sweden (Östbergand Andersson, 2013: 16) as neoliberal policies and ideas begin to take hold in a county which in only a few years as shifted from one of the most centrally controlled to one of the most deregulated in sectors such as education and health care. Such reality TV shows play an important role in the naturalization and legitimation of these discourses.

The chapter looks at three sequences from one episode of *Böda Camping*. In this particular episode the topic is rules of the campsite. They show the way that characters are set up as overly obsessive, petty and small minded, especially given the fairly modest and often cluttered setting of the campsite. Unrelated sequences are edited together, or resequenced, to create 'drama' and comedy and to make the participants appear silly. Music and sound editing here play an important role in providing character definitions and continuity. And this forms the key part of the analytic focus. We draw on the wider literature on film music, on music and meaning in psychology, and from social semiotics and bring this together to carry out a multimodal CDA of these sequences.

Rusty Barrett's contribution examines the ways in which Mayan hip hop music challenges colonial and racist discourse. The emergence of Mayan hip hop is part of the Maya Movement, a linguistic and cultural revitalization movement that emphasizes indigenous rights and the preservation of Mayan languages and culture in Guatemala. This chapter focuses on the music of Tz'utu Baktun Kan, who raps in Tz'utujil Maya and performs in a musical style that draws heavily on global forms of hip hop. Hegemonic colonial discourse in Guatemala represents the contemporary Maya as disconnected both from their pre-Columbian ancestors and from modern society. Maya music that is viewed as authentic or traditional reproduces this discourse. This music is played on colonial era instruments, rarely involves singing, and involves dances with highly restricted movement. Tz'utu's music challenges this discourse by combining the conventions of modern hip hop with pre-Columbian musical and linguistic forms. For example, the linguistic structure of this music uses traditional forms of Mayan poetry similar to those found in pre-Conquest hieroglyphic texts. Similarly, the music incorporates pre-Columbian instruments, such as conch shells and deer-skin drums. The structure of Tz'utu's music is viewed as authentically 'Maya' because the songs are composed in collaboration with traditional Mayan shamans, or daykeepers. The daykeeper performs a burning ritual asking the Mayan ancestors and natural spirits to send him hip hop lyrics, which Tz'utu then puts to music. The belief that the lyrics are written by pre-Columbian ancestors is reinforced by the highly traditional poetic structure found in the lyrics. The lyrics of Tz'utu's music reflect the discourse of the Maya movement in promoting awareness and respect for cultural traditions, such as understanding the Mayan calendar or being familiar with works of Mayan literature. The songs are taught to children in a hip hop school that Tz'utu helped found. The school aims to teach traditional Mayan cultural values and promote the use of Mayan languages while also teaching art, rapping and break dancing. The various art forms taught in the school produce a multimodal discourse that challenges the racist and colonial discourses that dominate understandings of Maya identity in Guatemala.

Matthew Ord's chapter uses the notion of sonic metaphor to consider the contribution of recording techniques such as echo, reverb and panning to the construction of countercultural meanings in the folk-rock recordings of the 1960s and 1970s. The performance of folksong in the United Kingdom was intimately associated with leftist cultural-political movements in the early 1960s, figuring prominently in the Campaign for Nuclear Disarmament and the trade union movement. In the folk-club, revivalists developed a performance aesthetic which emphasized directness and personal authenticity and tacitly critiqued the conventions of mainstream pop.

With the emergence of folk labels such as Topic, the revival produced recorded texts which sonically translated revivalist values, using the semiotic resources of recording to express counterhegemonic subject-positions. The starkly realist sound of these recordings contrasted significantly with the increasingly complex sonic texts produced in pop, which frequently used the latest studio techniques to explore affect and inner experience. As pop's status as a popular art form rose, this experimental approach to sound became strongly associated with the progressive aims of the global counterculture.

In the folk-rock records of the late 1960s, traditional texts were interpolated into multimodal texts which combined textual, musical and sonic discourses to create rich imaginative spaces. This chapter applies the concept of modality as outlined by van Leeuwen to explore how the management of sonic detail afforded by mic placement and processing techniques affects the interpretive affordances generated by recorded song. This approach is then developed using Zbikowski's work on conceptual blending to explore the construction of meaning in the blended conceptual 'spaces' – musical, textual and sonic – that combine in song texts, and how folk-rock records used mixing and processing techniques to reinterpret traditional song in ways which reflected countercultural values and identities.

Lyndon C. S. Way and Simon McKerrell
March 2016

Acknowledgements

There are many people to thank for contributing in one way or another to this book. We would both like to thank the good people at CADAAD, such as Chris Hart, who organize great conferences and were receptive to a panel on 'Music as Discourse'. Without that opportunity, the idea of this book would never have taken root. We would also like to thank all the individual contributors to the book who have contributed interesting, insightful, challenging chapters, and those other scholars whose interest in music as an essential part of social discourse have contributed to the ideas and intellectual foundations of this volume.

We would also like to thank Theo van Leeuwen whose ideas have inspired much of what is written in this book. He is one of few scholars, who have taken discourse analysis beyond the confines of studying written language and explored other modes of communication. We would also like to thank David Machin not only for his ideas about music as discourse but also for his advice through most stages in this book. Many thanks also to all those at Bloomsbury including Gurdeep, Paul and Andrew who happily committed to publishing this edited collection in the *Advances in Semiotics Series*.

And on a personal level, we would like to thank our families, the Ways – Ayla, Erim and Kerem – and the McKerrells – Stephanie, Niamh and Kinnon – for their patience and (mostly good) humour in the gestation, consultation, production and dissemination of this volume. As ever, any errors, factual or critical that remain, are ours (collectively).

Understanding Music as Multimodal Discourse

Simon McKerrell and Lyndon C. S. Way

Introduction

Music has been studied from a wide variety of perspectives across fields as diverse as anthropology, ethnomusicology, musicology, semiotics, sociology, philosophy, popular music studies and psychology, amongst others. Each field has its own approaches, advantages and interests, sometimes taking music as the object of study, and sometimes using music to examine other, often social, topics such as class, race or gender. This book, however, provides what is a relatively unique approach to music stemming from the perspective of the broader principles and concerns of Critical Discourse Analysis (CDA) and social semiotics. Essentially, CDA examines linguistic choices to reveal broader ideological discourses articulated in texts to reveal what kinds of social relations of power, inequalities and interests are perpetuated, generated or legitimated both explicitly and implicitly in text (van Dijk, 1993; Kress and van Leeuwen, 2001). Some scholars of CDA have pointed to the need to look more at how ideologies are communicated not only in political speeches and news reports, but also through more cultural media like video, posters, computer games and toys (van Leeuwen, 1999; Machin and Richardson, 2012). These same scholars have also drawn on certain tools, approaches and assumptions in multimodality to show how discourse and ideology can be revealed by closer analysis of communication in images, visual design, television, newspapers, monuments, toys and also in and through music. Approaching music as multimodal discourse is a relatively recent innovation which is not only informed by various disciplinary perspectives, but is also embedded within CDA which views music as a part of communication often inextricably set within a variety of other modes used to articulate ideology. In this book therefore, we seek to contribute to this body of work through a set of chapters which considers music as a communicative element embedded within multimodal discourse alongside modes such as text, still images, moving images, colour, gesture and other sounds, all of which contribute to articulating ideological discourses in society.

Music, discourse and meanings

The literature on the study of music and social ideas is contested, plural and messy, drawing on many different theoretical and ideological frameworks. However, the study of musical sounds in the social sciences has a long yet thin strand of scholarship. There has of course been much more research focused upon the social positioning, uses and interpretation of music in society, but the strand of work that engages with musical sound itself in the social science tradition has been a rather narrow one. A number of scholars have noted this trend (Frith, 1993), with Goodwin for instance remarking that musical sound is '. . . usually relegated to the status of sound track' (1993: 4). Indeed since the development of the 'New Musicology' and the increasing prevalence of various types of cultural musicologies in the 1990s and throughout the 2000s, musical sound itself has been in retreat in the published outputs across most musicological disciplines. Often for very good reasons, mostly tied to the shift towards relativism from modernism, and with the spreading conviction across genres, that musical meaning is made in the mind of the listener(s). This was undoubtedly necessary to rebalance music studies away from its restrictive focus upon classical music and the musical work as an object (often simply analysed as a visual object via the musical score), and can be witnessed in the massive growth of culturally sensitive analyses of musical communities, nations, scenes, genres, politics, commodification, and globalization across music studies.

We think there is now the beginnings of a slow pivot back towards musical sound and its role in understanding music in society, but with a relativist's understanding and attention to the importance of analysis that places musical sounds and structures within the complexity of social life (see for instance Berger, 1999; Tenzer and Roeder, 2011; Tagg, 2012; Moore, 2013). Although a broad essentialization, much of musicology's focus as a discipline has been on the 'what' and the 'why' of music as a cultural object, whereas considering music as multimodal communication shifts the emphasis firmly onto the 'how' and the 'when' of music as communication. That is to say that this collection takes a position that approaches musical sound as just one part of human communication, and as such opens up musical discourse within a broader framework focused upon how different modes relate and communicate discourses of power, agency and social positioning.

Allan Moore in his (2013) *Song Means* and elsewhere in his publications (see e.g. Moore, 1993; Moore and Dockwray, 2008; Dockwray and Moore, 2010) offers a robust consideration of music as a form of discourse. Moore's position is not that of a social semiotician, but that of a musicologist of popular music whose work engages very broadly with analytical traditions across and beyond musicology, narrative, metaphor, embodiment and discourse. Moore's approach is perhaps closest to our own in terms of understanding how the mechanism for musical meaning works; he recognizes that the body is foundational for meaning and that cross-domain mapping shows us that we have the ability to make sense of the world by understanding unfamiliar ideas or sounds in terms of familiar ideas. Moore shows that this therefore destabilizes any notion of formalism in musical analysis because he undermines the idea that music is best understood in and of itself (Moore, 2013: 14). As he suggests, musical sound is more semantically ambiguous than other modes like still images or written text. It affords certain meanings in society, and it affords some meanings over others, and not all meanings are possible. Some songs afford a narrow range of possible meanings through their interrelationship of music and language, while others are 'under-coded' and afford many more possible meanings. Moore's own system of analysis, is a very strong model for understanding music as a communicative act. This volume takes a stance that is different from that of Moore's because we approach music as a communicative affordance from a discourse analytical tradition, valuing musical sound primarily for its communicative power and as an attempt to better understand its collocation and relations with other modes as part of wider multimodal discourse.

On the subject of the relationship between popular music (hereinafter pop) and politics specifically, there is considerable debate which has produced no real consensus among scholars (Hesmondhalgh and Negus, 2002: 7). Some scholars have been highly optimistic as regard the ability of music to represent and promote socio-political interests or particular cultural values (Shoup, 1997; Lorraine, 2006; Korczynski, 2014). However, other scholars have rather pointed to its limitations. Frith (1981, 1988) and Street (1986) highlight how production and promotion, by large corporations, along with social and consumption contexts constrain potential meanings in pop. Though constrained by its institutional context, the music industry does not necessarily control music 'unless the stock market is offended' (Street, 1986: 107), resulting in subversive politics being a part of some pop. Though countercultural pop is incompatible with conventional politics (Street, 1986; Frith, 1988: 472), it can articulate some politics better than others such as nationalist struggles (some Black music), the politics of leisure (youth cults and gay disco) and has been powerful in particular ways such as in shifting the social discourse on gender (Frith, 1988: 472). Even when pop is political, it tends to be highly populist rather than about specific issues (Street, 1986; Way, 2016). These studies suggest lyrics are highly ambiguous and the way they are performed, and marketed, plays a big role in how they are received. Pop musicians often allow a sense of being anti-mainstream and anti-authority within an ambiguous counterculturalism, where this is indirectly connoted rather than specified, knowing that their fans will value this counterculturalism whilst simultaneously holding down mainstream jobs and with broader personal investments in 'mainstream' capitalist society.

Researchers from various disciplines note that much of pop's political power lies with listeners, meanings being ambiguous and open to individual interpretation. Hebdige (1979) demonstrates how music is used by some as part of a self-imposed exile from mainstream culture. Street (1986: 7) claims that pop's politics are related to 'the way private feelings are tapped by the song [and] are linked to the public world'. Grossberg (1987) argues that pop's politics are played out in the activities associated with different tastes of music. Similarly, Huq (2002: 96) argues that rave music is less about conventional politics and more about the politics of pleasure.

There is also much debate concerning pop and authenticity. To understand the discourses of authenticity, which are particular to each genre of music, is to understand the deeply emotional shared connections we have to music. Today, authenticity across many musical genres has shifted from being understood as located in musical objects, to being constructed in and through music as a social discourse. Much has been written on the subject including its usefulness (see for instance Redhead and Street, 1989; Taylor, 1991; Peterson, 1997; Moore, 2002; Burns, 2007). Recent studies have found it useful to view authenticity as the quality of 'sincerity' or 'playing from the heart' that listeners ascribe to performers (Moore, 2002: 210). How this is assigned is socially, historically and genre contingent. Historically, the scholarship of authenticity had its roots in the Romantic tradition where artistic creativity was seen as coming from the soul, as opposed to something which emerges from society (see Machin, 2010). These beliefs contributed to the dichotomy of authentic versus 'establishment', allowing some pop to link authenticity with anti-establishment discourses. Rock's authenticity, for example, is still very often located in countercultural ideologies (Frith, 1981; Machin, 2010). Gilbert and Pearson (1999: 164–165) note that 1980s' authentic rock entailed singers speaking the truth of their (and others') situations representing the culture from which s/he comes and the presence of a specific type of instrumentation. Indie rock differs, where authenticity is about purity not found in 'high-tech manipulations of large scale production' and 'defined in opposition to the commercially influenced (Hibbett, 2005: 64). Alternatively, hip hop authenticity is articulated through lyrics which reveal personal truths, representing a geographical background linked to lived experiences in predominantly Black urban neighbourhoods (Fraley, 2009: 43). Artists, record companies and their managers use semiotic resources such as music, looks and styles to articulate these discourses. Musical authenticity, then, is today properly conceived of as a social process of continual renegotiation of the shared 'truths' and canonical values of a particular musical community. In this collection, we position authenticity as a still essential concept for understanding music as multimodal communication and Way (this volume) examines various types of authenticity articulated in a protest music video. We believe well-informed CDA can add to the study of music through the systematic analysis of music inherent in CDA's approach to textual analysis. So it is this approach we turn to next.

Critical Discourse Analysis

CDA and Halliday's functional grammar starts with the idea that liguistic choices made by text producers reveal obvious and not so obvious discourses in texts. By discourses, we mean 'complex bundle[s] of simultaneous and sequential interrelated linguistic acts', which are thematically interrelated (Wodak, 2001: 66). These discourses can be thought of as models of the world and project certain social values and ideas which contribute to the (re)production of social life. Compositional choices in texts have political repercussions (Kress, 1985: 3). For example, naming a member of the Palestinian Liberation Organization a 'freedom fighter' or a 'terrorist' carries with it political significance. Texts recontextualize social practice (representations) which are transformed dependent 'on the interests, goals and values of the context into which the practice is recontextualised' (van Leeuwen and Wodak, 1999: 96). CDA also emphasizes an examination of context. This is because CDA perceives discourse as a form of social practice or action, something people do to, or for, each other (van Leeuwen, 1993). It is closely interconnected with other elements of social life (Fairclough,

2003: 3) where '... discourse constitutes social practice and is at the same time constituted by it' (van Leeuwen and Wodak, 1999: 92). Due to this close dialectical relationship, both text and context are important in any conception of CDA (Fairclough, 1995: 62; Fairclough and Wodak, 1997).

CDA also has a political stance: one which is critical to those who abuse power. It has been argued that all scholarly discourse and textual analysis are socio-politically situated, selective, limited, partial and thereby biased (Fairclough, 2003; Richardson, 2007). Choosing a critical approach provides a scientific basis for a critical questioning of social life in moral and political terms, e.g. in terms of social justice and power' (Fairclough, 2003: 15). So, research should question and not support unjust aspects of social life. According to Wodak,

> CDA may be defined as fundamentally concerned with analysing opaque as well as transparent structural relationships of dominance, discrimination, power and control as manifested in language. In other words, CDA aims to investigate critically social inequalities as it is expressed, signalled, constituted, legitimised and so on by language use (or in discourse). (2001: 2)

Here we see CDA's concern with relations between language and power, a sentiment echoed by many CDA scholars (van Leeuwen, 1993; Fairclough and Wodak, 1997; Bishop and Jaworski, 2003; Richardson, 2007). In fact, CDA prioritizes a political commitment. Van Dijk (1993) highlights that scholars who apply CDA start by identifying a social problem with a linguistic aspect, choose the perspective of those who suffer the most, and then critically analyse those in power, those who are responsible and those who have the means and opportunity to solve such problems (cited in Richardson, 2007: 1; Wodak, 2001: 1).

Most CDA studies concentrate on news and political speeches. It has been argued that political discourses should be investigated not just in these but in entertainment media (Machin and Richardson, 2012) where they are also disseminated and legitimized. This is because the press, broadcast news and internet news websites are only some of the outlets through which political ideology is circulated. Research using CDA has demonstrated how cultural texts (broadly defined) such as war monuments (Abousnnouga and Machin, 2010), video games (Machin and van Leeuwen, 2005), sound (Roderick, 2013), colour (Zhang and O'Halloran, 2013), clothing (Bouvier, forthcoming) and television reality programmes (Eriksson, 2015) can construct ideology. In fact, in 1920s Europe, 'art and architecture, as well as music, were used as central parts of communicating fascist ideology' (Machin and Richardson, 2012: 331). These studies and others use CDA for examining not just written language, but other modes of communication as well.

As far back as 1996, Kress and van Leeuwen in *Reading Images* (1996) and *Multimodal Discourse* (2001) demonstrated how meanings in texts are created from not just written language but through other semiotic resources such as visual features, material objects and architecture. According to Machin (2013), these two works were groundbreaking because they introduced the idea to linguists that visual features, material objects and architecture create meaning, not just written and spoken language. These books also emphasize that communication was moving from monomodal to multimodal, partly due to technology. Overall, their work is attributed with pointing 'to the possibility of a social semiotic approach to different forms of communication that allowed not only deeper analysis, but as in linguistics, a more systematic level of description. And this is where its strength lies' (Machin, 2013: 348).

Multimodal Critical Discourse Studies (MCDS), with its origins in CDA and Halliday's (1985) functional grammar, assumes linguistic and visual choices reveal broader discourses articulated in texts (Kress and van Leeuwen, 2001). In this collection, we define a mode not to be corollarous with a channel of human perception (sight, hearing, touch, taste, smell) but as a socially agreed channel of communication. Analysing texts multimodally can reveal how various semiotic resources, or modes, play a role in articulating ideological discourses (Kress, 2010; Machin, 2013). In practical terms, MCDS gives us a chance to take advantage of CDA's systematic analysis, that is, by 'taking the power of description so useful for drawing out buried ideologies in linguistic-based CDS to be applied to other communicative modes' (Machin, 2013: 348). MCDS has the advantage of revealing the way each mode works to articulate discourses 'on a particular occasion, in a particular text' (Kress and van Leeuwen, 2001: 29). Machin and Mayr argue that the task of MCDS is to draw out the details of how broader discourses or the 'scripts', the 'doings' of discourse are communicated and how the different modes play different roles (2012). According to Machin, 'What is of foremost importance in MCDS is the way that different kinds of semiotic resources can be used to communicate the scripts of discourses in this process of deletion, addition, substitution, and evaluation, that is recontextualisations (2013: 353). It is our belief that musical sounds also play a role in recontextualizations'. In this book, the various chapter authors use the MCDS approach in various ways and to varying degrees, though each have one factor in common: analysing music critically and in great detail. This allows the study of music to harness the critical analytical potential of CDA.

Music and multimodal analysis

Until very recently, there has been very little attention paid to the social semiotics of sound within multimodal texts. Multimodal analysis and indeed social semiotic treatments of music have been theorized primarily upon the static and interrelated modes of written text and image. Much of this work in multimodality has relied on homologous relationships frozen in time, although embedded in complex social life. While we acknowledge that our own role as interpreters of signs changes in different contexts and times, much of the literature of multimodality considers fairly static texts such as posters, paintings or road signs. This is one reason why sound, and more specifically music, has not been fully theorized in multimodality and its significant social semiotic power is largely absent from many analyses of important social discourses such as those about power, ethnicity, race, gender and nationalism. Musical experience is very often multimodal, has a powerfully affective role in contemporary society, and has inspired a wide range of semiotic, aesthetic and mystical theories of how it makes meaning in people's lives. Moreover, much of the discourse of multimodal semiotics has until recently, relied upon linguistic models of musical meaning.

Much of music's power lies in its use as multimodal communication. It is not just lyrics which lend songs their meaning, but images and musical sound as well. The music industry, governments and artists have always relied on posters, films and album covers to enhance and make specific, music's semiotic meanings. This book considers musical sounds as one element of larger multimodal texts, examining the interacting meaning potential of semiotic resources such as rhythm, instrumentation, pitch, tonality, melody and their interrelationships with lyrics, written text, image, colour and other modes of communication, drawing upon, and extending the conceptual territory of social semiotics. And it is social semiotics which reminds us of the importance of context in the making of meanings. It is context and our personal auditory experience which shape the sonic affordances in multimodal communicative acts. We believe that music and sound are not trivial concerns for scholars of communication and media, but that they play an important role both as a discrete mode(s) in itself, but perhaps even more crucially, in dialogue with other modes of communication such as image and written text. In some ways, music and sound as a mode of communication allows multimodal texts to account for the limitations of linguistic affordances, often bringing the most affective aspects to multimodal texts. Music can produce broad 'unnuanced' emotions in us such as joy and fear, as well as simultaneously signal more nuanced memories and emotions attached to individual people and relationships in our lives (see Cook, 2001). Therefore, music within multimodal communication often brings with it particular affordances that are either difficult to express via more propositional linguistic texts or images, or in some cases, impossible to express in other modes.

The literature that examines music as, and within, multimodal discourse is still a relatively novel area of research. However there have been some significant texts in this direction that in our view begins with van Leeuwen's examination of *Speech, Music, Sound* (1999). Van Leeuwen (1999) identifies six major domains of sound which contribute to meanings. These domains do not dictate what listeners hear but identify experiential meaning potential of the sounds listeners experience (van Leeuwen, 1999: 94). This points to the importance of context in being able to make sense of semiotic affordances (meaning potentials), something critics of video analysis also note (Goodwin, 1993; Shuker, 2001; Railton and Watson, 2011). Musicians manipulate such domains as perspective, connoting social distance, music's adherence (or not) to regularity, how sounds interact with each other, melody, voice quality, timbre and the modality of sounds. Machin (2010) focuses on these ideas and on some of his own and examines how music operates within multimodal texts. Elsewhere, Machin and Richardson (2012) analyse two pieces of music associated with two pre-1945 European fascist movements – the German NSDAP and the British Union of Fascists. Through an analysis of melody, arrangements, sound qualities, rhythms and lyrics, they demonstrate how semiotic resources communicate discourses of a machine-like certainty about a vision for a new society based on discipline, conformity and the might of the nation including unity, common identity and purpose. Their article identifies how sounds communicate specific ideas, values and attitudes. McKerrell (2012) analyses the role of the lyrical content, context, performance and subsequent reception and mediatization of a football song in the press to demonstrate how cultural performance can construct sectarian difference in the Scottish public imagination. McKerrell (2015) then goes on to examine the construction of social semiotic space and social distance in sectarian YouTube videos. He offers a theoretical model for the metaphorical understanding of melodic and harmonic musical sounds in relation to social distance where proximity to the root chord, or most diatonically stable chords, construct notions of Self and the Other. This shows how the musical sound using the harmonic or melodic distance from the tonic or root of the music as a reading of social distance can be multimodally collocated with the text and images to produce a multimodal text whose combined social semiotic meaning is geater than the sum of its parts. Similarly, musical motifs can be so strongly correlated with textual or visual signs that they can become a 'multimodal synecdoche'; where a discreet sign in one mode can signify a specific semantic meaning in another. For example, the Nokia message alert is now widely heard as a multimodal synecdoche that signifies the owner has a new message on their mobile phone, recognizable to many, simply through a unique combination of musical notes.

Van Leeuwen (2012b) argues that music can, and should, be analysed as discourse. He examines a range of sonatas, advertising jingles and news signature tunes. Power, Dillane and Devereux (2012) explore how the singer Morrissey has represented the struggles of the proletariat in a deep textual reading that reveals a complex counterhegemonic stance on the issue of social class. This is illustrated through a detailed semiotic, musical and contextual reading of a Morrissey song, examining the harmonic and melodic structure, tempo and instrumentation in the recorded song and the visuals in the video, as well as a socio-historical and political contextualization of the era and the performer himself. Way (2012, 2013, 2014, 2015, 2016) applies van Leeuwen's (1999) categorization of sounds to a wide range of political popular music videos. These studies demonstrate how music commodities work multimodally to articulate not only political discourses, but also discourses of authenticity. This short list of key articles and books in the arena of music as multimodal discourse studies shows that there is much work to be done both in bringing the best conceptual territory of the various disciplines to bear in considering music as part of a larger multimodal communicative discourse, but also that musically, the analysis has been thus far limited to popular, hip hop, protest, folk, vernacular and advertising or incidental musics, and that the social semiotics of sound within multimodal discourse of many musical genres have not yet been considered. It is timely therefore to begin to think about what music does uniquely as a mode and relate this more overtly to CDA. This will have the dual benefit of both rehabilitating music into wider scholarly debates about social power and communication and simultaneously open up social semiotics and MCDS to powerful new ways of understanding human communication.

Talk and text in musicology

Musicology itself has a long and highly complex historiography that places text and talk alongside, or sometimes entirely distinct from music. There have been various attempts to understand the relationships between music and other modes in musicology (see e.g. Tagg, 1979; Middleton, 1990; Feld and Fox, 1994; Leppert, 1995). But crucially, because of its focus on music as an object, the formalism inherent in the musicological inheritance from analytic aesthetics and musicological analysis is fundamentally at odds with much CDA and *social* semiotic approches to analysis. Much has been made of the semiotic connections between music and language (e.g. Feld and Fox, 1994), and they share some systemic attributes. However, fundamentally, our position is that music is not a language and as such we must pay careful attention to the particular modal attributes in music that mark it out from other modes and give it such emotional and affective power in multimodal texts.

Much semiotic theory of music has started from the position that music can either be treated as a form of linguistic communication or is analogous to the extent that it should be treated with linguistic models (Powers, 1980; Feld, 1984; Feld and Fox, 1994). Good examples of this lie in much of the work on deep and surface structures in musical grammars, Schenkerian analysis, Bakhtinian applications of narrative to musical scores, and almost all structuralist approaches to formal analysis that derive from Saussurian ideas. Musicology has had a very long history of treating music as an object, which has largely been enabled by visual analysis of musical scores. This focus on the visual has encouraged the belief that '...what is in the score wholly specifies music's identity and content' (Leech-Wilkinson, 2013: 219). In fact, the evidence from discourse about music, as well as the affective experience of musical discourse itself, supports the idea that music is not 'a language' in the linguist's sense. That is, the commonly accepted sense of a language as a form of communication of propositional concepts and ideas (Cross, 2011), but that music and language share foundational sensorimotor and somatic processes that produce understanding, meaning and emotions.[1]

If one therefore regards musical sound as a distinct mode from sung language (i.e. in a song or a music video) another problem arises which is whether sounds we hear are always part of the same musical mode: Do two separate, contrary tunes heard simultaneously suggest two different modes, or are they part of the same complex mode? Can non-pitched, non-lexical vocal sound count as 'music' or part of the linguistic 'text'? One critical and certain aspect of musical sound however is that, when audible, it is always heard through time, making it entirely subject to our notions of temporality, and also forcing us to recognize that musical sound, unlike an image or a written word, cannot be perceived statically *through* time, but is always heard *in* time. Long climaxes in music or the build up of dynamic tension in a film soundtrack really do matter in a way that means that understanding what has come before, and what may come in the immediate future, all figure in the multimodal understanding of the present. It is always disappearing from our semiotic perception and is constantly in a changing dialogue with other modes. Music's very immateriality makes it both powerful and deeply temporal, meaning that no multimodal analysis that includes music can really ignore the narrative semiotics of how time, and our semiotic perception of it, changes our perception of a multimodal text. This supports a definition of musical sound as a single mode of communication, because it can always be analysed in relation to other modes in a multimodal text and despite the complexities of the aural perception, we always perceive it as one aspect of a multimodal text, constantly moving through time.

However, it is important to note that in certain contexts there may be two modes operating in the audible semiotic space of a multimodal text. For instance, diegetic music in films and television is that music which refers explicitly to something visible on screen such as a door slamming or a bell ringing. But music can also construct the affective aspects of multimodal texts as non-diegetic music such as an orchestral soundtrack, and thus the audible aspects of a film, television programme or online video can include both diegetic and non-diegetic sounds as different modes in the same communicative moment. The auditory channel of perception can also be inherently multimodal in and of itself, when someone is singing (or shouting) over diegetic background music. In these contexts, we must accept that the sounds, although heard simultaneously in time, are part of two distinct socially accepted channels of communication and that the audible elements of the multimodal text can be multimodal in addition to whatever might be going on visually or linguistically. When someone sings a song, however, we have essentially the conjoining of language with melody. This makes song an inherently multimodal form of communication. Therefore, in this book, we recognize that even the audible aspects of a multimodal text, such as a film or an online video, may be multimodal even before considering how these relate to the spoken language or moving images elsewhere in the text. The analyst must use their common sense to decide which audible aspects of the text are within the musical mode, and which are part of another mode, and more importantly, how do they respond to each other in the total semiotic space of the text?

It follows therefore that we must also be careful not to simply ascribe the same semiotic or discourse analytical methods and concepts transplanted wholesale from linguistic CDA. For instance, we cannot forget that music has many more affordances than language for semiotic meaning, because of its lack of propositional or referential meaning. In other words, we cannot simply make straightforward metaphorical analyses of multimodal metaphors between language and music: rising pitches do not always signify increasing tension; thickly textured musical sound does not always connote semiotic complexity; loud sounds often imply something very public, but not always; and people understand vocal timbre and meaning in many different and contradictory ways across the globe. As in most text-based CDA, context and collocation are crucially important in any consideration of music in multimodal communication.

Like language, music is not always an aural phenomenon. It can form part of a multimodal text without sound, via musical notation or other visual representations of musical sound. Indeed, there are interesting junctures between language and music particularly focused around linguistic onomatopoeia such as 'boom', 'cough' and 'click', where phonetic meaning is foregrounded. Music and sound can also be heard in different ways depending on the multimodal context. That is to say that unlike language, to a certain extent what some might recognize as 'music' is not universally shared, whereas in general, most human beings can recognize a foreign language even if they cannot speak it. But importantly, if we regard language as a complex mode of communication that includes signs, signifiers, referents and important characteristics such as double articulation, then in general, music cannot be considered a language, because of its semiotic ambiguity. It is therefore important to understand that music's meaning is not straightforwardly causal within a multimodal text, but is often more constitutive; just in the same way that verbal discourse constructs emergent socio-cultural identities and meanings, so too does music within complex multimodal texts. This assumption is fundamental to CDA and social semiotics; yet the emergent and social nature of discourse is not incompatible with more structural analyses of how meaning is made. Just as Cameron (1997) has pointed out that the key shift in understanding 'women's talk' and gender relations as social discourse was to move from gender as a causal function of 'women's talk' towards the now widely accepted position of gender as constructed performatively within social discourse (Cameron, 1997: 28), so might we move to a more processual understanding of musical meaning in multimodal discourse, whereby music's meanings are emergent and performative, depending largely upon the social and cultural bodies that hear them. Our bodies are cultured; we feel music in different ways according to class, gender, ethnicity, race, place and personal experience.

There is today a growing consensus in musicology, popular music studies, music psychology and cognitive musicology that is placing embodiment at the centre of musical meaning. Johnson supports this view when he says that: 'Music is meaningful in specific ways that some language cannot be, but it shares in the general embodiment of meaning that underlies *all* forms of symbolic expressions, including gesture, body language, ritual, spoken words, visual communication, etc.' (Johnson, 2007: 260). Furthermore, Zbikowski recognizes this too when he reflects that 'musical meaning is on the whole much less precise than linguistic meaning' (Zbikowski, 2009: 395). Music does not have a finite number of signs with propositional meaning that can be combined in a particular syntax for more complex systematized meaning. Therefore, music is not a language in the conventional sense, but it is very definitely a mode of human communication that 'does' emotion and affective meaning particularly powerfully. On this point we find various points of view that conflict. Philip Tagg (2012) for instance suggests that there has been too much logocentric analysis of music, and that for him, music should be understood *musically*, because it is a different sort of sign system to verbal language: 'Music is an alogogenic [essentially the "opposite of logogenic"[2]] sign system whose semantic precision relies largely on connotation and on indexical signs' (Tagg, 2012: 160–161). But what this view of communication suggests is that somehow music is a special mode, different from any other type of mode of communication such as verbal language, written text, colour, image, gesture etc. Tagg's own view of music is useful across much social semiotics but we disagree with the notion of music as a special form of communication. As Moore so aptly points out in response to Tagg's ambitious methodological research, the problems lie not so much in a logocentric view of music, or in the difference between shared and individual meanings for musical listeners, but

> the problem, I believe, lies not in Tagg's aim, nor in Kennett's critique, but in the assumption of the initial arbitrariness in semiotic meaning, an arbitrariness that then becomes (sometimes) fixed through practice. It is only the least interesting meanings that bear an arbitrary relationship with the sounds of music, and the fixity of meanings that is taken to ensue is illusory. (Moore, 2013: 221)

Moore is correct in pointing out the importance of intertextuality and in the maleability of musical meaning in society. Indeed, this book can in part be read as an attempt to rehabilitate music into a more holistic analytical system that regards music as just one other mode of communication in a multimodal world. We also suggest that if the cognitive theories of embodiment and conceptual metaphor theory are correct, then all semiosis itself is done in and through our embodied minds via embodied conceptual metaphor and cross-domain mapping, which would undermine any kind of special argument for music as a distinct and entirely separate semiotic mode of understanding than other modes. Our point here however is to emphasize that music is not a language in the linguistically normative sense, but that it is a communicative mode, and that its very semantic ambiguity and sonic presence lends it a particularly powerful affective role in communication, where it has very fluid affordances, which are highly adaptable in multimodal texts. In essence, then, this is the same position as outlined by Moore; however where we differ from his rich conceptual treatment of music as semiotic communication is essentially in what is considered 'music'. Moore considers the sung text of songs as part of the musical mode; we consider songs as essentially multimodal texts because they combine sung or spoken text with musical sound; music with words. In this way then, it is possible to consider the text of a song as part of a larger multimodal whole, especially for instance when watching a music video or a film where other modes such as moving images and still images, and gesture and colour are also often present. And this is why we take issue with Tagg's position, because we consider musical experience to be almost always a multimodal experience anyway, and that, as analysts, it is worth understanding the ways in which musical sound interacts with other modes and because a multimodal approach can bear rich insights into the socio-cultural understanding and significance of human communication. All this is important therefore because it affects not only the methodological approach to analysing how music does ideological and cultural work in multimodal texts, but also because it is crucial to understand that musical sound, because of its very malleable affordances, offers a particularly emotionally powerful aspect of many texts: The film soundtrack can reinforce or destroy a sense of intimacy in a scene between two lovers depending on how we understand the sonic aspects of the text; music has been shown to make us buy more (or less) in supermarkets and is now increasingly used in online retailing; the music associated with political campaigns is often a shorthand way for politicians to acquire cultural capital from artists for their own political gain. Music is important in our lives because we often share values embodied in sound, however tacit these may be, and multimodal critical discourse analysis is emerging as a novel, interdisciplinary and multifaceted method for deconstructing these power relations in text.

Notes

1   We take meaning (after Johnson, 2007: 268) to indicate embodied semiotic experience that includes qualities, emotions, concepts, propositions, abstract

reasoning, feelings, metaphors, image schemata, etc., which acts across modal domains.

2 See Philip Tagg's own definition on his website: http://tagg.org/articles/ptgloss.html [accessed 7 December 2015].

References

Abousnnouga, G. and Machin, D. (2010), 'Analysing the Language of War Monuments', *Visual Communication* 9(2): 131–149.

Auslander, Philip. (2008), *Liveness: Performance in a Mediatized Culture*, 2nd edition. Abingdon, Oxon: Taylor & Francis.

Berger, Harris M. (1999), 'Death Metal Tonality and the Act of Listening', *Popular Music* 18(2): 161–178. http://dx.doi.org/10.1017/S0261143000009028, [accessed 13 November 2015].

Bishop, H. and Jaworski, A. (2003), '"We Beat'em": Nationalism and the Hegemony of Homogeneity in the British Press Reportage of Germany versus England during Euro 2000', *Discourse and Society* 14(3): 243–271.

Blacking, John. (1982), 'The Structure of Musical Discourse: The Problem of the Song Text', *Yearbook for Traditional Music* 14: 15–23. <http://dx.doi.org/10.2307/768068> [accessed 13 November 2014].

Bouvier, G. (forthcoming), 'The Role of Clothing in Materialising Ideologies: A Social Semiotic Study of Women's Abaya', *Visual Communication*.

Burns, Robert G. H. (2007), 'Continuity, Variation, and Authenticity in the English Folk-Rock Movement', *Folk Music Journal*: 192–218.

Cameron, Deborah. (1997), 'Theoretical Debates in Feminist Linguistics: Questions of Sex and Gender', in Ruth Wodak (ed.) *Gender and Discourse*, pp. 21–36. London: Sage.

Cohen, Sara. (2012), 'Live Music and Urban Landscape: Mapping the Beat in Liverpool', *Social Semiotics* 22(5): 587–603.

Cook, Nicholas. (2001), 'Theorizing Musical Meaning', *Music Theory Spectrum*, 23(2): 170–95.

Cook, Nicholas. (2012), 'Anatomy of the Encounter: Intercultural Analysis as Relational Musicology', in Stan Hawkins (ed.) *Critical Musicological Reflections: Essays in Honour of Derek B. Scott*, pp. 193–208. Farnham: Ashgate Publishing Ltd.

Cross, Ian. (2011), 'Music and Biocultural Evolution', in Martin Clayton, Trevor Herbert and Richard Middleton (eds) *The Cultural Study of Music: A Critical Introduction*, 2nd edition, pp. 17–27. London: Routledge.

Cross, Ian. (2012), 'Music as a Social and Cognitive Process', in Patrick Rebuschat, Martin Rohrmeier, John A. Hawkins and Ian Cross (eds) *Language and Music as Cognitive Systems*, pp. 315–328. Oxford and New York: Oxford University Press.

Dockwray, Ruth and Moore, Allan F. (2010), 'Configuring the Sound-Box 1965–1972', *Popular Music* 29(2): 181–197. <http://dx.doi.org/10.1017/S0261143010000024> [accessed 19 September 2015].

Eriksson, G. (2015), 'Ridicule as a Strategy for the Recontextualization of the Working Class: A Multimodal Analysis of Class-making on Swedish Reality Television', *Critical Discourse Studies* 12(1): 20–38.

Fairclough, N. (1995), *Media Discourse*. London: Edward Arnold.

Fairclough, N. (2003), *Analysing Discourse: Textual Analysis for Social Research*. London: Routledge.

Fairclough, N. and Wodak, R. (1997), 'Critical Discourse Analysis', in T. A. van Dijk (ed.) *Discourse Studies. A Multidisciplinary Introduction, Vol. 2. Discourse as Social Interaction.* pp. 258–284, London: Sage.

Faudree, Paja. (2012), 'Music, Language, and Texts: Sound and Semiotic Ethnography', *Annual Review of Anthropology* 41: 519–536.

Feld, Steven. (1984), 'Communication, Music, and Speech about Music', *Yearbook for Traditional Music* 16: 1–18.

Feld, Steven and Fox, Aaron A. (1994), 'Music and Language', *Annual Review of Anthropology* 23(1): 25–53.

Fraley, T. (2009), 'I Got a Natural Skill: Hip-Hop, Authenticity, and Whiteness', *Howard Journal of Communications* 20(1): 37–54.

Frith, S. (1981), *Sound Effects*, New York: Pantheon books.

Frith, S. (1988), 'Art Ideology and Pop Practice', in L. Grossberg and C. Nelson (eds) *Marxism and the Interpretation of Culture*, pp. 461–475. Chicago: University of Illinois Press.

Frith, S. (1993), 'Youth/ Music/ Television', in Goodwin Frith and L. Grossberg (eds) *Sound and Vision*, pp. 67–84. New York: Routledge.

Gilbert, J. and Pearson, E. (1999), *Discographies: Dance Music, Culture, and the Politics of Sound*. London: Routledge.

Goodwin, A. (1993), *Dancing in the Distraction Factory: Music Television and Popular Culture*, London: Routledge.

Grossberg, L. (1987), 'Rock and Roll in Search of an Audience', in J. Lull (ed.) *Popular Music and Communication*, pp. 152–175. Beverly Hills: Sage.

Halliday, M. A. K. (1985), *An Introduction to Functional Grammar*. London: Edward Arnold.

Hebdige, Dick. (1979), *Subculture: The Meaning of Style*. Suffolk: Metheun & co.

Hesmondhalgh, D. and Negus, K. (2002), 'Popular Music Studies: Meanings, Power and Value', in David Hesmondhalgh and Keith Negus (eds) *Popular Music Studies*, pp. 1–10. London: Arnold.

Hibbett, R. (2005), 'What Is Indie Rock?', *Popular Music and Society* 28(1): 55–77.

Huq, Rupa. (2002), 'Raving not Drowning: Authenticity, Pleasure and Politics in the Electronic Dance Scene', in Hesmondhalgh and Negus (eds) *Popular Music Studies*, pp. 90–101. London: Arnold.

Johnson, Mark. (2007), *The Meaning of the Body, Aesthetics of Human Understanding*, Chicago and London: University of Chicago Press.

Korczynski, M. (2014), *Songs of the Factory: Pop Music, Culture, and Resistance*. Ithaca, NY: Cornell University Press.

Kress, G. (1985), *Linguistic Processes in Sociocultural Practice*. Oxford: University Press.

Kress, Gunther. (2010), *Multimodality: A Social Semiotic Approach to Contemporary Communication*. London: Taylor & Francis.

Kress, Gunther and van Leeuwen, Theo. (2001), *Multimodal Discourse*. London: Bloomsbury Academic.

Leech-Wilkinson, Daniel. (2013), 'Tonality and the Cultural', *Empirical Musicology Review* 8(3–4): 219–222.

Leppert, Richard. (1995), *The Sight of Sound: Music, Representation, and the History of the Body*. Berkeley: University of California Press.

Lorraine, L. (2006), 'Music and National Culture: Pop Music and Resistance in Brazil', *Portuguese Cultural Studies* 1(1): 36–44. <http://scholarworks.umass.edu/p/vol0/iss1/4> [accessed 8 January 2013].

Machin, David. (2007), *Introduction to Multimodal Analysis*. London: Hodder Arnold.

Machin, David. (2010), *Analysing Popular Music: Image, Sound and Text*. London: Sage.

Machin, David. (2013), 'What Is Multimodal Critical Discourse Studies?' *Critical Discourse Studies* 10(4): 347–355.

Machin, David and Richardson, John E. (2012), 'Discourses of Unity and Purpose in the Sounds of Fascist Music: A Multimodal Approach', *Critical Discourse Studies* 9(4): 329–345.

Machin, D. and van Leeuwen, T. (2005), 'Computer Games as Political Discourse: The Case of BlackHawk Down', *Journal of Language and Politics* 4(1): 119–141.

McKerrell, Simon. (2012), 'Hearing Sectarianism: Understanding Scottish Sectarianism as Song', *Critical Discourse Studies* 9(4): 1–12. <http://dx.doi.org/10.1080/17405904.2012.713315>.

McKerrell, Simon. (2015), 'Social Distance and the Multimodal Construction of the Other in Sectarian Song', *Social Semiotics* 25(5): 1–19. <http://dx.doi.org/10.1080/10350330.2015.1046216>.

Middleton, Richard. (1990), *Studying Popular Music*. Buckingham: Open University Press. <http://dalspace.library.dal.ca/handle/10222/44667> [accessed 9 September 2014].

Moore, Allan. (1993), *Rock: The Primary Text – Developing a Musicology of Rock*, *Ashgate Popular and Folk Music Series*. Farnham: Ashgate Publishing, Ltd.

Moore, Allan. (2002), 'Authenticity as Authentication', *Popular Music* 21(2): 209–223.

Moore, Allan. (2013), *Song Means: Analysing and Interpreting Recorded Popular Song*. Farnham: Ashgate Publishing, Ltd.

Moore, Allan F. and Dockwray, Ruth. (2008), 'The Establishment of the Virtual Performance Space in Rock', *Twentieth-Century Music* 5(2): 219–241.

O'Halloran, Kay L., Sabine Tan, Bradley A. Smith and Alexey Podlasov. (2011), 'Multimodal Analysis within an Interactive Software Environment: Critical Discourse Perspectives', *Critical Discourse Studies* 8(2): 109–125. <http://dx.doi.org/10.1080/17405904.2011.558687>.

Peterson, Richard A. (1997), *Creating Country Music: Fabricating Authenticity*. Chicago: University of Chicago Press.

Power, Martin J., Dillane, Aileen and >Devereux, Eoin. (2012), 'A Push and a Shove and the Land Is Ours: Morrissey's Counter-Hegemonic Stance (s) on Social Class', *Critical Discourse Studies* 9(4): 375–392.

Powers, Harold S. (1980), 'Language Models and Musical Analysis', *Ethnomusicology* 24(1): 1. <http://dx.doi.org/10.2307/851308>.

Railton, D. and Watson, P. (2011), *Music Video and the Politics of Representation*. Edinburgh: Edinburgh University Press.

Redhead, Steve and Street, John. (1989), 'Have I the Right? Legitimacy, Authenticity and Community in Folk's Politics', *Popular Music* 8(2): 177–184.

Richardson, J. E. (2007), *Analysing Newspapers: An Approach from Critical Discourse Analysis*. London: Palgrave Macmillan.

Roderick, I. (2013), 'Representing Robots as Living Labour in Advertisements: The New Discourse of Worker–Employer Power Relations', *Critical Discourse Studies* 10(4): 392–405.

Shoup, J. (1997), 'Pop Music and Resistance in Apartheid South Africa', *Journal of Comparative Poetics* 17(17): 73–92.

Shuker, R. (2001), *Understanding Popular Music*. London: Taylor & Francis.

Street, J. (1986), *Rebel Rock: The Politics of Popular Music*. Oxford: Blackwood.

Tagg, Philip. (2012), *Music's Meanings, a Modern Musicology for Non-Musos*. New York: Mass Media Music Scholars' Press Inc.

Tagg, Philip. (1979), 'Kojak: 50 Seconds of Television Music': Toward the Analysis of Affect in Popular Music'. <http://search.ebscohost.com/login.aspx?direct=true&db=rih&AN=1979-01928&site=ehost-live 80>.

Taylor, Charles. (1991), *The Ethics of Authenticity*. Cambridge: Cambridge University Press.

Tenzer, Michael and Roeder, John. (2011), *Analytical and Cross-Cultural Studies in World Music*. New York: Oxford University Press.

Turino, Thomas. (2008), *Music as Social Life: The Politics of Participation*. Chicago: University of Chicago Press.

van Dijk, T. (1993), 'Principles of Critical Discourse Analysis', *Discourse and Society* 4(2): 249–283.

van Leeuwen, Theo. (1993), 'Language and Representation – The Recontextualisation of Participants, Activities and Reactions', *Discourse and Society* 4(2): 193–223.

van Leeuwen, Theo. (1999), *Speech, Music, Sound*. Basingstoke, London: Palgrave Macmillan.

van Leeuwen, Theo. (2012a), 'Multimodality and Rhythm', in Carol A. Chapelle (ed.) *The Encyclopedia of Applied Linguistics*, Oxford: Blackwell Publishing Ltd. <http://onlinelibrary.wiley.com/doi/10.1002/9781405198431.wbeal0832/abstract> [accessed 15 May 2014].

van Leeuwen, Theo. (2012b), 'The Critical Analysis of Musical Discourse', *Critical Discourse Studies* 9(4): 319–328.

van Leeuwen T. and Wodak, R. (1999), 'Legitimizing Immigration Control: A Discourse-historical Analysis', *Discourse Studies* 1(1): 83–118.

Way, Lyndon. (2012), 'Pop's Subversive Potential: Turkish Popular Music Videos as a Multi-modal Site of Resistance', *Multimodal Communication* 1(3): 251–275.

Way, Lyndon. (2013), 'Discourses of Popular Politics, War and Authenticity in Turkish Pop Music', *Social Semiotics* 23(5): 715–734.

Way, Lyndon. (2014), 'Özgünlük ve Direniş Hikayeleri: Popüler Müzikte Protesto Potansiyeli', *Kültür ve İletişim Dergisi* 17(1): 39–68.

Way, Lyndon. (2015), 'Youtube as a Site of Debate Through Populist Politics: The Case of a Turkish Protest Pop Video', *Journal of Multicultural Discourses* 10(2): 1–17.

Way, Lyndon. (2016), 'Protest Music, Populism, Politics and Authenticity: The Limits and Potential of Popular Music's Articulation of Subversive Politics', *Journal of Language and Politics* 15(4).

Wodak, R. (2001), 'The Discourse-historical Approach', in R. Wodak and M. Meyer (eds) *Methods of Critical Discourse Analysis*, pp. 63–94. London: Sage.

Zbikowski, Lawrence M. (2009), 'Music, Language, and Multimodal Metaphor', in Charles Forceville and Eduardo Urios-Aparisi (eds) *Multimodal Metaphor*, pp. 359–381. Berlin: Mouton de Gruyter. <http://humanities.uchicago.edu/faculty/zbikowski/pdfs/Zbikowski_Multimodal_metaphor_2009.pdf>.

Zhang, Y. and O'Halloran, K. L. (2013), 'Toward a Global Knowledge Enterprise: University Websites as Portals to the Ongoing Marketization of Higher Education', *Critical Discourse Studies* 1–18.

2

The Role of Music in Ridiculing the Working Classes in Reality Television

Göran Eriksson and David Machin

Introduction

In this chapter we are interested in the ideological use of music in a Swedish television reality show called *Böda Camping* – how it is deployed to communicate a very specific discourse linked to wider socio-political shifts in Sweden. Critical scholars have revealed how such programmes tend to morally evaluate and ridicule working-class people (Skeggs and Wood, 2012). It has been argued that this has been one part of a legitimation of the discourse of a moral underclass, who are undeserving in a neoliberal society where there is a shift away from an emphasis on welfare, investment in education and healthcare and abandonment of collective responsibility for disenfranchised sections of society (Eriksson, 2015). Critical work so far has shown clearly how such discourses are communicated through spoken language and how visually, for example, the participants are placed in situations which point to their lack of education, restricted cultural experience or their lack of taste (Lyle, 2008). Here we show how music plays an important role in realizing these discourses.

There is a rich tradition of music analysis in film studies, although not in television studies, upon which we draw in our analysis. But this has tended to point to the broader uses and role of music rather than taking a critical stance. Film music scholars themselves have argued the need for greater detail in analysis to reveal the more precise meanings carried by sounds and music. We explore how we can address this issue by drawing on work from the social semiotics of sound (van Leeuwen, 1999; Tagg and Clarida 2009; Machin, 2010). This combined approach allows us to show how, as with the detailed analysis of language and visual analysis, critically engaged scholars can analyse sound and music to draw out more detailed meanings that are communicated. It has been observed that we must be aware, in analysis, how different semiotic resources can work in very different ways due to their specific affordances (Ledin and Machin, 2015). Much of the delegitimization of the working classes in *Böda Camping*, we show, is accomplished by the clever and precise deployment of music, which can operate in a way that language and images cannot, providing ideas about, and evaluation of, characters, actions, setting and activities. In this chapter we analyse three typical sequences from *Böda Camping* and carry out a detailed analysis of the music that forms part of each.

Critical studies of reality television

Reality TV has attracted attention from a broad mix of scholars, although not with regard to the role of music. Researchers have explored how audiences evaluate the programmes' truth claims and what they think they learn from them (Hill, 2007) or, like Andrejevic (2004) notes, have discussed the exploitative dimension of reality TV and how value can be extracted from the commodification of surveillance. Reality TV has been analysed from a gender perspective (e.g. Negra, Pike and Radley, 2013) or with respect to the issue of race (e.g. Orbe, 2008). There has been an immense scholarly interest in the makeover genre, often starting from Foucault's ideas on governmentality and treating television as cultural technology aimed at fostering people to be good citizens (e.g. Heller, 2007; Murray and Ouellette, 2009; Ouellette and Hay, 2009). During the past decade researchers have also begun to more explicitly address questions related to reality TV and social class (see e.g. Lyle, 2008; Tyler, 2008; Wood and Skeggs, 2011; Skeggs and Wood, 2012; Eriksson, 2015) looking at how people are set up in situations and represented in ways which make them appear as crude and morally problematic. What has yet to be studied, both specifically for reality television and more broadly for television, however, is the way that music can play a major part in the process of representation. Here we explore how this kind of analysis can be carried out in order to show music is one semiotic resource that can be used to define setting, characters, emotional states and to create continuity. If these reality shows are one way by which viewers can be tutored in understanding society, in fostering particular views of citizenship, we show that in this case music plays a crucial role in helping to load this with particular ideologies about the nature of working-class people and the kinds of ideas, values and identities that society should esteem.

The programme we examine is a Swedish docu-soap titled *Böda Camping*, aired by Swedish Channel 5 since 2010. This programme follows the activities at a busy campsite in Sweden during the summer and focuses on the campers' daily life at the site. *Böda Camping* is part of a trend of reality TV appearing in the late 2000s in Sweden characterized by the use of representational strategies that ridicule working-class participants' behaviours, ideas and lifestyles (Eriksson, 2015). This trend can be linked to wider political and ideological shifts which represent the poor and unemployed as a moral underclass (Levitas, 2005). Rather than these people being viewed as part of wider structural inequalities where government policy and economic systems have responsibility, it is their negative characteristics and flawed characters that are foregrounded as part of legitimizing a neoliberal ideological climate where the individual is increasingly responsible for his or her own welfare. This regular representation of working-class people can be contrasted, for example, with instances where the authorities have deliberately fostered positive media representations in times where social unity is required and where there have been fears of workers' movements, as in the case in films by John Grierson and Humphrey Jennings in 1930s Britain where all working-class people were represented as honest and hard-working who enjoy simple pleasures.

In fact this discourse is something rather recent in Sweden which has for many decades celebrated a culture of 'Folkhemmet' which emphasizes the absolute centrality of social equality, social welfare and social interdependence. This newer discourse is part of a process of the legitimization of a shift away from welfare and equality. It is then no coincidence that this is taking place now in Sweden as neoliberal policies and ideas begin to take a hold in a country which in a matter of few years has shifted from being a centrally controlled to a deregulated economy, especially in sectors such as education and health care (Östberg and Andersson, 2013: 16). These reality TV shows play an important role in the naturalization and legitimation of these discourses. Swedish people cease to see themselves as part of a society defined by social interdependence and equality, supported by strong welfare, but one rapidly shifting to sweeping privatization in public services, increasing unemployment and individualization.

Methodology: studying music in film and television

In this chapter we draw on a set of analytical tools from what has become known as Multimodal Critical Discourse Analysis (Machin and Mayr, 2012;

Machin, 2013). This is a form of critical analysis that has its origins in Critical Discourse Analysis (CDA) but which has extended its principles and concerns to include the analysis of visual representations, design, material objects and also sound. Central to this kind of analysis is the notion of discourse. Here the broader ideas communicated by a text are referred to as discourses (Fairclough, 2003; van Dijk, 1993). These discourses can be thought of as models of the world (Foucault, 1977) and can include kinds of participants, ideas, values, goals and settings (van Leeuwen and Wodak, 1999). In CDA, texts are analysed for the details of their linguistic and grammatical choices in order to reveal what these broader discourses are. Since the groundbreaking work of Hodge and Kress (1988) and Kress and van Leeuwen (2006), scholars have also begun to analyse how discourses along with their values, participants, actions and settings can be communicated both in language and visually through images and design. A number of scholars have also begun to extend this to the study of sound and music (Machin, 2010; Machin and Richardson, 2012; Way, 2013; McKerrell, 2015).

Van Leeuwen and Wodak(1999) argue that it is through discourse that social actors constitute knowledge, roles and identities. These discourses represent a kind of knowledge or 'script' about what goes on in a particular social practice, ideas about why it is the way it is, who is involved and what kinds of values they hold. Discourses tell us why these scripts are reasonable ways of acting in the world. And as we show in the analysis that follows, music can be seen to be one important way that the parts of scripts are communicated. 'Scripts' in this case can refer to the smaller scale social practices and meanings of a camping holiday or the wider discourses as to how we organize our societies, such as around mutual responsibility and support, or through individualization and the prioritization of a neoliberal idea of the economy.

We also draw on the notion of the 're-contextualization of social practice' (van Leeuwen and Wodak, 1999). This is useful for thinking about the way that reality shows represent the actions and identities of their participants. Van Leeuwen and Wodak (1999) argue that social practices can be recontextualized, in the interests of individuals or institutions, in language through substitutions, additions, deletions and in reordering the sequences that comprise that social practice. A social practice can be thought of as including the following kinds of elements: participants, ideas, values and attitudes; activities; social relations; objects and instruments; time and setting; and causality. In this chapter we are interested in the way that the social practice of a camping holiday can be recontextualized, for ideological purposes.

There has been little scholarly attention to the use of music in television. There is, however, a strong body of work on film music from within film studies, which while not critical, provides a basis for thinking about how music is used alongside film (Manvell and Huntley, 1957; Gorbman, 1987; Kassabian, 2001; Chion, 2009). These studies point to a number of communicative uses of music in film which we will use to organize our observations in this chapter. Music can contribute to action, for example, by indicating tension or danger. It can follow action closely such as by following footsteps, or it can be used more broadly to suggest adventure or speed. It can also contribute by suggestion that action is about to commence or to be resolved. Music can be used to indicate the state of mind of a character, to suggest love, or, fear, for example. It can, in the tradition of vaudeville theatre, be used to indicate kinds of stock characters, such as evil or comedic. It can also be used to represent kinds of settings such as geographic places or moments in history, mainly using a limited range of cliches. Music can also be used for continuity and creating links between scenes. A handful of authors (Chion, 2009; Donnelly, 2005) have focused in slightly more detail on sound qualities and signification, and they have called for more work in this area.

Analyses of the meaning of sound and music are often made through vague adjectives (Barthes, 1977; van Leeuwen, 1999) such as 'scary', 'romantic', 'lively', etc. But adjectives point more to the effect of the music rather than telling us what, exactly, is in the music that communicates these meanings. Due to the vagueness of such terms, we may miss out on meanings that can be drawn out by more systematic analysis. Just as linguistic texts can be critically analysed, in order to pinpoint the kinds of semiotic choices in language that realize particular discourses, so too can a more systematic analysis of music and sound reveal forms and structures that may have been missed by the more casual listener.

Tagg (2009) has argued that there has simply been a lack of emphasis on studying the semantics of music (the relationship between sounds and what they stand for), or its pragmatics (the cultural and social aspects of production and reception). Tagg has himself produced pioneering work in this area, taking an interest in film and television music, looking, for example, at sound patterns that are used to represent particular kinds of settings and characters in movies.

In order to draw out the way that music can be used to communicate quite specific ideas, attitudes and identities, Tagg (1984) discusses the emergence of sounds and music as communicative acts in hunting and gathering type societies in terms of the way they could be used to communicate about the nature of activities such as initiation rites, marriage ceremonies, harvests and the hunt. Tagg suggests:

> Obviously, the pace required in conjunction with a hunt – intensity of heart-beat, speed of eye, of hands, arms, feet and breathing – will be far greater than that needed for singing a child to sleep… In the case of the hunt, quick, sudden movements enacted with the precision of split seconds are vital ingredients of the activity, but they would be detrimental when trying to send a child to sleep. (1984: 8)

What Tagg makes clear here is that there are much more precise and predictable aspects of sound as communication than we tend to assume and that these can convey quite clear ideas, attitudes, sequences of events and identities. So we cannot use sharp sounds to mean relaxed, nor soft lingering sounds to convey urgency. These are useful observations to take on board if we wish to understand the kinds of movements, activities and attitudes that music can attribute to persons and events in television. It is not just that music is 'scary' or 'fun', but that it can communicate specific things about what goes on in a social practice, about how it should be evaluated and what kinds of identities are involved.

The musicologist Cooke (1959) showed that it was possible to document how the shapes of melodies and rhythms are used in a predictable way to communicate different kinds of ideas attitudes and identities in classical music and opera – a kind of musical vocabulary that has been built up and established over time. He demonstrates how qualities like higher pitch ranges in melodies relate to emotional expansiveness whereas restricted pitch ranges relate to emotion containment. He establishes how specific rhythmic qualities can be tied to different kinds of bodily movement which connote quite specific ideas, attitudes and identities.

In the field of social semiotics, a handful of scholars have taken up the ideas of Tagg and Cooke with a view to providing more predictive models of the use of sound to create meaning. Van Leeuwen (1999), drawing on Hallidayan (1978) linguistics, showed how it is possible to identify basic underlying building blocks of sound quality in the sung voice, for example. Machin (2010) followed this work to look at meaning-making in popular music compositions and also how the details of melody types, such as those that are more expanded or restricted, more sharply or gently articulated, tend to be found used in quite predictable ways. Machin and Richardson (2011), Griffiths and Machin (2014), Way (2013) and McKerrell (2015) have applied these models to think about the way, therefore, that music and sound can be used for ideological purposes.

In this chapter we take the basic uses of music identified in film studies – setting, character motifs, emotional states, and action/ continuity – but draw on the tools for analysis proposed by van Leeuwen (1999) and Machin (2010), which themselves owe much to Tagg (2009) and Cooke (1959). Through this approach we want to identify how music and sound are used as part of the process of ridicule in *Böda Camping* and in the process of recontextualizing the everyday life of a set of campers to suit particular ideological purposes. In the fashion of Tagg, we look at the way rhythms, melodies, articulation and sound arrangements realize discourse.

Analysis of *Böda Camping*

Each episode of *Böda Camping* deals with one particular theme. In the episode we analyse, the topic is the 'rules of the campsite'. We begin with the introductory sequence that is shown at the start of each episode and then move on to two sequences from the contents of the programme.

Music and setting

When each episode of *Böda Camping* starts there is the same opening sequence. This shows a montage of people at the campsite. This is shot with a high quality camera as seen in Example 1 (see Figure 2.1). Production values are high. People are shown in a flattering way, all laughing heartily as they put up tents, make food, cycle past, and so on. There are uses of fast edits, close-ups, playful angles, and slowed-motion, with a slight effect of over-exposure suggesting a glorious summer day. People engage with each other in their laughter and also look confidently and warmly at the camera, and therefore with the viewer (Kress and van Leeuwen, 2006). They appear to regard the view of the camera confidently and with trust, which is something we do not find in the later sequences. Here summer must be understood as having a highly significant and almost mythical role in Swedish culture, given the long and dark winters. Importantly, the film and editing style in this opening sequence contrasts greatly with the realism and lingering, unflattering, more Cinema Direct, shooting style of the of the sequences that comprise the content each week.

On the one hand, while this opening sequence represents people in a flattering way visually it appears to have an ironic aspect. The voice-over comments: 'Every

Figure 2.1. *Böda Camping* opening sequence

year two million Swedes take their pack and go to their own paradise. And the biggest paradise of them all is Böda Sands Camping'.

For many, particularly middle-class viewers, to call the campsite a paradise is indeed ironic, and, as we find in many of the sequences in the programme, this points to the tastelessness and crudeness of the campers. However, the sequences do have a positive feel. Different kinds of people enjoy simple things and there is a sense of the older values of the Swedish Folkhemmet, of co-independence as we see an array of people enjoying the same thing. We show that both of these sets of associations are partly communicated by the music.

The music in these opening sequences gives meaning to the setting and provides continuity by linking the fast sequences of edits. But importantly it also provides important meanings about the social relations between the persons depicted.

The opening piece of music is a kind of 1950s style rock'n'roll piece. On the one hand this points to the campsite being something from the past, something slightly out of fashion. And this is one important part of what Lyle (2008) calls the 'middle-class' gaze that is imposed upon working-class people in such reality shows – that they have no sense of style. But on the other hand the music communicates a number of less obvious meanings. We begin by looking at rhythm, then move onto other aspects of the way the music communicates.

Rhythm

To begin with, the rhythm of the opening sequence, in terms of adjectives, is 'light' and 'flowing' and has a 'side-to-side' carefree feel. This is, as we shall see, very different from the rhythms used to represent persons within the content of the programme. We can draw out the meaning of these choices in rhythm through the observations on rhythm and meaning made by Cooke (1959). We spend a little time to explain these, returning to them in later analyses.

Cooke (1959) has discussed the way that different rhythms are associated with different kinds of bodily movement. So rhythms can be even (in pop music) or uneven (as may be the case in jazz). Uneven rhythms can communicate a sense of difficulty, or if the unevenness is repeated a sense of being prevented from moving forwards or remaining in one particular place. Unevenness can also suggest creativity as it can imply something changing, reacting and refusing to conform. Rhythms can be fast or slow which can suggest energy or relaxation or

Table 2.1 Meaning potentials for rhythms

Rhythmic quality	Meaning potential
Even/uneven	conformity versus creativity; ease versus difficulty
Fast/slow	hurry versus leisurely; energy versus its lack of; rush versus patience
Lightness/heaviness	mobility or clumsiness; important versus unimportant; strength versus weakness
Stasis/motion	restriction versus freedom; marking ground versus progress, hesitation versus certainty

sluggishness. Rhythms can suggest lightness or weight due to light or heavy bass drum beats respectively; they can suggest stasis through constant beat tones (such as a single bass drum pulse) or forwards motion through alternating tones (such as between a snare and bass drum), hesitation (as in Reggae) or progress. They can also suggest a side-to-side swaying motion (as in Swing) as opposed to a forward action like that found in some pop ballads or more relentless and forceful forward motion in military marches. We summarize these meaning potentials in Table 2.1.

Such a list should not be considered a set of rules, and rhythm is just one part of how meaning is created. But, in the fashion of Tagg, as regards his hunt and lullaby, we can begin to think about what attitudes, ideas and identities are communicated.

We can think about the rhythms in the introductory rock'n'roll through these terms. In the first place there is a sense of lightness. We find no heavy bass drum or heavily accented notes. This is certainly not a laboured slow movement. The kind of movement suggested is side-to-side and carefree movement, rather than one which suggests driving forwards motion. It is certainly not a restricted, hesitant or uneven movement. This effect is created by the guitar and drums playing a choppy rhythm on alternate beats. These observations are important when we start to link this with other meanings in the song. But for present purposes we begin to see how this edited sequences of smiling people are not 'hurried', 'clumsy' or 'restricted', but move easily and lightly.

Melodies

There are two aspects of melody, or tune, that we analyse here. The first is the way that the melody changes or moves around in pitch, and the second is

Table 2.2 Meaning potentials of pitch

Pitch	Positive meaning	Negative meaning
High	Bright/energetic/happy	Lightweight/trivial/flighty
Low	Important/solid/relaxed/closer	Clumsy/depressed/danger

how the melody is articulated. In both studies of music and of inguistics, both aspects have been shown to have important and specific communicative meaning potentials. Again we can relate this to the difference between Tagg's hunt and lullaby: One might allow much more variation in pitch and require more abrupt articulation, whereas the other might require a more moderate shift in pitch and more measured, or gentle articulation. Pitch relates to how high or low a sound is: a scream would be a high note, thunder a low note. What is of importance to us here is the meaning both of pitch itself and in shifts in pitch.

In the first place, higher pitches can mean higher energy, excitement or even agitation, whereas lower pitches can mean lower levels of energy, danger or even despair. Cooke shows that classical composers have used high pitch to suggest 'up and away' due to its energy and low pitch to suggest 'closer, down and relaxation (1959: 103) (Table 2.2).

In our rock'n'roll song we find the very deep voice of the lead singer suggesting something solid, relaxed and intimate. Behind this we find much higher pitched bright and energetic backing singers. The female singers bring bright energy and optimism. We can begin to see here that the music, through rhythm and pitch, helps to indicate that the visuals, showing the happy, flatteringly represented, people and the lovely sunshine, are bright and carefree and that there is both bright energy, but also relaxation and intimacy. This signifies a wonderful Swedish summer.

In addition to whether pitch rises or falls there is important meaning potential in the range of these changes – a large pitch range communicates a sense of letting more energy out whereas a small pitch range can mean holding more energy in. Newsreaders always speak using a restricted pitch range to suggest a neutral stance. Once can imagine the difference were they to use a large pitch range. Soul singers use a large pitch range to communicate the expression of emotions. Brazil, Coulthard and Johns (1980) note that pitch range in speech is akin to excitement, surprise or anger. In contrast, smaller pitch ranges can be associated with emotional constraint or even modesty. The meaning potential of pitch range is summarized Table 2.3.

Table 2.3 Meaning potential of pitch range

Pitch range	Meaning potential	Effect
High	Emotionally expansive	Emotionally open/subjective
Low	Emotionally contained	Repressed/contained/objective

In fact all of the three levels of singers in this arrangement sing over a relatively narrow pitch range. So while it has bright, high pitches, each is measured and constant as regards outpouring of emotion. This is about having simple, measured fun with the light, side-to-side, beat and the closeness of the deep-voiced singer. It is not about the expression of intense feelings. In the final scene, one of the campers is edited in slow motion to appear to say the closing words of the song 'My love' sung in the deep voice of the lead singer (see Figure 2.1). This in itself is playful through editing, but also plays an important part in connecting the participants to the music.

Social relations and composition

One important meaning potential of sound is to do with how the different voices or components in the music interrelate. A number of scholars have shown that arrangement in music can indicate different kinds of social organization or social relations (Schafer, 1977). This is highly significant for this particular song in the context of *Böda Camping*.

Van Leeuwen (1999) points to the way that unison in musical arrangements can have important meaning potential. The different voices in an arrangement can sing together in unison which can suggest conformity or shared purpose. Or voices can sing at different levels suggesting a hierarchy. They can also compete suggesting conflict. In national anthems voices are heard almost as one. A simple way to subvert a national anthem would be to break rhythm and sing out of unison with other voices. Contrastingly however, in beer commercials, we might hear the melody being sung to suggest cohesion but still hear individual voices. In some polyrhythmic music different voices weave around each other (Ibid., 1999). This suggests an accommodation of difference, yet the need to operate around one another (Machin, 2010). The different members of the society here are different yet not hierarchically. Tagg (1994) suggests that we analyse this as regards the way, for example, the singer in rock music must shout to be heard out of the noise, something he relates to social organization in industrial society. Chanan (1994) notes that in later Gregorian chants voices would sing the same flat melody in a call and response fashion. In this case a monotonous subjection of all people to the word of God, mutually communicating these values back to each other.

We can relate such observations to our rock'n'roll music, and later to other pieces in the episode. In the rock'n'roll song we have three layers of voices: the lead singer, male backing and female backing. These are allowed to do their own thing and are not required to be absorbed by the unity of the melody as in a national anthem. Yet they happily work together to contribute to the whole, each taking their place. Each has their place in the overall fun and energy. While the voice-over appears to point to the irony of the campsite being a paradise and visually it may be seen as inappropriate to be quite so overjoyed at being there, the music nevertheless points to a kind of act of unison, perhaps of mutual inter-dependence – along with the meanings of brightness, carefree and relaxed. We might argue that while the following sequences are entirely about ridicule the opening sequence combines irony with an older sense of Folkhemmet, which here is indeed rather old fashioned in the contemporary world of style and individualism.

Music, character motif and narrative

Moving on to the sequences within this particular episode we begin with one of the male campers, Lasse, who has visited the site for many years. He is asked about the rules of the campsite. He is given a musical motif which is then heard throughout the programme each time he appears (his 'leitmotif'). This plays a narrative role in telling a story about obsessive and petty behaviour. Verbally Lasse tells the interviewer that he has told other campers about obeying bounda-ries of the pitches, pointing to his pettiness. Visually there is an emphasis on editing and shots that suggest that he patrols the campsite looking for rule trans-gressions, although closer inspection of the footage reveals he in fact remains in the same place, close to his own trailer.

When we first see Lasse we see him as if he is patrolling the campsite look-ing for transgressions of rules (Example 2; see Figure 2.2). This is done by shooting him from behind as if the camera follows and Lasse takes the lead. Other sequences, where apparent rule breaking is shown, are then inter-spersed with sequences of Lasse. The music begins (indicated by these signs

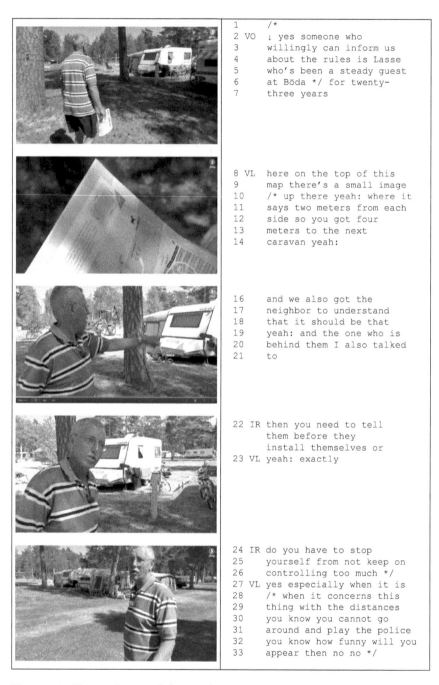

```
1      /*
2 VO   ↓ yes someone who
3      willingly can inform us
4      about the rules is Lasse
5      who's been a steady guest
6      at Böda */ for twenty-
7      three years


8 VL   here on the top of this
9      map there's a small image
10     /* up there yeah: where it
11     says two meters from each
12     side so you got four
13     meters to the next
14     caravan yeah:


16     and we also got the
17     neighbor to understand
18     that it should be that
19     yeah: and the one who is
20     behind them I also talked
21     to


22 IR  then you need to tell
       them before they
       install themselves or
23 VL  yeah: exactly


24 IR  do you have to stop
25     yourself from not keep on
26     controlling too much */
27 VL  yes especially when it is
28     /* when it concerns this
29     thing with the distances
30     you know you cannot go
31     around and play the police
32     you know how funny will you
33     appear then no no */
```

Figure 2.2. Veteran-Lasse and the march-music
VO=Voice-over L=Veteran-Lasse IR=Interviewer

/*) as we see Lasse (Line 1) but is slightly tuned down (indicated by ↓) when the voice-over starts (Line 2). It is a drum roll on a snare drum in the fashion of parade ground drums. There is no forward motion, it is as if preparing to march. The snare drums are high pitched and tense. Brass instruments begin to play and the drums change to suggest a forwards march. Clearly this is about military precision. The brass instruments play deep notes suggesting gravity and menace. These play in complete unison. Unlike the rock'n'roll song with its space for different voices, there is singularity and certainty in this music. The melody rises in pitch a step at a time, in the fashion of military music or national anthems suggesting the rising of spirits and energy, possibly Lasse's anger. This is played in a minor key which brings a sense of foreboding.

But there is also a lightness in this music. As the march develops we hear fifes that first play whimsically at a high pitch and then with rapid trills going up and down in pitch. In the first place there may be a sense of the sadness or thoughtfulness of heading off to battle which then shifts where such rapid tempos and rises and falls in pitch represent emotional flux. Here it would be the nerves, and butterflies in the tummy, either representing the feelings of the enemy or purely the emotional highs of marching to battle. However, the fifes themselves, which have their origins in march-music in the American civil war, here suggest not a modern twentieth- or twenty-first-century type war but something, historical and perhaps therefore a little quaint.

Phrasing and articulation in melodies

An important part of melody is the phrasing. Bell and van Leeuwen (1993) have noted in speech that shorter phrases are associated with sincerity, certainty, weight and therefore with authority. In contrast longer, lingering articulation suggests the opposite, so emotion, subjectivity. Newsreaders use such short phrases for this reason. Folk singers use short bursts in their lyrics to communicate sincerity. The opposite case, where singers produce longer lingering statements, suggests rather slow burning internal emotion as in the case of many jazz or soul singers. The melody played in our march-music is clearly composed of bursts rather than lingering notes. There is a sense of certainty and authority here. In fact the speaker himself speaks quite smoothly and certainly not in short bursts. He does, however, use a restricted pitch range in his sentence

Table 2.4 Meaning potentials of note articulation

Articulation of notes	Meaning potential
Shorter dotted notes	Abrupt, lively, hurried, certain, objective/clumsy if played in deep pitched brass or woodwind
Longer lingering notes	Emotionally lingering, subjective

articulation. But viewers also hear the stepped, ascending and shorter phrased melody of the march-music.

Importantly, there are different kinds of shorter abrupt articulations to be found in music. McClary (1991) observed that traditionally in opera masculine characters have been represented through harsher staccato notes as might be associated with military music which conveys liveliness and certainty, whereas women are represented through longer legato articulation which is more emotionally lingering and less assertive. The masculine staccato notes would be played on brass instruments and with percussion while the feminine, more lingering, legato notes are played on strings. Again, as regards the march-music here, the motif given to the man is brisk, assertive and unemotional, although the softer and whimsical fife helps to bring something less serious and lighter. We summarize the meaning potentials for articulation in Table 2.4 since we return to these later in the chapter.

Important for meaning-making in the use of the march-music as a character motif here is the way it is edited into the sequence. We hear the music just before we first see Lasse and before any voice-over begins. We hear the preparation to march on the snare drum. This sets the scene for something taut, tense and regimented. However, just before the voice-over ends the presentation of Lasse the music stops (indicated by */, Line 6) completely as Lasse begins to answer. He speaks one sentence: 'here on the top of this map there's a small image' (Lines 8–9), and then the music starts again, this time building up as he is seen pointing things out around the site.

The technique of the music stopping, that is allowing the man to begin an answer and then the music starting again, is an interesting feature. First, it is often the case that a lack of music in films is used to indicate realism, or a serious moment. It is where the viewer attends to the actual diegetic sounds produced in the moment represented. So, at this level we can think about the way that while music is used, as part of the programme as 'entertainment' and 'fun', these moments without music connote realism and the 'reality' of the show. In Derick Wiseman's own accounts of documentary film he expressed that it was longer sequences of silence that gave the impression of 'being there', of unmediated reality (Nichols, 1991).

We can draw on Halliday's (1978) account of clause relations to think about the way music is added at this specific point. Put simply, clauses in sentences can expand on preceding ones in three different ways. The first is 'extension' where the expanding clause adds something new or offers an alternative. The second is 'enhancement' which provides circumstantial features such as time, place, reasons, and so on. The third is 'elaboration' which exemplifies, or speci-fies in greater detail. We can apply these to help us think about the way that Lasse speaks first without and then with the musical accompaniment. When Lasse speaks he first provides an enhancement by providing circumstantial details to say what he means by the tents being pitched together pointing to the site leaf-let: 'it says two meters from each side so you got four meters to the next caravan yeah'. He then moves on to elaboration giving an example involving the neigh-bour. 'And we also got the neighbor to understand that it should be that.'

The reinsertion (Line 10) of the music appears to work at the same time as a kind of enhancement, providing information and evaluation for his reasons and motifs. Lasse, at this point, is not really allowed to explain his reasons, although later he does mention the issue with fire risk. Yet the music here provides an evaluation. The reason is his controlling, petty nature. These are not added by the voice-over, or the interviewer, or by Lasse himself. The effect of the pause in the music means that he is allowed to speak; we listen to him briefly, but we quickly return to the enhanced level of meaning of his military precision and the forward march around the campsite.

Music and internal states of mind

We now move on to our third use of music, which is linked to the sequence with Lasse. The next sequence involves a man named Micke, with his family, who is presented as being overly obsessed with finding the best position for his tent (Example 3; see Figure 2.3). From the shot of Lasse we cut to a generic scene of the campsite as if we, or Lasse, is searching. Just before we cut to the scene of Micke we hear a pasodoble (bullfighting music) begin, which acts as a kind of conjunction (Line 1) between the scenes. We then see a family, in a medium shot sitting at their campsite. At the end of this sequence we again return to Lasse who appears to be looking out across the site (Lines 52–58). In fact from what Micke says this is not really related to Lasse's concerns regarding the distance between pitches. It is clear that he wants to move his tent as it is too close to the road: 'if we have the table and the chairs here then the cars can run over the table.'

It is the editing and the music which play an important role in making this appear to be of the same order. Music again appears to play a role in enhancement here. We are given evaluation about circumstance and reason, before we see Micke.

The pasodoble music points to a man's battle with his tent, so here it is ironically intended. Again, looking a little more carefully at the semiotics of the piece we can draw out more meanings to show why it indicates a battle, and specifically what kind of battle. This too helps to give a sense of irony to the scene.

The pasodoble has military origins. It is written in 2/4 time which deliberately imitates the steps of a march and was timed for troops to take 120 steps each minute. It was later introduced into bullfighting where it was used when the bullfighter enters the arena or just before the kill. Unlike the militaristic march discussed above, however, this is more flamboyant. The backing instrumentation plays a lively, bouncy repetitive rhythm, almost suitable for a party. The melody is played by a single trumpet that glides over this backing thus suggesting the lone bullfighter. This plays a melody that combines more dotted notes with more legato notes and rises and falls in melody, with the characteristic regular rolls or turns which produce a flamboyant and showy effect. The pitch range is quite expansive suggesting excitement and emotional turns.

Compared to the regulated minor melody of the former military pieces, this has not only a regulated rhythm but also a playful and exotic emotional duel as the bullfighter circles, performs and struts. The backing music here suggests the context of the celebration, that is the bullfight, while the melody is used to depict the calculated yet showy performance. It is at the semiotic level here that we can draw out these more detailed meanings.

The pasodoble music stops when the voice stops (Line 12). This is coordinated with the moment Micke gets up from the chair, and it stops in the exact moment when he is on his feet. He then starts explaining (Line 13) and a new piece of music starts (Line 14). We shift away from the flamboyant battle of the pasodoble to a tune played on a banjo and acoustic guitar. The banjo shifts from irony to communicating something silly. In Anglo-American culture the banjo tends to have associations of simple, or inward looking, country folk. But again looking at it a little deeper points to more specific meanings.

With regard to the rhythm, the banjo music moves along very quickly. It is rapid and slightly chaotic. The rhythm is created by the circling of the melody,

```
1        /Bullfighting music starts/
2    VO  Some other people having a
3        problem with the distances
4        is Micke and Milla


5        on spot twohundred and
6        sixty-seven

7    Ml  move a tent that sounds
8        tough


9    VO  just after breakfast
10       they're not quiet pleased
11       with the tent's position


12       (Micke gets up) *
13   Mi  look here we sit here
14       /banjo music/ when the
15       evening comes and a little
16       cozy then we sit here
17       a bit sheltered
18       if we have the table and
19       the chairs here then the
20       the cars can run over
21       the table

22   Ml  yes and we don't wont that
23       to happen no
```

Figure 2.3. Sequence to show how music help to construct internal states of mind include VO=Voice-over, Mi=Micke (male), Ml=Milla (female), L=Veteran-Lasse, IR=Interviewer

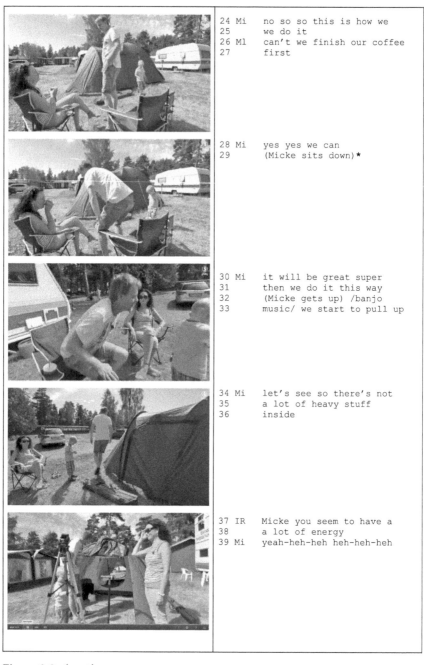

	24 Mi	no so so this is how we
	25	we do it
	26 Ml	can't we finish our coffee
	27	first
	28 Mi	yes yes we can
	29	(Micke sits down)*
	30 Mi	it will be great super
	31	then we do it this way
	32	(Micke gets up) /banjo
	33	music/ we start to pull up
	34 Mi	let's see so there's not
	35	a lot of heavy stuff
	36	inside
	37 IR	Micke you seem to have a
	38	a lot of energy
	39 Mi	yeah-heh-heh heh-heh-heh

Figure 2.3. (*cont.*)

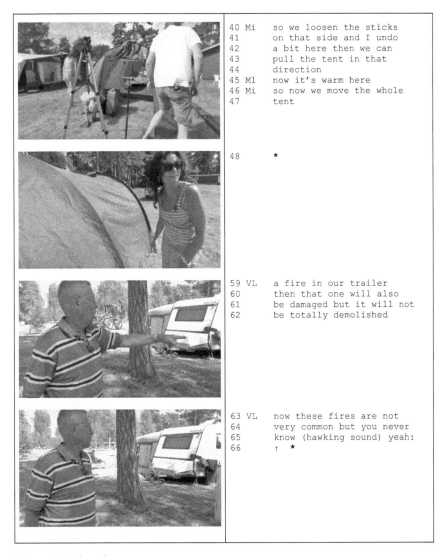

40	Mi	so we loosen the sticks
41		on that side and I undo
42		a bit here then we can
43		pull the tent in that
44		direction
45	Ml	now it's warm here
46	Mi	so now we move the whole
47		tent
48		*
59	VL	a fire in our trailer
60		then that one will also
61		be damaged but it will not
62		be totally demolished
63	VL	now these fires are not
64		very common but you never
65		know (hawking sound) yeah:
66		↑ *

Figure 2.3. (*cont.*)

which creates a slightly frivolous, directionless, unplanned feel. The pitch as it rises and falls, and skips around rapidly suggests emotional unevenness. All of this takes place at a fairly high pitch, thus suggesting something unsubstantial or lightweight. The banjo itself creates a hollow, insubstantial sound. We could say this is the opposite of the slower, highly regular and ascending notes of the march-music. Importantly the banjo sits here in an arrangement as a lone instrument, joined only by a single guitar chord which is placed abruptly at the conclusion when Micke sits down (Line 29), to only start again as he again gets up to fuss around the tent (Line 32). This also suggests his isolation, and slight madness, which is supported by shots of his wife looking awkward and making ironic comments edited in with shots where he adjusts the tent (Line 22–23, 49–51).

At the end of this sequence we cut immediately back to Lasse. The march-music starts when Milla is still talking (Line 50) indicating that Lasse will appear, thereby creating the connection between the two sets of events. The camera resumes following him when he appears (Line 52). The sequences with Lasse frame the tent moving sequence as if they are temporally linked, as if Lasse patrols the site seeking out such transgressions.

Returning briefly to Halliday's (1978) categories of clause relations, music is not really used to provide extension, in other words to create something new or alternative. In the case of the pasodoble and banjo, the music is used for elaboration, in other words to exemplify. So the instance of Micke is set up by Lasse's comments and through visual continuity as an example of what he is talking about. Here too the music allows the link to be created. But it is mainly used as enhancement as the circumstances and the reasons are indicated. In this sense these people become trapped by the music. With the banjo playing how can Micke explain his concerns about the proximity to cars and having a child playing so close by? The music has established the setting and form of social relations – his battle with the tent as his wife with embarrassment. And it has set up his reasons, his state of mind, which is silly and obsessive. These sequences of music are punctuated by the silences and the bearing witness, the unmediated reality.

Conclusion

In this chapter we suggest an approach based on Multimodal Critical Discourse Analysis for analysing the way that music can play a crucial part in the processes of representation. Here we have worked with examples from the Swedish reality programme *Böda Camping*, which is a part of a wider trend of reality shows ridiculing working-class people and their pastime activities. In the analysis, we show how participants are associated with musical motifs which help represent them with particular characteristics; how music plays the role of constructing internal states of mind and can help to create narrative; how music is indicating certain actions and creates continuity where there is none. Using Halliday's (1978) clause relations we were able to think about the way music helps to trap participants within the definition of the narrative and discourse set up visually and linguistically. Overall, these examples demonstrate that it is necessary to take the previously often overlooked role of television music seriously in order to reveal otherwise hidden discourses. In *Böda Camping* as well as in other Swedish reality shows (see Eriksson, 2015), music plays a key role in communicating particular discourses that tend to delegitimize the working classes. Such discourses are part of a wider political trend in which the Swedish working classes are being devalued.

References

Andrejevic, M. (2004), *TV: The Work of Being Watched*. New York: Rowman and Littlefield Publishers.

Barthes. (1977), *Image, Music, Text*. London: Fontana.

Bell, P. and van Leeuwen, T. (1993), *The Media Interview*. Kensington, NSW: University of New South Wales Press.

Brazil, D., Coulthard, M. and Johns, C. (1980), *Discourse Intonation and Language Teaching*. London: Longman Higher Education.

Chanan, M. (1994), *Musica Practica: The Social Practice of Western Music from Gregorian Chant to Postmodernism*. London: Verso.

Chion, M. (2009), *Film a Sound Art*. Columbia: Columbia University Press.

Cooke, D. (1959), *Language of Music*. Oxford: Clarendon Paperbacks.

Donnelly, K. (2005), *The Spectre of Sound: Music in Film and Television*. London: BFI.

Eriksson, G. (2015), 'Ridicule as a Strategy for the Recontextualization of the Working Class: A Multimodal Analysis of Class-Making on Swedish Reality Television', *Critical Discourse Studies* 12(1):20–38.

Fairclough, N. (2003), *Analysing Discourse: Textual Analysis for Social Research*. London: Routledge.

Foucault, M. (1977), *Discipline and Punish: The Birth of the Prison*. New York: Pantheon Books.

Gorbman, C. (1987), *Unheard Melodies: Narrative Film Music*. London: BFI.

Griffiths, F. and Machin, D. (2014), 'Communicating the Ideas and Attitudes of Spying in Film Music: A Social Semiotic Approach', *Sign Systems Studies* 42(1): 72–97.

Halliday, M. A. K. (1978), *Language as Social Semiotic: The Social Interpretation of Language and Meaning*. London: Arnold.

Hodge, R. and Kress, G. (1988), *Social Semiotics*. Cambridge: Polity Press.

Heller, D. (2007), *Makeover Television: Realities Remodelled*. London: I.B. Tauris.

Hill, A. (2007), *Restyling Factual TV: Audiences and News, Documentary and Reality Genres*. London: Routledge.

Huntley, J. and Manvell, R. (eds) (1981), *The Technique of Film Music*. London: Focal Press.

Kassabian, A. (2001), *Hearing Film: Tracking Identification in Contemporary Hollywood Film Music*. New York and London: Routledge.

Kress, G. and van Leeuwen, T. (1996), *Reading Images: The Grammar of Visual Design*. London: Routledge.

Kress, G and van Leeuwen, T. (2001), *Multimodal Discourse: The Modes and the Media of Contemporary Communication*. London: Arnold.

Kress, G. and van Leeuwen, T. (2006), *Reading Images*, London: Routledge.

Ledin, P. and Machin, D. (2015), 'How Lists, Bullet Points and Tables Re-contextualize Social Practice: A Multimodal Study of Management Language in Swedish Universities, *Critical Discourse Studies* 12(4): 463–481.

Levitas, R. (1998), *The Inclusive Society? Social Exclusion and New Labour*. London: Palgrave Macmillan.

Levitas, R. (2005), *The Inclusive Society? Social Exclusion and New Labour*. 2nd edition. London: Palgrave Macmillan.

Lyle, S. (2008), '(Mis)recognition and the Middle-class/Bourgeois Gaze: A Case Study of Wife Swap', *Critical Discourse Studies* 5(4): 319–330.

Machin, D. (2010), *Analysing Popular Music: Image, Sound, Text*. London: Sage.

Machin, D. (2013), 'What Is Multimodal Critical Discourse Studies?', *Critical Discourse Studies* 10(4): 347–355.

Machin, D. and Mayr, A. (2012), *How to Do Critical Discourse Analysis*. London: Sage.

Machin, D. and Richardson, J. E. (2012), 'Discourses of Unity and Purpose in the Sounds of Fascist Music: A Multimodal Approach', *Critical Discourse Studies*, 1–17.

Manvell, R. and Huntley, J. (1957), *The Technique of Film Music*. London: Focal Press.

McClary, S. (1991), *Feminine Endings: Music, Gender, and Sexuality*. Minneapolis: University of Minnesota Press.

McKerrell, S. (2015), 'Social Distance and the Multimodal Construction of the Other in Sectarian Song', *Social Semiotics* 25(4).

Murray, S. and Ouelette, L. (2009), *Reality Television: Remaking Television Culture*. New York: New York University Press.

Nichols, B. (1991), *Representing Reality: Issues and Concepts in Documentary*. Bloomington, IN: Indiana University Press.

Negra, D., Pike, K. and Radley, E. (eds) (2013), 'Gender and Reality TV [Special Issue]', *Television and New Media* 14(3).

Orbe, M. (ed.) (2008), 'Race and Reality TV [Special Issue]', *Critical Studies in Media and Communication* 25(4): 413–443.

Östberg, K. and Andersson, J. (2013), *Sveriges Historia 1965–2012 [The History of Sweden 1965–2012]*. Stockholm: Norstedtsförlag.

Ouellette, L. and Hay, J. (2008), *Better Living through Reality TV*. Oxford: Blackwell Publishing.

Schafer, M. (1977), *The Tuning of the World*, New York: Knopf.

Skeggs, B. and Wood, H. (2011), 'Introduction: Real class', in H. Wood and B. Skeggs (eds) *Reality Television and* Class, pp. 1–29. London: Palgrave Macmillan.

Skeggs, B. and Wood, H. (2012), *Reacting to Reality Television: Performance, Audience and Value*. London: Routledge.

Tagg, P. (1982), *Nature as a Musical Mood Category*. Nordens working paper series. <http://www.tagg.org/articles/xpdfs/nature.pdf>.

Tagg, P. (1994), 'From Refrain to Rave: The Decline of Figure and the Rise of Ground', *Popular Music* 13(2): 209–222.

Tagg, P. (1984), *Understanding Musical Time Sense. In Tvarspel – Festskrift for Jan Ling (50 ar)*. Goteborg: Skriften fran Musikvetenskapliga Institutionen. <http://www.tagg.org/articles/xpdfs/timesens.pdf>.

Tagg, P. and Clarida, B. (2009), *Ten Little Tunes*. New York: The Mass Media music scholars press.

Tyler, I. (2008), ' "Chav mum chav scum": Class disgust in contemporary Britain', *Feminist Media Studies* 8: 17–34.

van Dijk, T. (1991), 'Discourse and the Denial of Racism', *Discourse and Society* 3: 87–118.

van Dijk, Teun. (1993), 'Principles of Critical Discourse Analysis', *Discourse and Society* 4(2): 249–283.

van Leeuwen, T. (1999), *Speech, Music, Sound*. London: Macmillan.

van Leeuwen, T. (2005), *Introducing Social Semiotics*. London: Routledge.

van Leeuwen, T (2008), *Discourse and Practice: New tools for Critical Discourse Analysis*. Oxford: Oxford University Press.

van Leeuwen, T. and Wodak, R. (1999), 'Legitimizing Immigration Control: A Discourse-Historical Analysis', *Discourse Studies* 1(1): 83–118.

Walser. (1993), *Running with the Devil: Power, Gender, and Madness in Heavy Metal Music*. Front Cover. Middletown, CT: Wesleyan University Press.

Way, L. (2013), 'Discourses of Popular Politics, War and Authenticity in Turkish Pop Music', *Social Semiotics* 23(5): 715–734.

Wingstedt, J., Brändström, S. and Berg, J. (2010), 'Narrative Music, Visuals and Meaning in Film', *Visual Communication* 9(2): 192–210.

Wood, H. and Skeggs, B. (eds) (2011), *Reality Television and Class*. London: Palgrave Macmillan.

3

'Shame Makes the World Go Around': Performed and Embodied (Gendered) Class Disgust in Morrissey's 'The Slum Mums'

Aileen Dillane, Martin J. Power and Eoin Devereux

Being a member of society is an essential condition for becoming a conscious being and creating music.

(John Blacking, 1995: 51)

Introduction

This chapter explores how a pop song can become (and remain) a critical site for counterhegemonic expression, through the creative manipulation of discursive, structural, sonic and somatic elements. 'The Slum Mums', by popular music artist Morrissey, deals with the contempt felt for lone female mothers on welfare in the United Kingdom under the New Labour governments of the 1990s and 2000s. Rather than providing a straightforward critique of this 'contempt', Morrissey deftly creates a song whose meaning relies on the ambiguous interrelationship between the socio-political context, the lyrical content, and musical structure and sound as they relate to issues of gendered embodiment in particular. To this end, we locate our work within what might be understood as a social constructivist approach, leaning into scholars who argue for embodied perspectives. We argue that it is through the careful subversion of expectations that the song provides a powerful critique of gendered, class disgust.

We begin by exploring gendered class discourse in the United Kingdom at the time of the song's release in 2004, rather than going straight to the song, as we believe it needs to be fully contextualized in order to be 'read' critically. This is followed by an introduction to Morrissey, an artist who demonstrates a strong track record in championing the marginalized and in offering counter-hegemonic stances on a variety of contemporary social, political and economic issues. We begin our analysis of the song with a close reading of the lyrics. Because of the possible ambiguity in interpreting Morrissey's lyrics (which on face value may seem to support as opposed to counter, prevalent, negative discourses on female welfare recipients), we then examine the song's structure to illustrate (on the macro structural and discursive level and the micro textual and somatic level), how this is not actually the case. We conclude that as 'The Slum Mums' pre-empted the intensification of gendered and classed disgust discourses (cf. *Benefits Street*, Channel 4 Television, 2014) and the ever increasing demonization of welfare recipients, the song is potentially even more important and efficacious now.

Interpreting 'Slum Mums'

'The Slum Mums'[1] was released as a 'B Side' to Morrissey's single 'I Have Forgiven Jesus' (Sanctuary Records, 2004). Its lyrics were written by Morrissey and its music co-composed by Boz Boorer[2] and then bassist Gary Day. The placement of the song on the B Side of the single perhaps indicates Morrissey's understanding that this song would never be a hit in its own right; yet he was nonetheless ensuring its further circulation. The song received little more than a lukewarm reception (Goddard, 2009: 397) largely failing to impress fans or music critics. Whether it was the song structure itself, or the challenging message it carried that proved unpopular, is difficult to establish. From our perspective, however, it is these very elements that make this song a prime example of social critique that resonates beyond its date of creation.

In *Music for Pleasure*, Frith (1998: 103) argues that it is 'possible to read back from lyrics to the social forces that produced them' (see also Frith and Goodwin, 1990). While we engage in a close lyrical reading of 'The Slum Mums', we adhere to Brackett's cautionary note (2000: 192) to 'consciously avoid considering the lyrics in isolation which often forms 'the basis for the interpretation of popular songs' and which can end up producing a reductive and incomplete analysis. At the same time, we accept that signification can, depending on the lyricist, most directly occur through words, at least initially, and that it is through language that subjects are most obviously discursively produced and reproduced.

To this end, we focus first on the lyrics for 'meaning' but then later explicate the role of music, instrumentation and, crucially, the grain of Morrissey's voice, to underscore how these discrete elements operate as part of an efficacious complex. Such an interpretation also involves, as Brackett (2000: 171–172) explains, 'explicating both a "primary" level of signification such as "positional values" and the interconnection of this level with "secondary" levels such as "positional implications," "emotive connotations" and "rhetorical connotations"'. Layers of meaning and feeling are created through the interconnectedness of text, context, sound and embodied performance.

In other words, a song, even one as replete with social commentary as 'The Slum Mums', does not simply comprise or represent a particular verbalized discourse. A song is, first and foremost, a musical event with sonic and lyrical-melodic components. Obviously, different listeners focus to varying degrees on different aspects of a given song. For some, the lyrics take precedent, while for others, the words may not even register with the focus instead, perhaps, on the bass line or the harmonic movement of the rhythm guitar, or simply on the sensuousness of the lead vocals.[3] A song is also meant to be performed. A pop song, as form and genre, has a melodic contour and harmonic topography, and like all music has a complex signification system of its own (Cooke, 1959; Middleton, 1990; Moore, 2003, 2012). This point cannot be overstated. Any musical analysis and criticism of a song has to consider both the lyrical and musical content in multimodal relation to each other, as their affective dimensions and their meaning are intertwined at numerous levels. Further, in the context of this specific analysis, both the music and lyrics of 'The Slum Mums' engage with gender and class discourses reflexively and reflectively in mutually constitutive ways. As Blacking argues, 'music cannot express anything extramusical unless the experience to which it refers already exists in the mind of the listener' (1995: 35).

Part of the larger argument we are making is that Morrissey is someone with considerable cultural and symbolic capital who has a keen sense not just of discourses around class disgust, but also of the manner in which songs can both underpin and rehearse *or* construct and subvert societal beliefs and behaviours. The structure and performance of 'The Slum Mums' may be interpreted as indicating Morrissey's appreciation of how music, on one hand, operates on a profoundly visceral and somatic level in bypassing cognition and interpretation (Ortony, Norman and Revelle, 1998, 2004), while on the other, is at its most potent when the emotions of a particular discursive stance become resonate and amplified through music systems that are also themselves culturally constructed. Adorno's (2001) argument that all popular music produced under capitalism is derivative and incapable of critique has, of course, been systematically challenged, though such a belief continues to persist with many aficionados of 'high art' forms. The message of 'The Slum Mums', wrapped up in a short, ostensibly musically unremarkable pop song of the early noughties suggests the opposite. The song demonstrates a keen awareness of its neoliberal, socio-historical moment and, by extension, the limits and potential paradoxes of its form (and its performance).

In the following section, we first examine the discourse of welfare and poverty at the time of the song's composition and release in the United Kingdom. Morrissey is then inserted into this socio-political context as a 'raconteur' of the marginalized, which leads us to an analysis of the lyrics in order to understand how two gendered, classed subjects, in the form of a male welfare officer and a female welfare recipient, are constructed lyrically/discursively.

The broader historical discourse on class and social welfare

It is impossible to understand 'The Slum Mums', a song in which a welfare officer castigates a single mother for being on welfare, without an understanding of the wider political and societal discourses that underpin it. Skeggs (2005: 45) argues that class disappeared from the academic radar at the exact moment that economic division reached unprecedented heights in the United Kingdom. Simultaneously there was an emergence of a political rhetoric of inclusion, classlessness, and social mobility (Skeggs, 2005: 47 cited in Tyler, 2008: 20). The problematic concept of the 'Underclass',[4] popularized by Charles Murray, ultimately created a 'moral panic' (Cohen, 1972) in an increasingly polarized society, and 'the subsequent neoliberal reordering of public policy under the aegis of Thatcherism, Reaganism and the ascendance of the New Right' (Hayward and Yar, 2006: 10).

As such, in political debate the Moral Underclass Discourse stresses 'moral' and 'cultural' sources of poverty and exclusion, and is primarily obsessed with the 'moral hazard' of welfare dependency (Levitas, 2000: 360), with the majority of the political establishment pontificating about how excessive resources are exhausted through such things as welfare payments (see, e.g. Allen, 2009). Such discourses reaffirm long established beliefs about the 'dangerous' working class who are professed to be a major hazard to the moral and social order (see Golding and Middleton, 1982; Skeggs, 1997; Lens, 2002; Wilson and Huntington, 2005; Tyler, 2008; Wood and Skeggs, 2008; Tyler, 2011; Devereux, Dillane and Power, 2011), non-contributors to affluence and over contributors to decline (Morris, 1994; Levitas, 2003; Skeggs, 2004, 2005; Hayward and Yar, 2006; Law, 2006;).

Over time, the New Labour governments of Blair and Brown created 'an implicit link between parenting and blame', stressing that parents needed to be given the 'skills' to enable social mobility and to make 'empowered' choices (Gillies, 2005). In recent times, young, single, working-class mothers have been subjected to stigma and hatred in the UK cultural context (Tyler, 2008: 26). The figurative function of the 'feral' 'chavette' slum mum is constructed through animalistic commentary as uncontrollably and immorally breeding (Gidley and Rooke, 2010 cited in De Benedictis, 2012: 11–12). As Tyler (2008: 26) remarks

> …the chav mum or pramface, with her hooped earrings, sports clothes, pony tail ('Croydon facelift') and gaggle of mixed race children, is the quintessential sexually excessive, single mother: an immoral, filthy, ignorant, vulgar, tasteless, working-class whore….

The widespread dissemination of such negative stereotypes ensures that these single mothers function as convenient scapegoats (Kelly, 1996 cited in Bullock, Fraser Whyche and Williams, 2001: 235) to deflect blame from the increasingly obvious shortfalls (i.e. the growing inequality between the very rich and the poor) of global capitalism (Jensen, 2012).[5] This is even more significant in the context of a move from 'redistribution to recognition politics' whereby those groups or individuals that are deemed to be 'disgusting'/not respectable are no longer 'entitled' to expect the state to provide for their welfare. In essence, those who do not conform to the idealized neoliberal citizen 'work as the constitutive limit; the limit to value' (Skeggs, 2005: 977). In these societies, further reducing access to welfare entitlements, or the amount of payment these individuals can claim, is seen to have a positive impact as it will force parents and their children to act responsibly and reintegrate into "normal" society (Barnes and Power, 2012: 7).

Morrissey as a raconteur of the marginalized

I am a social writer, a witness, and I cannot stand unfairness.
(Morrissey in interview with Araya, 2015)

As leader of The Smiths, solo-artiste, writer (2013) and most recently, novelist (2015), Morrissey is a figure whose influence and reputation looms large within the popular music scene and beyond.[6] Widely acknowledged as a complex, and controversial icon, Morrissey has become the focus of a growing body of academic research which seeks to make sense of his significant contribution to popular culture, particularly in terms of his often counterhegemonic stances on pertinent contemporary social and political issues (see Renyolds and Press, 1995; Zuberi, 2001; Martino, 2007; Bracewell, 2009; Hopps, 2009; Campbell and Coulter, 2010; Devereux, Dillane and Power, 2011; Power, Dillane and Devereux, 2012; Dillane, Devereux and Power, 2014; Power, Dilane and Devereux, 2015).

Emerging from a working-class background in Manchester, Morrissey has adopted a broadly critical left-wing and republican (in the European sense of the term) perspective. His often radical and challenging pronouncements have seen him provoke heated argument and debate among cultural commentators and his many fans. He has, for example, talked about not recognizing traditional gender binaries or sexual orientations such as 'straight' or 'gay' (referring to a 'Fourth Gender' and using the term 'Humasexual' to describe himself).[7] Although his more recent recordings have extended their focus by engaging with a wider range of themes including specific Chicano/a and Latino/a concerns (see Devereux and Hidalgo, 2015), Northern (White) English working-class life looms large in the Morrissey imaginary.[8] It is this understanding of the texture of working-class life that informs 'The Slum Mums'.

In terms of his presentational style, Morrissey's songs are written most often from the point of view of an outsider. In addition to writing carefully crafted poetic songs, which are rich in literary allusion (and irony), Morrissey manages to generate a wide appeal through semantic ambiguity combined with a semiotics of authentic working-class experience. Much of the authenticity which fans repeatedly refer to while explaining Morrissey's overall appeal is based on his creative use of social realism and his commitment to dealing with themes which are often rendered invisible or demonized within a popular culture or mass media setting. This is most in evidence in the myriad of references to working-class/blue-collar experience. As well as writing about geographically specific themes (focused on his own Irish Catholic Immigrant upbringing in Manchester and more recently on the Latino/a and Chicano/a experience in Los Angeles in particular) his lyrics and soundscapes express feelings of loss, alienation and *anomie.* As the perennial outsider, Morrissey is, in Power's (2011) words, 'a raconteur of the marginalized'. In the following section, we evidence how he embodies this position, initially through semantic ambiguity in his lyrics, and later, through his careful and deliberate use of structure and sound, all of which evidence his powerful, multimodal compositional and performance abilities at play.

Creating the classed subject through lyrics

The lyrics[9] of 'The Slum Mums' clearly rehearse a number of classed and gendered discourses, evidencing Morrissey's keen familiarity with such issues. Cleverly, the song is sung from the subject-position of a UK welfare officer castigating a welfare-dependent mother and subjecting her to his particular brand of classed and gendered vitriol. The 'irresponsible' poor and underclass are presented from the outset as overly sexually active – the mother is revealed as having six children by 'six absent fathers'. The welfare-dependent children are described as 'filthy' and in animalistic, scavenging terms as a 'rat-pack brood'. The slum is 'engrained underneath [her] finger nails', like something she cannot wash away. The welfare officer speaks of being 'paid to despise' her 'council house eyes', in a gesture that conflates poverty and stigmatized housing estates with her own bodily appearance and even genetic makeup. The lone mother is accused of being 'a slum mum', of breathing like one (her body having its own particular rhythms), of being unclean, and of 'breeding' like one, in terms of over-producing children. She is, in effect, viewed as physically producing the conditions of her own degeneracy.

The welfare officer questions the lone mother's audacity in trying to receive assistance from the state, by castigating that *'you turn to us for succour because you think we're just suckers'*. In addition he strongly expresses that he and others simply 'don't care', while simultaneously admonishing the lone parent and thereby, demonstrating the contempt that many people have for the 'undeserving underclass'. While a specific ethnicity is not mentioned, there is a passing reference to skin-bleaching in which the female lone mother is reminded that even a change of name, skin-colour or accent will not allow her to ever escape from her fixed class and racialized position. From the jaundiced perspective of the welfare officer, the poor and underclass regard the social welfare system as being there to be exploited. The officer goes so far as to imply that the welfare system deliberately sets out to discourage the legitimate claiming of welfare. The social services offices are:

> *Strategically placed in a rowdy, dowdy part of town*
> *To discourage you from signing*
> *We make you feel as if you're whining*
> *When you claim what's legally yours*

The welfare officer also states that the (New) Labour government has nothing but disgust for those on welfare. We are twice told that 'The Labour Government[10] can't stand "The Slum Mums"'. It is clear that the social and political matrix in which this mother is operating is a challenging one but one that receives little sympathy from the agents of the state.

The song reaches a dramatic climax when the welfare officer suggests the woman take her vermin children, her 'rat-pack brood', far away from the slums to a long-grassed meadow in order to 'administer seven doses lethal and illegal'. The welfare officer's shocking encouragement of 'The Slum Mums'' infanticide/suicide appears to suggest that she is better off killing her children, using her own illegally procured drugs, so as to save them from the indignities of a life spent as a member of the underclass.[11] The suggestion references earlier times in the United Kingdom where infanticide was used as a means of avoid shame.[12] She cannot easily access what is 'legally' hers (benefits) but the procurement of 'illegal' drugs to get rid of the problem seems simple, and she and her children will be quickly and efficiently rendered 'elsewhere'. At this point the lyrics end. Is that really the solution?

In spite of Morrissey's track record of speaking up for the marginalized or his 'authentic' positionality as working class, it might be argued that the lyrics alone do not seem to be delivering a counterhegemonic message.[13] In fact, arguably, this song could be understood as underscoring the neoliberal agenda with its powerful incitement of persuasive distaste, even hate. But this is not what we've come to expect of Morrissey, so clearly something is happening in the song's structure, in its very sonic textures, that leads us to an interpretation other than this obvious literal-lyrical one. We argue this is found in the song's structure, melodic lines, use of Morrissey's particular voice and instrumentation, all of which play into gendered discourse and emotional manipulation to creatively subvert the lyrical message with devastating effect. The result is a multimodal, nuanced and textured piece of work that manipulates the listener into potentially hating the slum mum, but in the end, realizing that the real disdain needs to be redirected towards those in power who would coldly cast her and her children aside. In order to come to this conclusion, we explore Morrissey's subversive processes by first looking at the social discourse of the working-class female body as deviant and other, examining how it has been constructed discursively and musically, and sometimes not without contradiction in terms of what female embodiment comes to mean.

Music, class and the gendered, singing body

There is a profound moment of recognition of the power of music in George Orwell's seminal novel *Nineteen Eight-Four* (2003[1949]), when the protagonist

Winston Smith hears a female 'prole' (the equivalent of a slum mum) singing a machine-generated and mass-distributed, government-sanctioned nonsense song as she hangs out clothes on her tenement washing line. Smith is struck by how the woman's voice somehow manages to transform the banal lyrics into something profoundly affective. The sensual female voice seems unaware of its potential to subvert the status quo and be the undoing of men. Significantly, Smith's only other experience of singing is while performing party propaganda songs in unison with his comrades, something that also incites his emotions, though in this case, of barely contained, disciplined and vehement violence and anger, things which are put to use for the good of the party. Both responses speak to the degree to which the affective and the ideological may be bedfellows in musical utterances. The example of the prole foreshadows in our musical analysis of 'The Slum Mums', the over-productive yet sensual, working-class female body, the *grain* of whose voice (Barthes, 1977),[14] though silenced in 'The Slum Mums', breaks beyond the bounds of hegemonic discourse captured in ideologically driven, commercial pop songs.[15] Morrissey, like many pop and protest singers, seems to recognize the latent power of the pop song as a vehicle of expression, par excellence, that can communicate on multiple levels to working-class and middle-class audiences, something explored by Bennett et al (2009). In terms of the UK context specifically, Bennett et al's *Culture, Class, Distinction* systematically assesses the relationships between cultural practices and the social divisions of gender, class and ethnicity in contemporary Britain. While much of this work is a reassessment of ideas of class and taste, especially in the digital age, what is particularly important is the manner in which the authors assess the relationship between cultural capital and inequality.[16]

When it comes to thinking about music and the working-class body, Fox's (2004: 152) exploration of the lexical trope of 'feeling' (a concept very prevalent in discussions on consuming popular songs) is particularly important – something he describes as seeking to connect 'sensory experience, embodied attitudes, and rational thought to the domain of social relations. This idea of feelingful qualities is particularly pertinent when one considers the degree to which social interactions may become 'generic and institutionalised' (Fox, 2004: 153), something which music *itself* is capable of producing and reproducing.[17] Music, then, is an ideological tool and in the discourse specifically on class disgust, a song like 'The Slum Mums' offers an insight into how and why the song might (subversively) perform and rehearse such negative feelings, providing a critique on class relations, from a distinctly gendered perspective, that remains as pertinent now as it did when the song was first written. But Fox's work also highlights the emotional capacity of working-class songs and the potential for the working class to construct the self. This tension between self-construction and creation by others is at the heart of any reading of 'The Slum Mums'.

In order to appreciate the efficacy of 'The Slum Mums' as a song form and performance act, particularly in relation to discourses on gendered, class disgust, it is necessary to briefly survey the manner in which music itself has been feminized as an art form. This in turn leads to a discussion of how feminist critiques of music scholarship in relation to popular music play into the ambivalence around the efficacy of Morrissey's critique within a populist, 'lower-class' genre that is often more concerned with stardom than seeking real social justice through sonic intervention (Brackett, 2000: 172). We insist that any critical analysis of gendered, class disgust *in popular song form* – a cultural artefact performed by a working-class singer – benefits from this perspective as it uncovers and lays bare often unquestioned attitudes around the rights of women, particularly working-class and unemployed women, while simultaneously revealing the gendered work that music does in creating women as sexual beings first and foremost.

In terms of the relationship between music and gender, feminist musicologist Susan McClary's pioneering work *Feminine Endings: Music, Gender, and Sexuality* (2002[1991]) challenged structural and empirical research in musicology at a time when scholarship declared 'signification' to be off-limits, yet where 'structures' as graphed by theorists, and 'beauty' (see Hanslick, 1995, for example) as celebrated by aestheticians evidenced violence, misogyny and racism. As part of her explorative critique, McClary identified the following ways in which musical discourses were gendered: *gender as musically constructed* (utterances based on gender, and musical codes containing social attitudes); *gendered aspects of music theory* (male cadences being 'strong', female cadences being 'weak', as well as binary discourses on attraction and repulsion); *gender and sexuality in narrative* (virile male protagonist, with lighter, wayward secondary female themes to be disciplined and contained); and finally, *music as gendered discourse* (music and musicians as effeminate, and male responses to music emphasizing objectivity, rationality and universality versus female responses as overwrought, emotional and even histrionic). McClary was focusing on the Western Music canon in *Feminine Endings* but many of her observations are applicable to popular music forms too, given that much of the language, conventions and practices come from that world.[18] In this and in her subsequent book *Conventional Wisdom* (2000), McClary has argued that because music can organize our perceptions of our gendered bodies and emotions, and it can tell us things about history and the contextualized, historical moment that are not always accessible through other mediums. But music doesn't just organize our perceptions. It profoundly shapes how we come to make sense of things, through our body, or senses and our emotions.

Shusterman (2008) explains, through somaesthetic means, that a person is configured by the social and cultural as well as the biological, and that the body and its emotional responses cannot be excluded from any engagement with 'meaning'. Feelings and emotions are both registered, negotiated and shared externally but also felt deeply and profoundly internalized, which feeds back into the society. This aspect of the operations of the feeling being in everyday life is examined at length in Tia De Nora's work (2003) which examines the manner in which we are moved, in terms of how aesthetics and performance can be manipulated. Music is therefore 'a cultural resource in the social construction of emotions' (Juslin and Sloboda, 2003: 17; also see Finnegan, 2003), particularly where that resource has been gendered. This social construction manifests in individual and collective bodies. For a song like 'The Slum Mums', its meaning and affective dimensions reside not just in social constructions of mothers on social welfare, but on how the protoganist (the welfare officer) sings his disgust which is not just discursive, but is deeply felt and embodied in the song structure. It manipulates us to feel the same disgust, and for that to inform our beliefs.

Popular music scholar Sheila Whitely has written extensively on the manner in which women are socially constructed through songs. Citing Simone de Beauvoir that one is not born a woman but rather becomes one, Whitely (2005: 65) points out that 'feminist would generally agree that girls, like women, are socially constructed rather than biologically given…in different ways in different social and historical contexts. Whitely (2005: 65) demonstrates how the conflation of …girl…babe, baby and mama (which has its origins in the blues) in Joplin's late 1960s' live performance of 'Tell Mama' was essentially a 'sexually knowledgable exchange' between the singer and her audience. This point might be extended to Morrissey's 'The Slum Mums', a figure of a particular moment in time (and geographic space), configured by that very English of terms 'mum', who was very much in the public eye and therefore highly topical for the politically aware Morrissey.

Given his sexual ambiguity, Morrissey is an interesting figure as the performer of this song, but, of course, it is not he, per se, that is constructing the slum mum but rather the male civil servant Morrissey is envoicing. By giving all of the 'lines' to this man, Morrissey is actually underscoring the 'fiercely patriarchal basis for constructing appropriate codes for behaviour and identity of women' as Whitely puts it (2005: 67). The bottom line is that slum mum is a 'bad girl', thereby establishing 'the ideological terrain for the three as of abuse, abjection and alienation' (Whitely, 2005:. 67). There is only one moment where the slum mum attempts to construct her own identity, through changing her accent, a moment where she 'refuses to enact the ascribed identity/the codes we live by (Whitely, 2005: 69). As a creative artist, Morrissey would also be patently aware of the working women's bodies as sites of 'contradiction, conflict and tension' (Whitely, 2005: 69), the very elements that form the basis of Morrissey's critical, performance and singing style. Moreover, as someone who is also ambivalent about gender and sexuality, Morrissey is particularly well positioned to understand how emotions have been gendered in musical form too. 'Reason' is often constructed as masculine, and 'emotion', particularly in terms of musical form, is constructed as female, and where 'reasoned emotion' is about control, discipline and manipulation. The very fact that this song endeavours to be about control, discipline and manipulation but gradually reveals itself to be a song of uneven structure and instability is precisely why is works so well as a critique. Therefore, in the following section, we go back to the song once again, but this time take into account the manner in which the music and lyrics work together, along with the very specific 'grain' of Morrissey's voice, to generate potential reactions and meanings which ultimately culminate in a devastating critique.

'Structures of feelings'[19] in 'The Slum Mums'

A close musical reading of 'The Slum Mums' reveals multiple ways in which the music acts as a gendered matrix, drawing upon binary conventions in terms of structure and form, but especially in relation to the gendered, emotional aspect of music, which in this specific song act as an overwrought foil or contradiction to the neutrally delivered but altogether misogynistic lyrics of the song, underscoring the gendered, class disgust that is at the centre of the narrative. As Langer has argued (cited in Blacking, 1995: 36), 'music can reveal the nature of feelings with a detail and truth that language cannot approach.' The following section leans into a basic harmonic outline of the song (Figure 3.1) and our more complete transcription of the song (see Appendix 1) which displays the vocal melody line (with occasional lyrics inserted), the framing and underpinning chords in relation to the melody and the overall rhythmic and metric structure of the song. Our approach here draws upon Moore (2012) where the focus is on the interaction of music and everyday words and, in particular, on the consequences of such theorizations.

The Slum Mums (skeletal structure and chord sequences)

Intro

1+ 2 + 3 + 4 +	1+ 2 + 3 + 4 + 1+ 2 + 3 + 4 +		1+ 2 + 3 + 4 +
Dmin	Am7	Emin	F7
Amin	*Emin	F7	C G

Verse 1

....   Six filty...

Emin	G**	Emin	D7	[** or E7 1st inversion]

think...

Dmin	Amin	Emin	F7

welfare, oh yeah...

Amin	Emin	F7	C/G

Chorus

change your...

Emin	G	Emin	C

won't escape...

G	Bmin7	C	Amin

government...

Emin	F7	C	Amin

Verse 2

offices...

Dmin	Amin7	Emin	F7

-courage you...

Amin	Emin	F7	C/G

Chorus

change your...

Emin	G	Emin	C

won't escape

G	Bmin7	C	Amin

government...

Emin	F7	C	B+

Coda

...   take your ...

C	F7	Amin***	F7	***or F7 1st inversion

lethal...

C	F7	Amin***	F7	***or F7 1st inversion

Figure 3.1. 'The Slum Mums'

Figure 3.1. (*cont.*)

Instrumental Coda

Dmin	Amin	Emin	F7
Amin	*Emin		

[* pre-emptive chords, falling on the 4+ and not the 1 downbeat at the start and end of the song]

Like all clever 'emotional designs' (Norton, 2005), this song crafts and manipulates our emotional responses to devastating ends. From the very outset of the song, listeners are placed in an uncomfortable sonic world. The song opens with a distinct guitar riff in the minor, historically 'weak/female' key, over which is heard a shrill sound sample of children screaming and crying. It is a melodramatic start, meant to startle and irritate and literally somatically embody the disgust communicated in the virulent opening line, 'six filthy children…from six absent fathers'. These eight chords, moving from D minor to A minor (the tonic) then quickly to E minor and F7, have a somewhat destabilizing effect, starting on chord IV (which we don't necessarily know is chord IV at this point) but then getting to the tonic by the measure 5, only to be destabilized again with a sequence of Amin – Emin – F7 and C/G (this G foreshadowing the change of key in the 'chorus'). The listener knows and feels (s)he is in a moment of tension and instability.

In terms of the song's melody and execution, a ventriloquist-like Morrissey assumes the position of the welfare officer with what should be a vitriolic and scathing verbal assault on a female lone mother in terms of the content.[20] Yet his male subject voice, with its smooth, persuasive grain, is in stark contrast with the insidious message of the song. Staying within the five-note, contained range of A–E, he intones reasonably and seductively. He croons us on side and in doing so he seems to help us rehearse our disgust, almost unaware (and so, we become complicit in a neoliberal positionality, at least for the present). But something is amiss. The logic of the rhetoric is not clearly supported by a concomitant logic in the music, which itself is not in a clear and rational/structurally repetitive verse-chorus form with easily performed and repeatable lines throughout. The overall song can be broadly cast into a verse, chorus, verse, chorus with coda schema. The first 'verse' starts with 'six filty children' (bar 9) and the second with 'the offices' (bar 33). But it is important to note that the underpinning harmonic structures and the manner in which each of these verses starts and are subsequently constructed differs. While the first verse begins into the third beat of the bar and follows the E min, G, E min, D7 riff, the second verse actually starts with the harmonic material that precedes the opening verse, that is with the chord sequence found in measure 1–8. In other words, the opening harmonic sequence of the song is now integrated into the structure of the second verse. The first verse starts in a rather uncertain fashion but the second verse is more confident, with a growing sense of the rightness of the protagonist's voice. But there is another way to look at it. The first verse is technically a line longer or starts earlier than the second verse, which really has only two lines. So perhaps the arguments being made by the welfare officer are not holding up or are proving unsustainable or are dissipating the longer he goes on. Either way, the verses differ, eliding and causing confusion; seemingly the same but not the same really.

The 'chorus' starts, arguably, at bar 21 though it seems more fully fledged as a chorus from bar 25 – 'but you won't escape' – which seems to reach a logical conclusion four bars later, suggesting a closed unit on reaching the section 'because you live a breathe like one' (bar 28). But somewhat unexpectedly, it runs forward for another line wavering on the semi-quavers ('and the labour government'), climaxing on a grating tritone interval (D sharp – A) with an underpinning tonic chord of A min, which then moves back to chord IV for the second verse. The melodic contour of the (ostensible) chorus intoning slum mum (bars 26 and 46 respectively) with its downward, downbeat gesture, recalls a kind of derisive football chant, its long drawn out broad vowels inviting uncritical participation – 'slum mums, slum mums, slum mums'.

In its second iteration, from bar 41 (or really bar 45), the 'chorus' material, though for the most part the same, has a distinctly different character where it uses a B major chord to module up to C major, a half-step and harmonically illogical move, again underpinning the flawed 'logic' of the argument used by the welfare office. At this point the song moves into new terrain, into a kind of coda where the words are more slowly and deliberately rendered in a monotone, encouraging infanticide (bars 53–60), the I–IV chords dominating and the melodic materials moving in downward gestures, falling syllables, signifying termination.

In sum, there isn't a clean internal logic to the verse and the chorus, both of which change in each rendition and whose starting points are unclear. Undoubtedly, there is repetition of melodic lines present, but the overall song is actually quite difficult to sing, with is shift in tonal centres and variable word spacing, sometimes with syllables placed on long held notes, other times on rapid moving semi-quavers, changing, as Moore (2003: 43) notes, the 'verbal space' in terms of speed and intensity. Herein lies the emotional design where the song structure sets up a very interesting dialectic between *what* is being said (through the lyrics) as appearing to be reasonable, and *how* it is said (through the music), as betraying an illogical and emotional argument that is inconsistent, and additive, and rhythmically uneven, though a smooth voice tries to keep it all in check persuasively. The rhetoric powerfully and persuasively takes us along to what to all intents and purposes promises to be a logical conclusion – infanticide. This is boldly and calculatingly set within the texture of a IV–I plagal or 'Amen' chord – its religious connotations being brutally and deftly referenced here with great irony and ambiguity by Morrissey. The final moment of the coda hang, unresolved in terms of musical structure, a kind of McClary-esque 'feminine ending' that is followed by a guitar solo which mimics the screaming from the opening of the song as well as reproducing the wail of an ambulance. The song ends abruptly on the E minor chord, unresolved and terminated before its time, just like the mother and children. There is a strong structural suggestion of no escape, of being caught in a loop. Perhaps this gesture is meant to indicate the trap of the welfare system, but maybe the real trap is the discursive field in which this mother has limited agency.

And where is the 'slum mum' in all of this? Crucially, throughout the song we never get hear the woman's response. She has no voice here (unlike her prole counterpart in *Nineteen Eighty-Four*). The only place we get a glimpse of her subject-position is in the welfare officers patronizing comment about the 'slum mum' trying to hide her working-class voice with a higher status one that would belie her origins. The vocal line becomes a falsetto, leaping up sharply on the 'don't' of 'camouflage your accent, so that even you *don't* recognise it' (emphasis added), the welfare officer derisively imitating a false middle- or upper-class accent in the upward curve of the melody in measure 24, which reaches up as high as high G, the seventh note of the A minor scale (though the accidental F sharp signals a modulation to G, a different oppositional key). Not only is the slum mum, copper-fastened as deceptive, but also her overwrought emotionality, her histrionic shrillness performs very common gendered musical code for females.

Such a negotiated reading of the dominant or hegemonic codes or discourses (Hall, 1999, 2000[1997]), has the potential to evoke a more compassionate or understanding view of 'The Slum Mums' of this world. To borrow from Brackett (2000: 172), and interpolating the song under scrutiny here, 'the conditions of [The Slum Mums] production and reception exemplify many of the paradoxes between art and commerce, political integrity and financial practicality. We argue that in assuming the role of the welfare officer who taunts and blames the lone mother, Morrissey's envoicing/ventriloquism actually has the potential to force audiences to deal with their own prejudices (Rogan, 1993: 300). Further, as Keith Negus (1996: 220) writes (citing Lawrence Gossberg, 1992) 'music works "at the intersection of the body and emotions", and in doing so can generate "affective alliances" between people, which in turn can create the energy for social change that many have a direct impact on politics and culture'. The potential for song as social commentary to change our views, or, at the very least, reflect prevalent discourses, remains compelling.[21]

'The Slum Mums' today

When this song was first written, gendered and classed discourses surrounding welfare recipients were prevalent but in recent years this process has intensified. We are in agreement with Jensen (2014) who argues that what has become known as poverty porn has multiplied across the UK television landscape (as indeed is the case elsewhere), reinstating classification processes of moral worth and in the process 'produced "the welfare 'scrounger/skiver'", an abject figure whose existence seems to justify new forms of economic punishment and conditional welfare'. The widespread use of the Moral Underclass Discourse (Levitas, 2000) has seen the demonization of society's most vulnerable people become an endemic feature of contemporary political and popular discourse. In essence, 'the media, popular entertainment and the political establishment have gone out of their way to convince us that these are moral issues, an indiscipline that needs to be rectified' (Jones, 2011: 195). Discourses which talk of the 'spatialisation of whole areas of Britain' abound, implying that the slum mum is spreading 'her wayward ways generationally and infectiously through parenting (De Benedictis, 2012: 11–12). Indeed, former British Prime Minister David Cameron (cited in Jones, 2011: 77) champions an ideology in which mothers (in particular) are increasingly expected to take responsibility for engineering a way out of poverty and exclusion for themselves and their children (MacDonald et al, 2001 cited in Allen and Taylor, 2012: 1). Rather than framing women's poverty in terms of structural causes like inadequate child care and low wages, these discourses, which present the poor as undeserving of sympathy and public support, do little to improve public understanding of poverty and ultimately fuel anti-welfare sentiment (Gans, 1995). It is in this context that the work a song like 'The Slum Mums' does, in the current age of austerity, is therefore doubly important. It operates as a protest song in that it reminds us that we are making the same mistakes and falling back into the same poisonous rhetoric, while simultaneously showing us how easy it is to do just that and forget.

Blacking (1995: 35) may have asserted that 'music cannot instill a sense of fellowship' and that 'the best it can do is confirm the situation that already exists' but more recent work on somatic embodiment and music might argue otherwise. 'The Slum Mums' undoubtedly confirms, in stark terms, the prevalence of gendered and class discourses in relation to welfare mothers, but it also has the potential to dismantle commonly held prejudices. The song's surface simplicity belies a complex multimodal piece at work, enticing us to perform gendered, class disgust while simultaneously revealing to us, in shocking terms, just how easy it is to become complicit in an ideology and emotional narrative that can have dire consequences for real people. The shame resides not with the slum mum but with those in power and by exposing this, Morrissey reveals how manipulative this power is, effortlessly recreating this ugly discourse of gendered class disgust and creatively and musically harnessing it to fold back on itself to devastating effect.

Notes

1 Please see full transcription in Appendix 1.
2 As his band's musical director, Boorer, in particular, has been central to the establishment of the Morrissey sound.
3 This will depend, of course, on the manner in which a song has been recorded and how the various textures are foregrounded or submersed. For an extended discussion of this in relation to recorded popular music forms specifically, see Moore (2012). For a more extended discussion of the grain of the voice and the voice as sensuous/gendered, see Frith (1988) on 'playing with a different sex' and the voices of women.
4 A significant body of literature challenges these assertions (see, e.g. Nayak and Kehily, 2014, for an excellent overview).
5 See for example O'Flynn, Monaghan and Power for a discussion of the use of scapegoating as a deflective strategy in explaining the causes and impact of the financial crisis in Ireland.
6 See Devereux, Dillane and Power (2011) for a discussion of Morrissey fandom.
7 For further discussion see Dillane, Devereux and Power (2014) analysis on the song 'I Can Have Both' by Morrissey. Also see (1996) for an exploration of the 'fourth gender' and 'melodic contours'.
8 So too do an array of queer icons, most notably Oscar Wilde and James Dean. See Hawkins, 2009.

9 Copyright issues prevent us from printing the full lyric here, but they can be accessed at www.passionsjustlikemine.com, and a performance of the song (the performance that forms the basis for the music transcription we provide later), can be found at <https://www.youtube.com/watch?v=-LVYZ_m5_Ig>.

10 In the United Kingdom at that time New Labour was far more enthusiastic about the neoliberal agenda than even Thatcher dared to be (Byrne, 2005: 56 cited in Power, 2011: 110) In this regard, Morrissey further signaled his hostility to neoliberal policies with the lines 'I've been dreaming of a time when the English are sick to death of Labour and Tories' in 'Irish Blood, English Heart', which he released in May 2004.

11 An earlier Morrissey/Stephen Street song 'Interesting Drug' celebrated (or at the very least refused to condemn) the use of drugs by the underclass to escape the misery of their existence (see Power, Dillane and Devereux, 2012). The 'Slum Mums' is ostensibly far bleaker.

12 There is much evidence of this practice documented in British folk song. Gammon (2008) and Symonds (2004) both explore this particular gendered and classed topic in oral folk balladry, a form that feeds into British popular music more widely.

13 We are keenly aware that there is potential to misread the lyrics (particularly without the necessary cultural capital). Equally, a critique might be leveled that Morrissey is fetishizing poverty and the working class for his own financial gain, though this is not the conclusion we come to here.

14 As well as thinking about the voice as identified by its specific 'grain', there is another meaning at play here. A singer is often forced to sing 'against the grain' or contrary to expectation, by adapting and subverting traditions and expectations in creative and compelling ways. Moreover, the 'grain' of voice is a site of the 'dual production of language' (meaning) and 'of music' (Barthes, 1977: 181).

15 In terms of these party songs, Orwell (2003[1949]) devastatingly underscores the manner in which humans can be co-opted into rehearsing emotions that affect behaviours and practices, especially to towards others, often with serious consequences. Even Winton, with his ability to critique and understand the powerful somatic responses songs generate, would still find his body betraying him, allowing him to be manipulated by the strong physiological responses rhythm and pitch and sonority generated in him. We argue that 'The Slum Mums' has the capacity to act in the same way and that is the potency of its critique. While we do not make direct, causal links between the content of Orwell's book and Morrissey's 'The Slum Mums' (we do not have evidence Morrissey read Orwell, though we very much suspect he did), both Penguin Classic authors deal with the rhetoric of politicians in resonant ways. From our perspective, the allusion to *Nineteen*

Eighty-Four functions on multiple levels which undergirds our analysis and argument here about 'The Slum Mums'.

16 Also see Savage (2006) where the author shows that that age and ethnicity in particular, and gender, educational qualifications and occupational class, strongly condition taste for both musical genres and works.

17 Though Fox is specifically talking about American country music, his ideas are equally applicable here, particularly when married to approaches from Middleton (1990), Cook (1998) and Schuker (2001), with their respective neo-Marxist approaches to music scholarship.

18 For perspectives on gender in heavy metal music, see Walser's (1993) groundbreaking work in this area. Walser's work is also useful in the manner in which it shifts the focus squarely on the music, rather than emphasizing the lyrics.

19 A term attributed to Raymond Williams, 'structures of feelings' largely refers to the gap that emerges between official discourse and popular responses to such discourses (in relation to governance, policy, regulation), and so on. As such, a popular song can be viewed as, in itself, as a structure of feeling. Williams coined the phrase in 1954 and developed it in his 1961 publication (see Williams, 2001[1961]). That work has further significance in the context of this paper as it documents the rise of the popular press in Britain and made a significant contribution to the development of cultural studies which in turn has shaped popular music studies.

20 Morrissey's long-standing strategy of envoicing or acting as a ventriloquist has allowed him to adopt and explore a range of controversial positions and ultimately expose problematic discourses more effectively. He has, for example, used this device to expose racism ('Bengali in Platforms') and (Irish) religious institutional child abuse ('Children in Pieces').

21 There are a number of well-known contemporary popular culture treatments of the underclass, welfare benefit abuse, and stigmatization, such as the TV documentary series 'We All Pay Your Benefits', 'On Benefits and Proud', Benefits Britain 1949' and 'Benefit Street'.

References

Adorno, T. (2001 [1991]), *The Culture Industry: Selected Essays on Mass Culture.* J. M. Bernstein (ed.). London: Routledge.

Allen, K. (2009), *Ireland's Economic Crash: A Radical Agenda for Change.* Dublin: The Liffey Press.

Allen, K. and Taylor, Y. (2012), 'Placing Parenting, Locating Unrest: Failed Femininities, Troubled Mothers and Riotous Subjects', *Studies in the Maternal: Special Edition*

– *Austerity Parenting* 4(2): 1–25. <http://www.mamsie.bbk.ac.uk/articles/abstract/ 10.16995/sim.39/> [accessed 12 July 2016].

Barnes, C. and Power, M. (2012), 'Internalizing Discourses of Parental Blame: Voices from the Field', *Studies in the Maternal: Special Edition – Austerity Parenting* 4(2): 1– 12 <http://www.mamsie.bbk.ac.uk/back_issues/4_2/documents/BarnesPower_SiM_ 4(2).pdf> [accessed 12 July 2016].

Barthes, R. (1977), *Image, Music, Text*. Stephen Heath (trans.). New York: Hill and Want.

Bennett, T., Savage, M., Bortolaia Silva, E., Warde, A., Gayo-Cal, M. and Wright, D. (2009), *Culture, Class, Distinction*. Abingdon: Routledge.

Blacking, J. (1995), 'Expressing Human Experience through Music', in R. Byron (ed.) *Music, Culture and Experience: Selected Papers of John Blacking* Chicago: University of Chicago Press.

Bracewell, M. (2009), *England Is Mine: Poplife in Albion*. London: Faber and Faber.

Brackett, D. (2000), *Interpreting Popular Music*. Berkeley and London: University of California Press.

Bullock, H., Fraser Wyche, K. and Williams, W. (2001), 'Media Images of the Poor', *Journal of Social Issues* 57(2): 229–246.

Campbell, S. and Coulter, C. (eds) (2010), *Why Pamper Life's Complexities? Essays on The Smiths*. Manchester: Manchester University Press.

Cohen, S. (1972), *Folk Devils and Moral Panics: The Creation of the Mods and Rockers*. London: Martin Robertson & Co.

Cook, N. (1998), *Music: A Very Short Introduction*. Oxford: Oxford University Press.

Cooke, D. (1959), *The Language of Music*. Oxford: Oxford University Press.

De Benedictis, S. (2012), '"Feral" Parents: Austerity Parenting under Neoliberalism', *Studies in the Maternal: Special Edition – Austerity Parenting* 4(2): 1–21 <http:// www.mamsie.bbk.ac.uk/back_issues/4_2/documents/DeBenedictis_SiM_4(2)2012. pdf > [accessed 12 July 2016].

Devereux, E. (2006), 'Being Wild(e) About Morrissey', in M. Corcoran and M. Peillion (eds) *Uncertain Ireland*. Dublin: IPA.

Devereux, E. (2010), 'Heaven Knows We'll Soon Be Dust: Catholicism and Devotion in The Smiths', in C. Coulter and S. Campbell (eds) *Why Pamper Life's Complexities? Essays on The Smiths*, pp. 65–80. Manchester: Manchester University Press.

Devereux, E. (2009), 'I'm not the Man You Think I am: Authenticity, Ambiguity and the Cult of Morrissey', in E. Haverinen, U. Kovala and V. Rautavuoma (eds) *Cult, Community, Identity*, pp. 103–118. Finland: Research Center for Contemporary Culture of the University of Jyväskylä.

Devereux, E. and Hidalgo, M. (2015), 'Your Gonna Need Someone on Your Side: Morrissey's Latino/a and Chicano/a Fans', *Participations: Journal of Audience and Reception Studies* 12(2).

Devereux, E., Dillane, A. and Power, M. (eds) (2011), *Morrissey: Fandom, Representations and Identities*. Bristol: Intellect Books.

Dillane, A., Devereux, E. and Power, M. (2014), 'I Can Have Both: A Queer Reading of Morrissey', *Journal of European Popular Culture* 5(2): 149–163.

Finnegan, R. (2003), 'Music, Experience, and the Anthropology of Emotion', in M. Clayton, T. Herbert and R. Middleton (eds) *The Cultural Study of Music: A Critical Introduction*, pp.181–192. London and New York: Routledge.

Fox, A. (2004), *Real Country: Music and Language in Working-Class Culture*. Durham and London: Duke University Press.

Frith, S. (1998) *Music for Pleasure: Essays in the Sociology of Pop*. Cambridge: Polity Press.

Frith, S. and Goodwin, A. (eds) (1990), *On Record: Pop and the Written Word*. London: Routledge.

Gammon, V. (2008), *Desire, Drink and Death in English Folk and Vernacular Song, 1600–1900*. Aldershot, Hampshire, England , Burlington and VT: Ashgate.

Gans, H. (1995), *The War against The Poor: The Underclass and Antipoverty Policy*. New York: Basic Books.

Gillies, V. (2005), 'Raising the Meritocracy: Parenting and the Individualization of Social Class', *Sociology* 39(5): 835–852.

Goddard, S. (2009), *Mozipedia: The Encyclopedia of Morrissey and The Smiths*. London: Ebury Press.

Golding, P. and Middleton, S. (1982), *Images of Welfare: Press and Public Attitudes to Poverty*. Oxford: Martin Robertson.

Gutstein, D. (2012), 'Generational Conflict: Neo-liberalizm's New Bait-and-Switch Ploy', *Rabble*. <http://rabble.ca/blogs/bloggers/donald-gutstein/2012/02/generational-conflict-neoliberalism%E2%80%99s-new-bait-and-switch-plo> [accessed 12 July 2016].

Hall, S. (1999), 'Encoding, Decoding', in Simon During (ed.) *The Cultural Studies Reader*, 2nd edition, pp. 507–517. New York: Routledge.

Hanslick, E. (1995 [1974]), *The Beautiful in Music: A Contribution to the Revisal of Musical Aesthetics*, 7th edition. Gustav Cohen (trans. and rev.). New York: Da Capo Press.

Hawkins, S. (2009), *The Great British Pop Dandy: Masculinity, Popular Music and Culture*. Farnham: Ashgate.

Hayward, K. and Yar, M. (2006), 'The "Chav" Phenomenon: Consumption, Media and the Construction of a New Underclass', *Crime Media Culture* 2(1): 9–28.

Hopps, G. (2009), *Morrissey: The Pageant of His Bleeding Heart*. London and New York: Continuum.

Jensen, T. (2012), 'Tough Love in Tough Times', *Studies in the Maternal: Special Edition –Austerity Parenting* 4(2): 1–26 <http://www.mamsie.bbk.ac.uk/back_issues/4_2/documents/Jensen_SiM_4(2)2012.pdf> [accessed 12 July 2016].

Jensen, T. (2014) (2014) 'Skivers/Strivers and the Classificatory Politics of Welfare Reform', *Critical Perspectives on Youth, Community and Urban Regeneration* Seminar Series. University of Limerick, Limerick. 9 April.

Jones, O. (2011), *Chavs: The Demonization of the Working Class*. London: Verso.

Juslin, P. and Sloboda, J. (2003), *Music and Emotion: Theory and Research*. Oxford: Oxford University Press.

Law, A. (2006), 'Hatred and Respect: The Class Shame of Ned "Humour"', *Variant* 25: 28–30.

Lens, V. (2002), 'Public Voices and Public Policy: Changing the Societal Discourse on Welfare', *Journal of Sociology and Social Welfare* 29(1): 137–154.

Levitas, R. (2000), 'What Is Social Exclusion?', in D.Gordon and P. Townsend (eds) *Breadline Europe*, pp. 357–364. Bristol: The Policy Press.

Levitas, R. (2003), 'The Idea of Social Inclusion', *2003 Social Inclusion Research Conference Ottawa* 27–28 March, <http://www.ccsd.ca/events/inclusion/chapters/rlevitas.htm> [accessed 12 July 2016]

Martino, P. (2007), 'I am a Living Sign: A Semiotic Reading of Morrissey', *International Journal of Applied Semiotics* 6(1): 103–119.

McClary, S. (2000), *Conventional Wisdom*. Berkeley: University of California Press.

McClary, S. (2002[1991]), *Feminine Endings: Music, Gender, & Sexuality*, 2nd edition. Minneapolis: University of Minnesota Press.

Middleton, R. (1990), *Studying Popular Music*. Milton Keynes: Open University Press.

Moore, A. F. (ed.) (2003), *Analyzing Popular Music*. Cambridge: Cambridge University Press.

Moore, A. F. (2012), *Song Means: Analysing and Interpreting Recorded Popular Song*. Farnham: Ashgate.

Morris, L. (1994), *Dangerous Classes: The Underclass and Social Citizenship*. London: Routledge.

Morrissey, S. (2015), *List of the Lost*. London: Penguin.

Nayak, A. and Kehily, M. J. (2014), '"Chavs, Chavettes and Pramface Girls": Teenage Mothers, Marginalized Young Men and the Management of Stigma', *Journal of Youth Studies* 17(10): 1330–1345.

Negus, K. (1996), *Popular Music in Theory*. Cambridge: Polity Press.

Norton, D. (2005), *Emotional Design: Why We Love (or Hate) Everyday Things*. New York: Basic.

O'Flynn, M., Monaghan, L. and Power, M. (2014), 'Scapegoating During a Time of Crisis: A Critique of Post-Celtic Tiger Ireland', *Sociology* 48(5): 921–937.

Ortony, A., Norman, D. A. and Revelle, W. (2004), 'The Role of Affect and Proto-affect in Effective Functioning', in J. M. Fellous and M. A. Arbib (eds) *Who Needs Emotions? The Brain Meets the Machine*, pp. 173–202. New York: Oxford University Press.

Orwell, G. (2003[1949]), *Nineteen Eighty-Four*. New York: Plume.

Power, M. (2011), '"The Teenage Dad" and "Slum Mums" Are "Just Certain People I Know": Counter Hegemonic Representations of the Working / Under Class in the Works of Morrissey', in E. Devereux A. Dillane and M. Power (eds) *Morrissey: Fandom, Representations and Identities*, pp. 95–118. Bristol: Intellect Books.

Power, M., Dillane, A. and Devereux, E. (2012), 'A Push and a Shove and the Land Is Ours: Morrissey's Counter-Hegemonic Stance(s) on Social Class', *Critical Discourse Studies* 9(4): 375–392.

Power, M. Dillane, A. and Devereux, E. (2015), '"I Sing Out to the Youth of the Slums": Morrissey and Class Disgust', *Popular Music and Society*, 1–6 DOI: 10.1080/03007766.2015.1072871.

Renynolds, S. and Press, J. (1995), *The Sex Revolts: Gender, Rebellion and Rock 'n' Roll*. Cambridge, MA: Harvard University Press.

Rogan, J. (1993), *Morrissey & Marr: The Severed Alliance*. London: Omnibus Press.

Savage, M. (2006), 'The Musical Field', *Cultural Trends* 15(2–3): 159–174. <http://dx.doi.org/10.1080/09548960600712975>.

Schuker, R. (2001), *Understanding Popular Music*, 2nd edition. London and New York: Routledge.

Shusterman, R. (2008), *Body Consciousness: A Philosophy of Mindfulness and Somaaesthetics*. New York: Cambridge University Press.

Skeggs, B. (2005), 'The Making of Class and Gender through Visual Moral Subject Formation', *Sociology* 39(5): 965–982.

Skeggs, B. (2004), *Class, Self, Culture*. London: Routledge.

Skeggs, B., (1997), *Formations of Class and Gender: Becoming Respectable*. London: Sage.

Symonds, D. A. (2004), *Women, Ballads, and Infanticide in Early Modern Scotland*. State College: Penn State University Press.

Tyler, I. (2008), '"Chav Mum Chav Scum" Class disgust in contemporary Britain', *Feminist Media Studies* 8(1): 17–34.

Tyler, I. (2011), *Revolting Subjects*. London: Zed Books.

Walser, R. (1993), *Running with the Devil: Power, Gender and Madness in Heavy Metal Music*. Hanover, NH: University Press of New England.

Whitely, S. (2005), *Too Much Too Young: Popular Music, Age and Gender*. London: Routledge.

Williams, R. (2001 [1961]), *The Long Revolution*. Calgary: Broadview Press.

Wilson, H. and Huntington, A. (2005), 'Deviant (M)others: The Construction of Teenage Motherhood in Contemporary Discourse', *Journal of Social Policy* 35(10): 59–76.

Wood H. and Skeggs, B. (2008), 'Spectacular Morality: Reality Television, Individualization and the Re-making of the Working Class', in D. Hesmondhalgh and J. Toynbee (eds). *The Media and Social Theory*, pp. 177–193. London: Routledge.

Zuberi, N. (2001), *Sounds English: Transnational Popular Music*, Urbana: University of Illinois Press.

4

Recontextualization and Fascist Music

John E. Richardson

Introduction

The vast majority of work examining identity and politics in musicology, and in popular music studies in particular, presumes and sometimes explicitly argues that music is personally and socially therapeutic – that since music enacts social identities it is a force for good, particularly in relation to marginalized groups. This chapter brings together two areas of critical examination: the sociological analysis of fascist music; and the concept 'recontextualization', developed in discourse analytic literature, wherein the contents of one text reappear in another text. Meanings are formed in use; and so, through this process of 'textual borrowing', (partly) new meanings are produced. This chapter examines three ways in which this occurs in fascist song and music – through appropriation; through interpolation; and through ideological realignment – and will explore the functions that this, and the performance of song and music more generally, serves to fascist cultural projects.

Music, politics, identity

This chapter is, in a general sense, interested in exploring the ways that music can contribute to inegalitarianism and inequality, and to individual and collective identities that orientate towards these political goals. However, the vast majority of work examining identity and politics in musicology, and in popular music studies in particular, presumes and sometimes explicitly argues that music is 'personally and socially therapeutic' (Johnson and Cloonan, 2009: 1). In his conclusion to the book *The Sociology of Rock*, for example, Frith (1978: 209) argued that rock 'will remain fun and the source of. . . power and joy'. Cross (as cited in McKerrell 2015) has argued that music itself may have evolved to enable social cohesion: 'Music as a communicative medium, is likely to have a significant role in minimising within-group conflict or, to put it another way, in collaboratively establishing a degree of social equilibrium' (Cross in McKerrell, 2015: 4).

Equally, there is a well-established literature on music and politics, which examines music's political power – the ways in which it can inspire individuals and movements, give voice to minority voices and call for emancipatory change (Garofalo, 1992; Frith and Street, 1992; Street, 1988, 2012; Billig, 2000; Brown, 2008). Pedelty and Weglarz (2013: xi) summarize this consensus in the literature as follows: 'given the right historical circumstances, cultural conditions, and aesthetic qualities, popular music can help bring people together to form more effective political communities'. Here too, the predominant narrative is one of positivity. That even when song and music are instrumental in articulating, representing or contesting relations of power, music plays a beneficial role in, inter alia, articulating identities, building groups and communities, in producing pleasure, and in resisting alienation, conformity and capitalism (Denselow, 1989). Pedelty and Weglarz (2013: xiii) state that their edited collection on political rock music 'is about that rare part of the popular music world where musicians, fans, and critics operate in the belief music can do more than express teen angst, sell mini vans, or evoke nostalgia'. All 11 chapters in their edited collection examine left-liberal political artists – or, 'the musicians who move *us*' (xiv, emphasis added), and this personal deictic is vital in understanding the orientation of their book. Although they acknowledge this limitation and justify their editorial choice in two ways – that 'politicized rock has been much more connected to the Left than the Right' and that 'in comparison to mainstream songs extolling the virtues of parties, sex, romance, and conspicuous consumption' Right-Wing rock 'barely registers at all' (Ibid.) – one is left with a very definite sense of academics writing about their own record collections.

I should point out that I value the contribution of the publications cited above; I also agree with many of their claims. I agree that music and song inevitably invoke, interpolate and index individual and collective identities (Campbell, 2010; Slobin, 1993). Such ideational and interpersonal functions of music and song are always implicitly political (in the sense that 'the personal is political') and, when the collective identities invoked articulate hierarchies, inequalities and power struggle, music can be explicitly political too (Garofalo, 1992; Slobin, 1996). Such political/musical interventions do frequently concern struggles for rights and recognition, and in this area the research literature is sizable and sophisticated. Such analysis, again, tends to assume and sometimes to specifically argue that music is fundamental to human life and that music's capacity to build community is an unquestioned good. As Marie Korpe (2004: ix) puts it, 'when music is banned, the very soul of a culture is being strangled'.

However, there are a number of ways in which power can be contested, and a number of political projects to which music can be functionalized. When Blecha (2004: 137) describes political rock music positively, as songs that 'dare to question authority', I immediately think: which authorities are we talking about? What questions are being asked? And with what extremity are these questions posed? What if the musical culture we are examining is orientated towards the *denial* of human rights? Should a musical culture that resists egalitarian principles, encourages prejudice and, arguably, incites violence against individuals and communities be deemed inferior or objectionable? Should this stand unopposed? As Johnson and Cloonan (2009: 4) point out, ethnomusicology and popular music studies only infrequently recognize that 'every time music is used to demarcate the territory of self or community, it is incipiently being used to invade, marginalize or obliterate that of other individuals or groups'. The degree of invasion and marginalization differs between songs, scenes and (sub)cultures; but the demarcation of Self and Other, and the roles projected onto these collective identities, are entailed whenever music speaks to the social and cultural (Bohlman, 2003).

Scholars are now starting to consider the roles that music and song play in articulating exclusivist (or *bigoted*) collective identities and giving succour to inegalitarian political projects (McKerrell, 2012). Within conventional musicology there is a well-established literature on nationalism and music and how music 'acquired the potential to articulate nationalism by representing place' (Bohlman, 2003: 50). 'National peoples' were taken to 'give voice' to the nation through music and song (cf. Herder, 1778), particularly in folk song, which 'came to be venerated as the spontaneous expression of the national soul' (Grout, 1960: 497–498). This process of 'finding' (inventing) national music traditions frequently went hand-in-hand with the 'exoticization' and 'racialization' of music associated with national others (cf. Piotrowska, 2013). In ethnomusicology, there is also a small but growing literature on music and conflict (Pettan, 1998, 2010; Grant and Stone-Davis, 2013), and particularly how song and music participate in overt and covert forms of violence (Johnson and Cloonan, 2009; Gray, 2010; O'Connell and Castelo-Branco, 2010; Fast and Pegley, 2012). In popular music studies, Grossberg (1983) has argued against the presupposed idea that rock is inherently resistant, suggesting that in addition to political opposition, rock can also adopt alternative, independent and co-opted political viewpoints. Most recently, Shekhovtsov has written extensively on White power music across Europe (Shekhovtsov, 2009, 2013a; Shekhovtsov and Jackson, 2012), and edited a special issue for Patterns of Prejudice on *Music and the Other*, which argued that 'music has played an increasingly prominent role in constructing national identities and promoting various types of national projects' (Shekhovtsov, 2013b: 330). Together, these works constitute a significant contribution to understanding the roles that musical transactions can play in social conflict and power abuse.

Fascist music, fascist movement

Music has formed part of the artistic and cultural projects of virtually every European extreme-right party and movement (see Lowles and Silver, 1998; Shekhovtsov and Jackson, 2012; Shekhovtsov, 2013a). The European fascist movements that grew from the 1920s used the arts to help foster their moral and cultural order (Kater, 1992, 1997; Steinweis, 1993; Etlin, 2002; Griffin, 2004; Hirsch, 2010). In their magisterial edited collection on music and Francoism, Pérez Zalduondo and Gan Quesada (2013) examine 'the many ways in which, throughout more than forty years of Francoist rule, music and musicians, musical thinking and practices, both individual and collective, became linked to the society and ideology of the dictatorship' (p. ix). Their resulting book, examining music, ideology and politics in Franco-era artistic culture, is not merely an exemplary study of the relationships between music and power; through making a case for the central importance of music in social and political life, it also makes a crucial contribution to historiography of twentieth-century Spain.

In setting out to achieve their political project, British fascists are motivated by a number of assumptions and commitments that draw directly on Herder's concept of 'nationalbildung' and an accompanying powerful line of racial nationalism inherited from the late eighteenth century. Central of these is that 'the state of the arts was a direct expression of the "greatness" of the nation' (Griffin, 2004: 45). And, just as great art is assumed to be a manifestation of 'the national genius' or 'the essential spirit of the people', so social and cultural pathology is revealed through the production and especially the popularity of so-called degenerate art (Griffin, 2004: 46). In response, fascists aim 'to reverse this deplorable state of cultural collapse' (Ibid.), using 'music to underpin party mobilization strategies, to anchor choreographed set-pieces like meetings and marches, and to reinforce "collectives of emotion" among participants as well as unaligned spectators' (Macklin, 2013: 430). As an author writing in the British Union of Fascists' newspaper *Blackshirt* put it, 'Fascism will sweep away that cult of ugliness and distortion in art, music and literature which is the product of neurotic post-war minds' (Randall, 1934: 1).

Potter's (1998) study of Nazi Musicology shows it gradually acquiesced, and was implicated in, the radicalization of German cultural life. In 1933 Joseph Goebbels established the Reich Culture Chamber (Reichskulturkammer; RKK) with sections responsible for the different arts. There was a section especially for music, because Goebbels viewed music as a primary way to communicate directly with the people (Potter, 1998; Etlin, 2002). As he put it:

> Music affects the heart and emotions more than the intellect. Where then could the heart of a nation beat stronger than in the huge masses, in which the heart of a nation has found its true home? (Goebbels cited in Hirsch, 2010: 5)

There was the intention that 'good German music' would be promoted through-out the Reich, in schools, through the Hitler Youth, through social and leisure Nazi organizations such as Kraft durch Freude ('Strength through Joy') and at Party Rallies. Soldiers too were encouraged to participate in collective singing and music; many special soldiers' song books were published and such songs were participants in 'the cultural work of persecution and genocide' (Bohlman, 2003: 53). As Bohlman points out: 'The very horror of the Holocaust is amplified by the recognition that music was, in fact, omnipresent. Music mobilized the fascism and racism of the Nazis' (Ibid.).

While all fascist music is intended with this goal of a fascist political-cultural pseudo-revolution in mind (Bertola, 2013), the manner in which such a goal is encoded in music outputs varies according to time, place and the relation of the fascist movement to wider subcultural groups. Songs were written and sung by fascist parties and movements after World War II and through the 1960s, though the genre and delivery were very similar to the pre-war tradition. The largest far-right musical movement has for a long time been the Skinhead scene (Lowles and Silver, 1998; Shaffer, 2013). The Skinhead subculture originally developed in the 1960s listening to ska, rocksteady and early reggae, and was influenced by Jamaican rude boys. It was a working-class subculture, some of its biggest stars were Black, and the scene was racially mixed. The subculture died back, only to be reborn in the mid- to late-1970s with a radically different constituency and (political) alignment, having been infiltrated and gradually taken over by National Front (NF) supporters.

In 1979, the NF launched 'Rock Against Communism' to 'fight back against left-wingers and anti-British traitors in the music press' with 'concerts, road-shows and tours' (*Bulldog*, no. 14, March 1979). Initially short-lived, due to the collapse of the NF following the 1979 General Election, 'Rock Against Communism' was relaunched in 1983. The key to its revival 'was having Skrewdriver, a skinhead band that broke up in 1978, to reunite... the National Front established White Noise Records to release music that mainstream companies would not, and its first release was Skrewdriver's White Power EP, quickly selling out of its first pressing' (Shaffer, 2015: 143). Defined by racism and dominated by a new musical genre – *Oi* – that offered a stripped down, simplified version of punk, 'the NF's message of "whiteness" was spread to radicals in other countries through music' (Ibid.). Bands such as Skrewdriver and Brutal Attack used the visceral energy of punk in combination with openly White-supremacist and National Socialist lyrics. Their music, and that of other groups, thrived in the 'White Noise' racist subculture, through 'not simply providing texts for complaints about minorities competing for employment, but also instigating violence and memorializing it in forms eerily consistent with the century of unimaginable destruction' (Schwarz, 1997; Bohlman, 2003: 54).

However, this musical genre, and musical subculture, did not draw universal approval from fascists in the United Kingdom. For example, Colin Jordan, the unrepentant father of British National-Socialism, argued that this musical genre was the *opposite* of the vision promoted in fascist ideology:

> National-Socialism's pursuit of good order... pertains to every aspect of life, including all the arts... National-Socialism seeks a reflective *harmony* in all the affairs of man. It seeks this good order in, for example, a just and efficient eco-nomic structure, and sees it in good music which by definition is *harmonious*. In contrast to and in conflict with this good music of National-Socialism is the *discordant* din which skinheads delight in. Such cacophony... is the authentic death sound of Democracy. (Jordan, 1995: 11, emphases added)

Accordingly, National-Socialism seeks harmony in music as part of its project to bring 'harmony' to life. In contrast, discord in music is taken to be evidence of social degeneracy and decay which, in turn, are symptomatic of democracy. Such multimodal analysis – commenting on the social and ideological signifi-cance of tonality, harmonics and distortion – demonstrates not only the sig-nificance of music and musical scenes to fascist political projects, but also that fascists themselves are aware of its importance.

Recontextualization

My analysis of fascism, in general, focuses on continuities and change in fascist discourse since the 1920s and the dialectical relations to wider social and political life (Richardson, 2013, 2015). In relation to fascist music and song, that means relating the music written, recorded and performed at particular points in time to the preoccupations and cultural affordances of that particular period. The concept of recontextualization gives us some analytic traction, allowing us to consider this tension between continuity and change in discourse, and how they can be traced intertextually.

Intertextuality refers to the linkage of texts to other texts, both in the past and in the present. Such links can be established in different ways: through a specific reference to another text by name; by referring to the contents of another text; through reference to the same events as another text; or through the reappearance of a text's contents in another text. The latter process is labelled *recontextualization*. Following Reisigl and Wodak (2001, 2009), if a textual element – a speech, a quote, a phrase and so on – is taken from a specific context we argue it is *de*contextualized; when this same element is inserted into a new context, we argue it is *re*contextualized. Meanings are formed in use and so, through this process of 'textual borrowing', (partly) new meanings are produced. As van Leeuwen and Wodak (1999: 96) have argued, 'Recontextualization always involves transformation, and what exactly gets transformed depends on the interests, goals and values of the context into which the practice is recontextualized.' There are four principal transformations employed in recontextualization: deletion; addition; rearrangement; and substitution. Taking each in turn: during de- and recontextualization of texts (and parts of texts), parts of these texts can be deleted (and the question, of course, is *what* is taken out and the rhetorical/discursive implications of this). Second, new elements can be put in, and van Leeuwen and Wodak (1999) argue that the most important additions during recontextualization are reaction, purposes and legitimations, since these all shift the significance of textual elements. Third, textual elements may be rearranged, or scattered throughout the new text. And finally, elements can be substituted, where a discursive choice is made to replace one element with an alternative from the range of possible choices (whether making the element more abstract or more concrete, more general or specific, mitigated or intensified, and so on).

Recontextualization is not limited to linguistic texts – images, songs and music can also be *de*- and *re*contextualized across successive texts and across

Table 4.1 Approaches and transformations in fascist musical recontextualization

	Addition	Deletion	Substitution	Rearrangement	Does recontextual-ization subvert connoted meanings?
Textual appropriation	no	no	no	no	yes
'Cover version'	rarely	rarely	yes	yes	not usually
Ideological realignment	rarely	rarely	yes	yes	yes
Interpolation	sometimes	sometimes	yes	yes	not usually

time. Indeed, music and song are particularly interesting to consider in relation to recontextualization, given the ways that lyrics, themes, motifs, melodies and complete songs can be reworked, remixed and rerecorded by successive composers (see Geary, 2014; Young, 2011). Fans of a particular song – whether amateur or professional – can signal their admiration through recontextualization; they can add elements of an old composition to a new one, whether through sampling, interpolation ('quotation' of musical content) or appropriation of thematic or structural aspects of a composition. Or else they can record a cover version of a song where the arrangement of the original recording – as a four-piece band or a full orchestra – is substituted for the fan simply singing into their laptop mic accompanied only by an acoustic guitar. YouTube is awash with such fan tribute recordings. Musical substitutions may involve rearranging a song in a particular way, changing the genre, changing the harmonics (monophonic to polyphonic, or vice versa), changing instrumentation or arrangement, changing the sex of the singer, and so on.

In this chapter, I will examine four ways that recontextualization occurs in fascist song and music: as textual appropriation; interpolation; cover version; and in ideologically realigned recording. These four approaches to recontextualization draw variously on the four principal transformations (deletion, addition, rearrangement and substitution) in different combinations. I have mapped these out in Table 4.1, above.

The remainder of the chapter will not provide extensive itemization of music and song that show widespread quantified evidence of appropriation, interpolation, cover version and ideological realignment. The numeric frequency of cultural phenomena is not the only, or even the most important, measure of discursive consequence; a single text, a single speech, a single image can (and do) send out waves of signification, that reverberate in and through (sub)cultural and social space. Accordingly, I will discuss qualitative instances of recontextualization of song and music, and explore the functions that they play in fascist cultural projects.

Recontextualization, 1: textual appropriation

In cases of what I am referring to as textual appropriation, a whole song is taken and incorporated into the fascist cultural project, either through material reproduction or through performance. In appropriating – and so recontextualizing – a song in this way, the party or movement attempts to reconfigure the connoted meanings of the song. Textual appropriation of this kind provides a clear instance of the maxim of discourse analysis that there is 'no meaning outside of context', and that the meaning of an utterance (or song, or whatever) is dialectically related to contexts of use. Imagine the fascist NF singing the British National Anthem, and you gain a sense of how this works in practice – the evocation of nationhood and the frequent use of the possessive 'Our' in the anthem ('Our Queen' and so on) gives us sense to pause, given the exclusive (racist) way that the NF defines who counts as British. And that's before we consider the second (or in some versions, third) verse of the National Anthem, which calls on God to 'Scatter her enemies, and make them fall'. McKerrell (2015) recently analysed a very similar discursive phenomenon, wherein the jingoistic-but-not-sectarian song 'Rule Britannia' was appropriated by Rangers football fans for sectarian political ends. McKerrell (2015: 1) shows that the way the song appears in a YouTube video – blended with Unionist flags, sectarian slurs and 'the "tonal gravity" of Rule Britannia where emphatic rhythm and musical harmonies act together in creating a very strong sense of Self positioned in opposition to an essentialised and simplistic Other' – means it emerges as sectarian.

In the 1970s, the NF produced a songbook that is interesting to consider in relation to these issues. The songbook itself is actually little more than a lyric book – there is no musical notation accompanying the lyrics, nor any indication of key, time signature or melody. This is itself quite interesting, and speaks to one of two possibilities: either the status of the songs was so well established, and their music was so well known, that the producers of the booklet felt they could dispense with any sheet music; *or*, that the function of the booklet was less about providing the party with a songbook to be used in collective singing, and more about implicitly claiming the songs as their own. The 14 songs in the songbook include traditional patriotic/jingoistic songs ('Rule Britannia', 'Land of Hope and Glory'), rousing hymns particularly associated with the Methodist tradition ('Battle Hymn of the Republic', 'Jerusalem'), marching songs associated with particular regiments ('Men of Harlech', 'Hearts of Oak'), and explicitly political songs of both paramilitary organizations in the North of Ireland and the NF. The choice to include 'Men of Harlech', in particular, shows the ways that songs can acquire additional implicit meanings through their incorporation in popular culture. Apparently written to commemorate the seven-year siege of Harlech Castle (1461–1468), the song is something of an unofficial anthem in Wales, associated with the country's determination to retain its identity *vis-a-vis* the English Other. However a version of the song, with rewritten lyrics, was also included in the film *Zulu* (1960). In this particular scene, the Zulu warriors are singing an (un-subtitled) 'war song'; panning over images of British soldiers, one retorts 'they've got a very good bass section, but no top tenors'; he then starts singing 'Men of Harlech' in defiant reply, and is gradually joined in chorus by the other soldiers.[1] So starts a call and response between the wild, loincloth wearing, spear-waving (Black) Zulus with their unintelligible shouting and chanting, and the uniformed, gun-holding (White) soldiers, singing in unison and perfect harmony. It may be this racialized scene – and its radical binary representation of Black/uncivilized vs White/civilized – that the NF wished to conjure up through the inclusion of the song in the songbook.

The book contains the lyrics of 'The National Front Calls', placed opposite those of the Ulster Defence Association song 'We'll fight in the Bogside' and, in so doing, indexes the way they share the same verse-chorus structure and are sung to the same tune. And this introduces a further way that we can examine some of the meanings inscribed into this booklet beyond the specific meanings of the lyrical content of each song: we can consider the co-textual intertextual relations established between songs, particularly those placed side-by-side. In other words, we can examine the meanings that are established through the choice to place two songs opposite each other on two-page spreads. I have recreated the contents of the songbook, and layout of the particular songs, in Table 4.2.

It is clear that the songs are being grouped together: the Victorian jingoism of 'Rule Britannia' and 'Land of Hope and Glory '; the two regimental songs 'Men of Harlech' and 'Hearts of Oak'; the two hymns 'Battle Hymn of the Republic' and 'Jerusalem'; and so on. To take two examples: pages 10–11 position the Unionist/Orangeman marching song 'The Sash my Father Wore' (which, among other things, celebrates the victory of William of Orange over King Charles II)

Table 4.2 Contents of the National Front songbook (n.d.)

Page		
1	[Cover piece]	
2–3	'Rule Britannia'	'Land of Hope and Glory'
4–5	'Men of Harlech'	'Hearts of Oak'
5–7	'Battle Hymn of the Republic'	'Jerusalem'
8–9 [centre pages]	'We'll fight in the Bogside'	'The National Front Calls'
10–11	'Here Lies a Soldier'	'The Sash my Father Wore'
12–13	'England Belongs to Me'	'Ye Mariners of England'
14–15	'Scarborough Fair'	'The National Anthem'
16	[Blank]	

opposite the explicitly pro-Ulster Volunteer Force (UVF) anthem, 'Here Lies a Soldier'. The UVF is a loyalist paramilitary organization; so placing these two songs opposite each other sets up a relation between the two, and helps pull the meanings of 'The Sash' more towards the violent, hardline form of Unionism espoused by organizations like the UVF. The songbook included the National Anthem but included it opposite the traditional ballad 'Scarborough Fair'. This unusual choice sets up an interesting co-textual relationship between the two songs – the ballad projecting a kind of traditional, folksy pastoralism onto the National Anthem; and, simultaneously, the National Anthem *nationalizing* the ballad, not only claiming it as part of an explicitly national musical tradition but also, in so doing, instilling it with a sense of patriotism obviously absent from the lyrics of the song itself.

Textual appropriation like this is frequently opposed, given that other individuals and groups tend to have a stake in ensuring that the connoted meanings of music and song (and sometimes *genre*, see Spracklen, 2015) remain compatible with their own political position. In 2009, for example, the British National Party (BNP) were selling a CD through their online shop. Entitled *A Place called England*, this was a compilation CD containing the music of Elgar and Vera Lynn, as well as contemporary British folk musicians such as John Spiers, Jon Boden and Steve Knightley. They had recorded songs for an album they were told would be sold through gift shops, and so were extremely upset to find that it was also being sold by the BNP to raise money for the party. Steve Knightley's song 'Roots' was featured on the CD, and it was, he argued, 'a betrayal of your invention' to see the BNP profiting in this way.[2] Jon Boden made a point specifically in relation to recontextualization: 'The CD was titled "a place called

England"', he said. 'But suddenly when you see it on the BNP's website, it takes on a darker significance that you never imagined.' The BNP went on selling the CD, but the event led to the establishment of the organization of 'Folk Against Fascism', launched at the Sidmouth Folk Festival in 2009; Jon Boden continues to play his fiddle with anti-BNP stickers stuck to it, to make his position clear.

Recontextualization, 2: cover versions and ideological realignments

As is well known, a *cover version* is a new performance or recording of a previously recorded song, by someone other than the original artist. A cover version frequently indicates esteem for either the original song or, especially in the case of fascist song, the original artist and their political motivation. Cover versions rework original compositions, principally through substitution and rearrangement. For example, Skrewdriver's acoustic ballad 'The Snow Fell' – which celebrates (and mourns) the deaths of German Wehrmacht soldiers on the eastern front during World War II – has been rerecorded by literally hundreds of amateur and (semi-)professional musicians, including the bands Rahowa, Sleipnir, Kolovrat, Ravensbrook, The Voice, Prussian Blue and the Swedish singer Saga. Whilst most cover versions reproduce the acoustic, 'singer-songwriter', arrangement of the original, others – such as the Noisecore version by 'DJ Panzerfaust and DJ Retaliator' (which, at points, samples Saga's cover version of the track) – are more radical reworkings. Cover versions are recorded and performed for a variety of reasons. For many of the young women who have recorded selfie-videos of them singing 'The Snow Fell', and uploaded these to YouTube (and young women singing this particular Skrewdriver song *vastly* outnumber men), the act appears to accomplish two things: it speaks to their political identity, and it provides an opportunity, in the words of 'angrygirl92', to give people 'a history lesson' about the Nazis and Stalingrad in accordance with their mythological fascist narrative of events in the 1940s.[3]

Cover versions exist in which music (or a musical 'quotation') is recontextualized in such a way that the meanings of the original are undermined or subverted. I refer to such cover versions as examples of 'ideological realignment'. Ideological realignment works in a similar way to a parody, except without the comedic intent/effect. In one particularly interesting case, Ian Stuart Donaldson, the lead singer of Skrewdriver, recorded several versions of 'Tomorrow Belongs to Me', which was written by John Kander and Fred Ebb for the musical *Cabaret*.

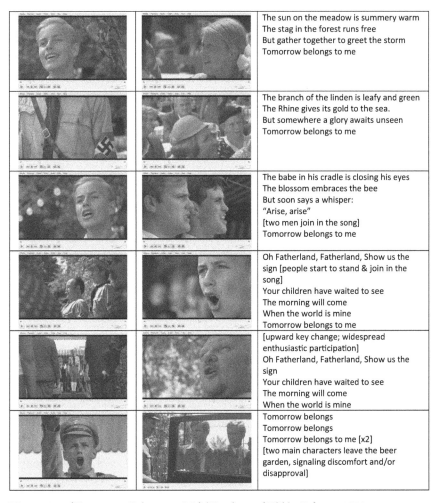

The sun on the meadow is summery warm
The stag in the forest runs free
But gather together to greet the storm
Tomorrow belongs to me

The branch of the linden is leafy and green
The Rhine gives its gold to the sea.
But somewhere a glory awaits unseen
Tomorrow belongs to me

The babe in his cradle is closing his eyes
The blossom embraces the bee
But soon says a whisper:
"Arise, arise"
[two men join in the song]
Tomorrow belongs to me

Oh Fatherland, Fatherland, Show us the sign [people start to stand & join in the song]
Your children have waited to see
The morning will come
When the world is mine
Tomorrow belongs to me

[upward key change; widespread enthusiastic participation]
Oh Fatherland, Fatherland, Show us the sign
Your children have waited to see
The morning will come
When the world is mine

Tomorrow belongs
Tomorrow belongs
Tomorrow belongs to me [x2]
[two main characters leave the beer garden, signaling discomfort and/or disapproval]

Figure 4.1. 'Tomorrow Belongs to Me' (Kander and Ebb), *Cabaret*, 1974

He recorded the song under the name of bands Skrewdriver and The Klansmen, as well as part of his double act Ian Stuart and Stigger; the Swedish White-supremacist singer Saga also recorded two versions of the song – and this despite it being written in *criticism* of Nazism, by two homosexual Jewish Americans. In the film version of *Cabaret* (1974), the song features in a scene set in a beer garden; a member of Nazi Youth spontaneously starts singing the song and the crowd gradually joins in, getting more exuberant as the song progresses; at the crescendo of the song, following an upward key change, the boy and others give the Nazi salute. I reproduce images of this scene in the sequence In Figure 4.1, above (the images on each row should be read from left to right).

We should note that there is nothing explicitly prejudicial or extremist in the lyrics of the song. Certainly, the lyrics evoke nationalist Germanic themes, of a bucolic pastoral paradise and an imminent future in which the Fatherland will arise and enjoy glory. But the mood of the song, whilst a little jingoistic, is nevertheless non-exclusionary. The political meaning of the scene, therefore, is created in context. First, through multimodal collocation in the scene itself where, at the start of the second verse ('The branch of the linden is leafy and green.') the camera pans down to reveal the boy's Swastika armband; second, it relies upon what we, in the film audience, know took place 'tomorrow', when the world 'belonged' to Swastika-wearing Brownshirts, their supporters and people like them. Even if we in the audience watching the performance on screen are emotionally or physiologically affected by the musical or lyrical content of the song – and it is undoubtedly an extremely well-crafted song, beautifully sung by both the soloist and the accumulating chorus – this affect is held in check by our understanding of the historic and immoral consequences of the worldview that the performance encapsulates. In other words, the scene creates a distance between us and the singers – we are meant to fear them, in their exultation, pre-cisely because what they declaim acts as a portent for what was to come: war; the death camps; mass murder on an industrial scale.

These levels of meaning, and the way they interpolate the audience, are all recontextualized and subverted in the realigned versions of the song, which take the same lyrics and sing them to a rock arrangement (or, later, as a pop ballad or in rockabilly style). If, when watching the scene from *Cabaret* (1974), we are meant to feel a sense of foreboding – a sense of fear in the terrible convictions of this group of people, and the way that song can be used to make these convic-tions more poetic and more palatable – this is embraced in the realigned versions of the song: yes, *you should fear*, fascist realigned versions of the song seem to say. Because while the fictional people in the film (and, at a stretch of the imagi-nation, the real-life Germans that they metonymically represent) may have been naïve or short-sighted in foreseeing what exactly was to come, the same cannot be said of Ian Stuart Donaldson or Saga or any other artist who has recorded an ideologically subverted version of the song. Fascists and other extremists who, through their performances, subvert the meanings of the song are aware of what happened next; they take pleasure in the prospect of control, in what they will do tomorrow when the world will, again, belong to them. And through reinter-preting and recording this *particular* song – a song sung by fictional Nazis at a particular historic juncture – they imply a very specific imagined future, a very specific sense of the (fascist) glory that 'awaits unseen'. One online commentary, written in praise of Ian Stuart Donaldson and what he aimed to achieve with this realignment, argues that Donaldson:

> . . .radically changed 'Tomorrow Belongs to Me' by substituting a driving rock beat for the ballad format of the original – a surprising decision. He also eliminated the song's sinister, repulsive, anti-white overtones. . . Ian Stuart's and Saga's interpretations of 'Tomorrow Belongs to Me' might be characterized as reverse engineering, or even reverse culture distortion: a song by Jews intended to convey an anti-white message has been transmuted into an explicitly pro-white anthem. (Hamilton, 2011)

As with all recontextualizations, it is the new context into which the prior text is inserted that is key to understanding the 'transmutation' of the song's meanings: a 'pro-White' (read: fascist) ideological agenda is imposed upon the song – a complete mirror-opposite of the original intentions of the composers – as a direct consequence of the ideological agenda of the singers and their fans.

Recontextualization, 3: interpolation

Interpolation is a form of musical recontextualization in which an element of a song or recording – typically a melody or refrain or (musical or lyrical) phrase – is incorporated into a new song. Interpolated elements are not samples or recordings, but selective rerecordings involving substitution and rearrangement of songs and parts of songs. Sometimes called musical 'quotation' in musicology, interpolation is a frequent feature of contemporary hip hop, wherein restrictive copyright laws which block artists sampling as little as a second of an original (copyright) recording can be sidestepped by rerecording the desired melody or refrain. Thus, the song 'Gangsta's Paradise' (1995) by Coolio and LV, interpolates the chorus and melody from 'Pastime Paradise' (1976) by Stevie Wonder; similarly 'Let's Stay Together' (2004), by Cee-Lo Green featuring Pharrell, interpolates a refrain from 'Live Forever' (1994) by Oasis.

One significant case in fascist music is a three-part recontextualization of the Nazi anthem 'Die Fahne Hoch' (Raise the Flag), later better known as 'The Horst Wessel Lied', after the lyricist. It is impossible to overstate the social and cultural importance of 'The Horst Wessel Lied' to Nazism. After 1933, the significance of 'The Horst Wessel Lied' steadily rose in Nazi Germany, to the point that the song ultimately stood as an unofficial second national anthem of the Reich. At the fall of France on 22 June 1940, after the French were read the terms of the armistice in the Forest of Compiègne, Hitler and his aides strode down the avenue whilst a Nazi band blasted out 'the two national anthems, Deutschland, Deutschland über Alles and the Horst Wessel Song' (Shirer, 1940: 263). Dedication to the cult of Horst Wessel could bring rewards to even the most out-of-favour party inductee. Take Josef Müller-Blattau for example, an associate professor of music at the University of Konigsberg who 'during the Weimar Republic had actually sympathized with the modernists' (Kater, 1997: 140). Müller-Blattau chose to write a 'pseudoscientific article' about Wessel in 1934 in which he described 'The Horst Wessel Lied' as:

> the 'never to be lost property of the people, a true *Volkslied*.' This calculated act won him advancement to Frankfurt (1935) and then Freiburg (1937). After publishing a book on 'Germanic music' in collaboration with the SS, he was given a Chair at the new Reichsuniversitat Strassburg in 1942. (Ibid.)

'The Horst Wessel Lied' remains such a symbol of Nazism that its sale and broadcast in Germany are still banned.

Throughout the 1930s and 1940s, fascist parties and movements across Europe adapted versions of the Horst Wessel song. These were not simply translations of the original German words, but rather were locally specific lyrics sung to what was essentially the same melody. It's difficult to make precise statements on the issues of discursive substitution and rearrangement of the *music* and arrangement of the song, given how many recorded versions there are of 'The Horst Wessel Lied'. But almost all versions (that I have heard) were recorded with a marching band and male voice choir; in all recordings, the melody and song structure remain the same: the rhythm is not fast, but rather is set at a metronomic walking-pace, as one would expect for a military march. There is no urgency, although there is a sense of relentlessness and forward motion; there is a *little* syncopation, which is used to create a slight 'skip' in each line, and helps to create lightness and ease of momentum. In pitch, the melodies bring both a sense of grounding and sincerity and increasing euphoria through a combination of frequent descending notes and sweeping escalations. Although the songs use a wide pitch range, notably, at its base, the pitch is low and deeply masculine bringing weight and size. The melodies use basic, simple grounding notes with lots of 4ths for building, 2nds to suggest a journey and something unresolved, with the use of 7ths to suggest emotional longing. The voice qualities through which these melodies are articulated include loud volume and taking up of social and physical space; we find open throats and relaxed, easy articulation. We find both longer phrasing suggesting emotional lingering but also some that is much more abrupt to suggest certainty and confidence. In arrangement we find the voices at the front of the mix above the instruments. The voices sing in unison,

Table 4.3 Recontextualization of song lyrics, 1

'Die Fahne Hoch'/'Horst Wessel Lied '	'The Marching Song' (British Union of Fascists)
The flag on high! The ranks closed tightly! SA marches with silent, solid steps. Comrades, shot by Red Front and reactionaries, March in spirit within our ranks. Comrades, shot by Red Front and reactionaries, March in spirit within our ranks.	Comrades, the voices of the dead battalions. Of those who fell, that Britain might be great. Join in our song, for they still march in spirit with us. And urge us on to gain the Fascist State! Join in our song, for they still march in spirit with us. And urge us on to gain the Fascist State!
The streets free for the brown battalions, The streets free for the stormtrooper! Millions look at the swastika full of hope, The day of freedom and of bread is dawning! Millions look at the swastika full of hope, The day of freedom and of bread is dawning!	We're of their blood, and spirit of their spirit, Sprung from that soil for whose dear sake they bled; 'Gainst vested powers, Red Front, and massed ranks of Reaction. We lead the fight for freedom and for bread! 'Gainst vested powers, Red Front, and massed ranks of Reaction. We lead the fight for freedom and for bread!
The last sound to charge is blown! We already stand prepared for the fight! Soon Hitler's flags will flutter above all streets. Our slavery will last only a short time longer! Soon Hitler's flags will flutter above all streets. Our slavery will last only a short time longer!	The streets are still; the final struggle's ended; Flushed with the fight we proudly hail the dawn! See, over all the streets the fascist banners waving – Triumphant standard of a race reborn! See, over all the streets the fascist banners waving – Triumphant standard of a race reborn!

following the melody of the instruments. The effect is a chorus of indistinct voices with just a few in the foreground that can be heard individually, but only just. This suggests social cohesion and unity although not to the point where the individual completely disappears – thus providing an ideological misrepresentation of the totalitarian crushing of individualism entailed in and through any fascist political project (see Machin and Richardson, 2012 for further analysis).

The British Union of Fascists (BUF) had a version of the song, called 'The Marching Song', whose lyrics were written by the Blackshirt E. D. Randall. The lyrics of both songs are reproduced in Table 4.3 above.

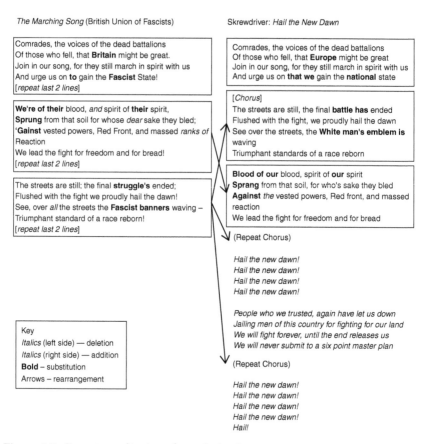

The Marching Song (British Union of Fascists)

Comrades, the voices of the dead battalions
Of those who fell, that **Britain** might be great.
Join in our song, for they still march in spirit with us
And urge us on **to** gain the **Fascist** State!
[*repeat last 2 lines*]

We're of their blood, *and* spirit of **their** spirit,
Sprung from that soil for whose *dear* sake they bled;
'**Gainst** vested powers, Red Front, and massed *ranks of*
Reaction
We lead the fight for freedom and for bread!
[*repeat last 2 lines*]

The streets are still; the final **struggle's** ended;
Flushed with the fight we proudly hail the dawn!
See, over *all* the streets the **Fascist banners** waving –
Triumphant standard of a race reborn!
[*repeat last 2 lines*]

Key
Italics (left side) — deletion
Italics (right side) — addition
Bold – substitution
Arrows – rearrangement

Skrewdriver: *Hail the New Dawn*

Comrades, the voices of the dead battalions
Of those who fell, that **Europe** might be great
Join in our song, for they still march in spirit with us
And urge us on **that we** gain the **national** state

[*Chorus*]
The streets are still, the final **battle has** ended
Flushed with the fight, we proudly hail the dawn
See over the streets, the **White man's emblem is**
waving
Triumphant standards of a race reborn

Blood of our blood, spirit of **our** spirit
Sprang from that soil, for who's sake they bled
Against *the* vested powers, Red front, and massed
reaction
We lead the fight for freedom and for bread

(Repeat Chorus)

Hail the new dawn!
Hail the new dawn!
Hail the new dawn!
Hail the new dawn!

People who we trusted, again have let us down
Jailing men of this country for fighting for our land
We will fight forever, until the end releases us
We will never submit to a six point master plan

(Repeat Chorus)

Hail the new dawn!
Hail the new dawn!
Hail the new dawn!
Hail the new dawn!
Hail!

Figure 4.2. Recontextualization of song lyrics, 2

The lyrics in the BUF's 'Marching Song' were clearly inspired by those of 'The Horst Wessel Lied'. We have the same open militarism; the same references to the spirits of soldiers, martyred for the greater good of the nation, who march alongside and strengthen the ranks of fascists; the same enemies of the fascist political project – 'vested interests' (capital), 'Red Front' (Communists) and reactionary conservatives – seemingly united in the traditional conspiracy. In both songs there is the same claim to be fighting for food and freedom as opposed to subjugation and terror; and a rousing declaration of imminent national rebirth. This *national* rebirth is substituted in the 'Marching Song' with an explicitly *racial* rebirth, and it was perhaps for this reason that Skrewdriver recorded a song which interpolated the 'BUF Marching Song'. Called 'Hail the New Dawn', and included on their 1984 album of the same name, Skrewdriver recontextualized the 'BUF Marching Song', rearranging and rerecording the song as a four-piece band (singer, drums, bass and guitar) in their preferred genre of Oi/punk. Figure 4.2 shows the extent of their recontextualization – not only in terms of what is added and taken away, but also the ways that the original song structure was transposed into the verse-chorus structure of popular song.

The notion of 'Finality' – whether 'the final battle' or the 'final solution' – is a particularly resonant watchword in fascist discourse. For a battle to be the *final* one, necessarily, the enemy needs to be not only defeated but denied the possibility of ever returning – that is, not only are their forces dead, but all possibility of others like them returning, and taking up arms, is also removed. Fascist discourse, particularly in the National Socialist tradition, ubiquitously identifies Jews (and/or 'International Jewry') as the enemy (Copsey, 2008; Richardson, 2013, 2015); victory in the 'final battle' is therefore tantamount to genocide; a second Shoah. It is therefore striking that Skrewdriver's interpolated song recontextualizes 'the final struggle' of 'The Marching Song' in two ways: first substituting 'struggle' for 'battle', and second, rearranging the song in such a way that this phrase is included in the newly created chorus. This repetition – it is sung three times in the Skrewdriver song – ensures it is given an emphasis lacking in the original. And, should listeners be unclear regarding who it is that this 'battle' is against, the additional final verse refers directly to a 'fight' against submitting to a 'six point master plan' – the six points implicitly indexing the six pointed Star of David, thus making it clear that this 'final battle' is, eternally, against *Der Jude*.

Conclusion

With each form of musical recontextualization, it is the changed social, political and interpersonal contexts in which a (new) song is performed or reproduced that are key to understanding how the meanings we associate with the song also change. With musical appropriation, a party/movement/individual attempts to colonize and incorporate a complete song (unchanged, unabridged) within, and as part of, a fascist political and cultural project. In so doing, the text remains the same, but its implied meanings partly shift according to this new context. With this form of recontextualization we see the clearest demonstration of both the dialectical links between text and context, and that there is no meaning outside of use. With interpolation, on the other hand, we see the greatest amount of discursive transformation – musical and lyrical elements can be deleted, added, rearranged and substituted, according to a range of textual, aesthetic and political functions. The political *meanings* of these transformations are related to the political *identities* of those interpolating the song, and their political motivations.

Ideological realignment is essentially a specific form of cover version – a cover version for a particular political purpose. In both cover version and ideological realignment, we tend to see little addition or deletion – the song remains lyrically and melodically 'intact'; but what we always see are substitution (one voice for another; one instrument for another) and rearrangement (the accordion and brass band of the song in *Cabaret* for the rock band of Skrewdriver; the simplification of key in the Skrewdriver realigned version, and so on). Mapping musical transformations in this way provides us with a starting point for analysing of the meaning potentials in each of the four transformations, and also the wider functions and discursive significance of recontextualization in (fascist) music and song.

In any musical culture, or subculture, music and song act to nurture intragroup solidarity. The sense of group identity that comes from shared pleasure of music and song, the role that music and song can play in delineating and differentiating group identities, and so the importance of music to individual and collective identity, are features common to any musical culture. But in a prejudiced musical subculture – like that which venerates a *fascist political tradition* – these individual and collective identities, this nurturing of In-group solidarity and radical rejection of the Outgroup, take on more ominous meanings. The recontextualization of prior texts (musical and other texts) in fascist songs is one way in which this historic tradition is indexed and celebrated; it signals continuity, connectedness and perpetuation of a political project translated into art and culture.

Notes

1   See <https://www.youtube.com/watch?v=0NuTaQsMNaE> for the scene in question [accessed 7 December 2015].
2   From the BBC report <http://news.bbc.co.uk/1/hi/uk/8191094.stm> [accessed 3 December 2015].
3   'angrygirl92' <https://www.youtube.com/watch?v=uOJhe-9SIhc> [accessed 3 December 2015].

References

Fascist sources

Bulldog, no. 14, March 1979.
Hamilton, A. (2011) Tomorrow Belongs to Me. <http://www.counter-currents.com/2011/11/tomorrow-belongs-to-me/> [accessed 7 December 2015].

Jordan, C. (1995) Gothic Ripples.

Randall, E. D. (1934) Fascism and Culture, Blackshirt.

Academic sources

Bertola, M. F. (2013), 'Defining a European "New Order" through Music: Ancient Music in Italian Radio Broadcasting during the Fascist Period', in M. J. Grant and F. J. Stone-Davis (eds) *The Soundtrack of Conflict*, pp. 25–42. Hildesheim: Georg Olms Verlag.

Billig, M. (2000), *Rock'n'Roll Jews*. Nottingham: Five Leaves Publications.

Blecha, P. (2004), *Taboo Tunes: A History of Banned Bands & Censored Songs*. San Francisco, CA: Backbeat Books.

Bohlman, P. V. (2003), 'Music and Culture: Historiographies of Disjuncture', in M. Claytron, T. Herbert and R. Middleton (eds) *The Cultural Study of Music: A Critical Introduction*, pp.45–56. New York and London: Routledge.

Brown, C. (2008), *Politics in Music: Music and Political Transformation from Beethoven to Hip-Hop*. Atlanta, GA: Farsight Press.

Campbell, S. (2010), 'Displaced Sounds: Popular Music-making Among the Irish Diaspora in England', in E. Levi and F. Scheding (eds) *Music and Displacement: Diasporas, Mobilities and Dislocations in Europe and Beyond*, pp.89–104. Lanham, Maryland: The Scarecrow Press.

Copsey, N. (2008), *Contemporary British Fascism: The British National Party and the Quest for Legitimacy*, 2nd edition. Houndmills: Palgrave Macmillan.

Denselow, R. (1989), *When the Music's Over: The Story of Political Pop*. London: Faber and Faber.

Etlin, R. A. (2002), *Art, Culture and Media under the Third Reich*. Chicago: University of Chicago Press.

Fast, S. and Pegley, K. (eds) (2012), *Music, Politics and Violence*. Middletown, CT: Wesleyan University Press.

Frith, S. (1978), *The Sociology of Rock*. London: Constable.

Frith, S. and Street, J. (1992), 'Rock against Racism and Red Wedge: From Music to Politics, from Politics to Music', in R. Garofalo (ed.) *Rockin' the Boat: Mass Music and Mass Movements*, pp.67–80. Boston, MA: South End Press.

Garofalo, R. (ed.) (1992), *Rockin' the Boat: Mass Music and Mass Movements*. Boston, MA: South End Press.

Geary, J. (2014), The *Politics of Appropriation: German Romantic Music and the Ancient Greek Legacy*. Oxford: Oxford University Press.

Grant, M. J. and Stone-Davis, F. J. (eds) (2013), *The Soundtrack to Conflict: The Role of Music in Radio Broadcasting in Wartime and in Conflict Situations*. Hildesheim: Georg Olms Verlag.

Gray, L. (2010), 'Can Music Kill?' *Index on Censorship* 39(3): 112–120.

Griffin, R. (2004), 'This Fortress Built against Infection: The BUF Vision of Britain's Theatrical and Musical Renaissance', in J. V. Gottlieb and T. P. Linehan (eds) *The Culture of Fascism: Visions of the Far Right in Britain*, pp.45–65. London: I.B. Tauris.

Grossberg, L. (1983), 'The Politics of Youth Culture: Some Observations on Rock and Roll in American Culture', *Social Text* 3(2): 104–126.

Grout, D. J. (1960), *A History of Western Music*. New York: W.W. Norton & Co.

Hirsch, L. E. (2010), *A Jewish Orchestra in Nazi Germany: Musical Politics and the Berlin Jewish Culture League*. Ann Arbor, MI: University of Michigan Press.

Johnson, B. and Cloonan, M. (eds) (2009), *Dark Side of the Tune*. London: Ashgate.

Kater, M. H. (1992), *Different Drummers: Jazz in the Culture of Nazi Germany*. New York and Oxford: Oxford University Press.

Kater, M. H. (1997), *The Twisted Muse: Musicians and their Music in the Third Reich*. Oxford and New York: Oxford University Press.

Korpe, M. (2004), 'Preface', in M. Korpe (ed.) *Shoot the Singer! Music Censorship Today*. London and New York: Zed Books: ix–x.

Lowles, N. and Silver, S. (eds) (1998), *White Noise: Inside the International Skinhead Scene*. London: Searchlight.

Machin, D. and Richardson, J. E. (2012), 'Discourses of Unity and Purpose in the Sounds of Fascist Music: A Multimodal Approach', *Critical Discourse Studies, Special Issue on Critical Analysis of Musical Discourse* 9(4): 329–346.

Macklin, G. (2013), 'Onward Blackshirts!' *Music and the British Union of Fascists*, *Patterns of Prejudice*, 47(4–5): 430–457.

McKerrell, Simon. (2012), 'Hearing Sectarianism: Understanding Scottish Sectarianism as Song', *Critical Discourse Studies* 9(4): 1–12.

McKerrell, S. (2015), 'Social Distance and the Multimodal Construction of the Other in Sectarian Song', *Social Semiotics*, 9(4): 363–374.

O'Connell, J. M. and Castelo-Branco, S. E. (eds) (2010), *Music and Conflict*. Urbana, IL: University of Illinois Press.

Pedelty, M. and Weglarz, K. (2013), *Political Rock*. Aldershot: Ashgate.

Pérez Zalduondo, G. and Gan Quesada, G. (2013), *Music and Francoism*. Turnhout (Belgium): Brepols.

Pettan, S. (1998), *Music, Politics and War: Views from Croatia*. Zagreb: Institute of Ethnology and Folklore Research.

Pettan, S. (2010), 'Music in War, Music for Peace: Experiences in Applied Ethnomusicology', in O'Connell and Castelo-Branco (eds) *Music and Conflict*, pp.177–192. Urbana, Chicago: University of Illinois Press.

Piotrowska, A. G. (2013), '"Gypsy music"' as Music of the Other in European culture', *Patterns of Prejudice*, 47(4–5): 395–408.

Potter, P. M. (1998), *Most German of the Arts: Musicology and Society from the Weimar Republic to the End of Hitler's Reich*. New Haven: Yale University Press.

Reisigl, M. and Wodak, R. (2001), *Discourse and Discrimination*. London: Routledge.

Reisigl, M. and Wodak, R. (2009), 'The Discourse-Historical Approach', in R. Wodak and M. Meyer (eds) *Methods of Critical Discourse Analysis*, pp. 87–121, London: Sage.

Richardson, J. E. (2013), 'Racial Populism in British Fascist Discourse: The Case of COMBAT and the British National Party (1960–1967)', in R. Wodak and J. E. Richardson (eds), *Analyzing Fascist Discourse: European Fascism in Talk and Text*, pp. 181–202. London: Routledge.

Richardson, J.E. (2015) ' "Cultural Marxism" ' and the British National Party: A Transnational Discourse', in N. Copsey and J. E. Richardson (eds) *Cultures of Post-War British Fascism*, pp.202–226. London: Routledge.

Schwarz, D. (1997), *Listening Subjects: Music, Psychoanalysis, Culture*. Durham, NC: Duke University Press.

Shaffer, R. (2013), *The Soundtrack of Neo-Fascism: Youth and Music in the National Front, Patterns of Prejudice*, 47(4–5): 458–482.

Shaffer, R. (2015), 'British, European and White: Identity in Post-War British Fascist Music', in N. Copsey and J. E. Richardson (eds) *Cultures of Post-War British Fascism*, pp.142–160. London: Routledge.

Shekhovtsov, A. and Jackson, P. (2012), *White Power Music: Scenes of Extreme-Right Cultural Resistance*. London: Searchlight.

Shekhovtsov, A. (2009), 'Apoliteic Music: Neo-Folk, Martial Industrial and "Metapolitical Fascism"', *Patterns of Prejudice*, 43(5): 431–457.

Shekhovtsov, A. (2013a), 'European Far-Right Music and Its Enemies', in R. Wodak and J. E. Richardson (eds), *Analyzing Fascist Discourse: European Fascism in Talk and Text*, pp. 277–296. London: Routledge.

Shekhovtsov, A. (2013b), 'Music and the Other', *Special Issue of Patterns of Prejudice*, 47(4–5): 329–501.

Shirer, W. L. (1940), 'Berlin Diary', in R. Stackelberg and S. A. Winklepp (eds) (2002) *The Nazi Germany Sourcebook: An anthology of texts*, pp.260–263. London and New York: Routledge.

Slobin, M. (1993), *Subcultural Sounds: Micromusics of the West*. Hanover and London: Wesleyan University Press.

Slobin, M. (ed.) (1996), *Returning Culture: Musical changes in Central and Eastern Europe*. Durham and London: Duke University Press.

Spracklen, K. (2015), 'Nazi Punks Folk Off: Leisure, Nationalism, Cultural Identity and the Consumption of Metal and Folk Music', in N. Copsey and J. E. Richardson (eds) *Cultures of Post-War British Fascism*, pp.161–176. London: Routledge.

Steinweis, A. E. (1993), *Art, Ideology and Economics in Nazi Germany: The Reich Chambers of Music, Theatre and the Visual Arts*. Chapel Hill, NC: University of North Carolina Press.

Street, J. (1988), *Rebel Rock: Politics of Popular Music*. Wiley/Blackwell: Oxford.

Street, J. (2012), *Music and Politics*. Cambridge: Polity.

van Leeuwen, T. and Wodak, R. (1999), 'Legitimizing Immigration Control: A Discourse-Historical Analysis', *Discourse Studies*, 1(1): 83–118.

Young, J. O. (2011), 'Appropriation and Hybridity', in T. Gracyk and A. Kania (eds) The *Routledge Companion of Philosophy and Music*, pp.176–186. New York and London: Routledge.

5

Authenticity and Subversion: Articulations in Protest Music Videos' Struggle with Countercultural Politics and Authenticity

Lyndon C. S. Way

Introduction

Turkey's 2013 protests started in Istanbul's Gezi Park on 28 May as a demonstration by a few city planners and environmentalists to save a public green space. By 31 May, approximately three and a half million people were protesting in over 80 cities. Protests attracted diverse groups who were against aspects of the ruling Justice and Development Party (Adalet ve Kalkınma Partisi; AKP) such as perceived infringements on democracy, freedom, repressive police tactics and government policies (Işik, 2013: 25–27). Police with the clear backing of the government responded with live ammunition, tear gas, water cannons, plastic bullets and beatings which resulted in over 3000 arrests, 8000 injuries and six deaths (Amnesty, 2013). Music played a key role in communicating these events to fans, protesters and the outside world. It is these which are of interest to us in this chapter.

During the month of June, over 100 cut and paste music videos which supported Turkish protesters were uploaded onto YouTube. Despite the violent end to most protesting by the middle of the summer, musicians have since made reference to the protests in sounds and images in their official videos to articulate subversion. Not surprisingly, this is notable in videos by Turkish bands such as Beyoğlu Kumpanya's 'Bu Daha Başlangıç', The Ringo Jets's 'Spring of War' and Ozbi's 'Asi', but also international pop group Placebo's 'Rob the Bank'. These were released after the protests as official promotional videos and are the focus of examination in this chapter. While in one sense these are political songs, this chapter closely examines what precise ideas and values they communicate about not only political issues, but also the bands themselves. Focusing in on one popular music video widely seen to communicate countercultural senti- ment, this analysis draws out the way that discourses of anti-establishment and authenticity are communicated through different modes in different ways. The countercultural message in fact appears to rest largely on discourses of being anti-establishment and authentic with an absence of any clearly identifiable issues. Analysis of videos is important because although it is common to criti- cally examine speech and news in CDA, it is less common to apply such analysis to popular culture, and popular music in particular, despite its ubiquity in soci- ety. In Turkey, with mainstream media all but silenced, popular music videos are one of the only remaining public spaces open to countercultural voices of subversion.

Music, politics and authenticity

Political expression in music is not new. In 1920s Europe, 'art and architecture, as well as music, were used as central parts of communicating fascist ideology' (Machin and Richardson, 2012: 331). Subversive articulations in popular music are as old as the industry itself, from Billie Holiday's 'Strange Fruit' (1939) to M.I.A.'s 'Born Free' (2010). Careers such as Bob Dylan's and The Red Skins' and whole books, such as *33 Revolutions per Minute* are devoted to protest songs which are described as 'a song which addresses a political issue in a way which aligns itself with the underdog' (Lynskey, 2010: ii). Songs of this nature not only enable musicians to express social concerns in the public domain, they also shape musicians' discourses of authenticity about themselves, their fans and pro- testers. Many musicians, for example Morissey (see Chapter 3 in this volume) and Billy Bragg, articulate discourses of authenticity for their countercultural identity granting them much needed cultural capital (Bourdieu, 1977).

Much has been written on authenticity generating considerable debate. It is attributed to musicians who are represented as true to themselves and sin- cere and 'genuinely express true emotion and feeling' (Machin, 2010: 14–15). Notions of authenticity have their roots in the Romantic tradition where artistic creativity was seen as coming from the soul, as opposed to something which emerged from society (Machin, 2010: 14). These beliefs contribute to the dichot- omy of authentic verses 'establishment', allowing some pop to link authenticity with anti-establishment discourses. How this is assigned is socially, historically and genre dependent. Rock's authenticity, for example, is determined by live performance and being anti-establishment (Machin, 2010; Frith 1981). Gilbert and Pearson (1999: 164–165) note that 1980s authentic rock entailed singers speaking the truth of their (and others') situations representing the culture from which s/he comes and the presence of a specific type of instrumentation. Indie rock differs, where authenticity is about purity not found in 'high-tech manipulations of large scale production' and 'defined in opposition to the commercially influenced' (Hibbett, 2005: 64). Alternatively, hip hop authenticity is articulated through lyrics which reveal personal truths, representing a geographical background linked to lived experiences in predominantly Black urban neighbourhoods (Fraley, 2009: 43). Alternatively, folk aesthetics and authenticity favour the rural outdoors which produce an 'invented geography. . . of a bygone natural environment' (Connell and Gibson, 2003: 39).

Despite varying criteria for authenticity all of which point to musicians being sincere and singing from the heart, studies highlight the central role of the listener (Moore, 2002; Hibbett, 2005; Fraley, 2009; Machin, 2010). Cook (1998: 14) claims authenticity values are 'not simply there in the music; they are there because the way we think about music puts them there'. So, authenticity is not inscribed in the music, but ascribed by the listener responding to choices music producers make in terms of musical sounds, images and styles. Moore (2002) identifies three types of authenticity. *First-person authenticity* 'arises when an originator (composer, performer) succeeds in conveying the impression that his/her utterance is one of integrity, that it represents an attempt to communicate in an unmediated form with an audience' (Moore, 2002: 214). This can be achieved through a wide range of semiotic choices such as vocal style, facial expressions and instrumental choices. *Second-person authenticity* 'occurs when a performance succeeds in conveying the impression to a listener that that listener's experience of life is being validated, that the music is "telling it like it is" for them' (Moore, 2002: 220). This authenticates listeners by articulating a place of belonging which distinguishes the music from other cultural forms. *Third-person authenticity*, according to Moore (2002: 218), 'arises when a performer succeeds in conveying the impression of accurately representing the ideas of another, embedded within a tradition of performance'. For example, Eric Clapton is a White Englishman renowned for authentically playing country blues music associated with Blacks in the Mississippi Delta in America. This chapter argues that post-protest videos multimodally authenticate not only musicians (first-person authenticity), but also protesters and their actions and fans' anti-establishment indie rock stance (second-person authenticity) through the use of semiotic resources by musicians, record companies and their managers.

Data

There were over 100 amateur and unofficial videos uploaded on to YouTube about the protests (see Way, 2016), but the focus here is on official videos produced after the peak of the Gezi protests in June. Common among this sample are visual and sonic reenactments, dramatizations, actuality and other representations of the Gezi Park protests. These strict criteria limit the sample to a handful of domestic videos and one international act. The small sample may reflect a lack of incentive on the part of producers to spend money on a promotional video which is guaranteed to get no domestic airplay. In fact, due to the sensitive nature of protest in Turkey, none of the videos about Gezi Park protests, official or otherwise, received any airplay on traditional media. However, the internet is an integral part of music fans' pop experiences and played an important role in distributing these music videos (Railton and Watson, 2011). One video typical of the sample namely Dev's 'Dans Et' which is analysed here in detail and can be found on https://www.youtube.com/watch?v=RFhAzSPIJpE.

Dev is an indie rock duo formed in Istanbul in 2008. The word 'dev' has two meanings in Turkish. It means 'giant, very large' and it is also a commonly used short-form for the word 'devrem' which means revolution. In the Gezi Park protests, it was common to see the words 'DEV-LİS' (revolutionary secondary school students) and 'DEV-GENÇ' (revolutionary youth) sprayed on the street. By choosing to call themselves Dev and singing about protests, the band articulates a discourse with obvious political sympathies towards subversion. 'Dans Et' was released on 20 July 2013, just after the peak of the protests. The accompanying video analysed here was not only censored by music channels in Turkey (Bianet, 2013), but erased twice from YouTube (The Official Twitter Account of Dev 2013).

Approach to analysis

Van Leeuwen (1999: 8) observes that researchers must '"contextualise" semiotic systems, to put them in their historical and social setting'. Critics of video analysis also note the importance of context (Goodwin, 1993; Shuker, 2001; Railton and Watson, 2011). For this reason, background to June's protests and a theoretical exploration of authenticity and Turkey's mediascape add context to the video analysis in order to understand the discourses it articulates. The video undergoes a multimodal analysis examining lyrics, images and musical sounds. This approach has the advantage of revealing the way each mode works to artic- ulate discourses 'on a particular occasion, in a particular text' (Kress and van Leeuwen, 2001: 29). It also addresses concerns that much video analysis ignores musical sounds which 'if discussed at all – [are] usually relegated to the status of sound track' (Goodwin, 1993: 4). Together, this examination of 'the range of non-musical factors' (Frith, 1999: 4) alongside a structured analysis of musical sounds clarifies the meaning potential of the video.

Videos are analysed as a multimodal site of communication where lyrics, images and music are viewed as semiotic resources. These modes not only con- tribute to meanings in music videos, but communicate 'discourses about their [musicians'] identities' (Machin, 2010: 77). For lyrics and images, analysis is carried out at three levels. At a basic level, the 'discourse schema' is examined to reveal 'the social values that underlie the song' (Machin, 2010: 78). Here, details are stripped to identify the generic role played by characters which 'tells us about the cultural values about identities and behaviours that lie deeper in a song' (Ibid., 81). At another level, representations of social actors and their actions are examined following the influential work of van Leeuwen (1995, 1996). Here questions such as who does what to whom and how participants are represented in more active or passive roles are examined. How social actions are recontextualized 'encode different interpretations of, and different attitudes to, the social actions represented', a significant factor in articulating discourses (van Leeuwen, 1995: 81). Social actors are analysed in the visuals based on Kress and van Leeuwen (1996) and Machin's (2007) three broad categories of partici- pant representations. These are how participants are positioned in relation to the audience, the 'kinds' of participants represented and how actions and agency are represented. Finally, representations of settings are considered. These affect our understanding of not only places, but also reinforce myths and provide listeners with a sense of identity (Forman, 2002). Analysing settings is 'highly revealing about the world being communicated' (Machin, 2010: 92), and 'can be used to understand broader social relations and trends, including identity, ethnicity. . . social activism, and politics' (Johansson and Bell, 2009: 2).

Musical sounds are analysed using a semiotic approach developed by van Leeuwen (1999) and Tagg (1983, 1984, 1990) and furthered by Machin (2010). This chapter considers how musical sounds articulate discourses based on van Leeuwen's (1999) six major domains of sound which contribute to meanings. These domains do not dictate what listeners hear but identify experiential meaning potential of the sounds listeners experience (van Leeuwen, 1999: 94).

Domains include perspective connoting social distance, music's adherence (or not) to regularity, how sounds interact with each other, melody, voice quality, timbre and the modality of sounds. These domains are considered, where relevant, to reveal how the music articulates discourses of protest alongside authenticity.

Turkey's mediascape, relations with the government and protest music

Turkish political pop has had its share of government control at the levels of production, distribution and performance with censorship (Bülent Ersoy, Dev), arrests (Grup Yorum, Fazıl Say) and exiles (Cem Karaca, Ahmet Kaya). Domestic music production is a multi-million pound industry involving both major global record companies and independents. The majors dominate the market while independent music production is confined to local record labels and distribution. AKP government music policies have had a detrimental effect on modernist composers such as Kamran İnce and Aydın Esen by trying to eliminate modern musical institutions whilst musicians and genres positioned against modernism such as Arabesk music performers Orhan Gencebay and Nihat Doğan who openly support AKP policies are granted their support (Way and Gedik, 2013).

Distribution of music is tightly controlled by the government. For a recording to be released, it must get a 'bandrol'. This is a sticker issued by the Ministry of Culture which indicates the product's manufacturer has paid the required tax. However, bandrol is used by the government to censor music. CDs can be refused a bandrol for 'language [being] objectionable to the government for its political content, such as song lyrics perceived to advocate violence, [or] political views the government would rather not see expressed' (Solomon, 2005: 6). Live performances are also under the watchful eye of the government. Sometimes authorities choose to not grant permission for concerts. When it is granted, concerts may be cancelled at the last minute despite being organized and paid for by bands and their supporters. These actions are usually accompanied by band members being arrested for spreading 'propaganda'.

Broadcasting music is also under direct and indirect government control. There are over 1100 radio and 200 television stations in Turkey. Despite these large numbers, Turkey's media are dominated by state-run Türkiye Radyo

Televizyon (TRT) and five private media conglomerates. Mainstream music broadcasting is in the hands of the government and these corporate holdings, some accused of 'broadcast[ing], rank[ing] and promote[ing] music-clips and in this way to a certain extent manipulate[ing] the music market in Turkey' (Barış, 2010: 1). Furthermore, corporate holdings are not necessarily independent of government control. Relations between media and politics are very close, characteristic of Hallin and Mancini's (2004) Mediterranean Model. Though Turkish media conglomerates achieve low investment returns on their media interests, they 'use the media to manipulate other economic or political interests' resulting in a 'notorious interlocking of interests between the media, politicians and the businesses' (Özguneş and Georgios, 2000: 414).

This relationship has taken on greater significance with AKP gaining more control over media than any of its predecessors (Jenkins, 2012). AKP has put pressure on existing media to become less critical whilst acquiring media outlets and initiating its own communication channels, resulting in AKP discourses dominating mainstream media output (Sümer and Yaşlı, 2010: 17). This dominance was seen in coverage of the 2013 protests where close ties to the government have been blamed on the under-reporting of the protests (Işik, 2013). Social media have also seen a crack-down by the government, it demanding the names of Twitter users who offended the government (Burch and Ozbilgin, 2013). Since the protests, the government has tendered huge fines on television channels which opposed their views, such as Ulusal Kanal, Halk TV, Cem TV and EM TV. According to Mehmet Özgenç from the government's media watch-dog RTÜK, the fines were given because 'these channels are encouraging the violence of the people' (Hürriyet, 2013). Turkey's pop industry is an integral part of this mediascape, magnifying the importance of videos on the internet as an alternative for countercultural musical voices.

Lyrics

With the exception of the song's opening two lines, the lyrics are nine repeated lines with no social actors identified (see appendix at the end of this chapter for the full lyrics). It is through the multimodal video text that we are able to identify the 'you' and 'your' as police and 'I' and 'me' as a protesting narrator. At a first level of analysis, we can identify the discourse schema, which is the basic structure of the song. By stripping 'away the details of [the] narrative in order to reveal its core structure', we can uncover the cultural values in lyrics (Machin,

2010: 80). This song's lyrical discourse schema may be read thus: 'There is an evil person(s) who is wrong, cowardly and does not help when s/he should. There is a narrator who questions and is brave.' Neither of these roles are particularly powerful. On the one hand, the evil person(s) is activated though negatively and with no agency (van Leeuwen, 1996). On the other hand, the narrator is activated positively though again with no agency. As such, this sets up a simple binary where we have two groups opposed to each other. Wright (1975) notes that such basic structures point to wider issues and anxieties present in society at particular times used to simplify far more complex issues.

Lyrics host a range of discourses which not only subvert, but also authenticate the band and fans. Though like most pop music there are few mentions of settings (Machin, 2010: 92), discourses of authenticity and subversion can be found. Here, we see settings of 'night', 'dawn', 'nightmare', 'dream' and the 'dark'. Nightmarish, dark and mysterious settings are common in heavy metal, including 'Enter Sandman' by Metallica, a band known to span the gap between heavy metal and indie music. Representing such settings serves to authenticate Dev as metal-influenced indie rockers. They also suggest a discourse opposed to the police. Darkness has the universal meaning potential of evil, a lack of clarity and untruths. With negative representations of police (see below) alongside settings of darkness and night, negativity surrounds the police. Though these representations of settings lack detail, they serve to authenticate Dev and legitimize a negative stance towards the police.

Collocations and activations also play a role in articulating a discourse of negativity towards the police. Police are collocated with 'nightmare', 'afraid' and 'darkness'. These collocations reveal a 'collocative pattern' of negativity surrounding the police, though no circumstances are represented (Fairclough, 2003: 131). When they are activated, these are vague. Police 'are not in your place', 'are even afraid of the darkness' and 'flee'. None of these actions are transactive material process activations which connote power (van Leeuwen, 1995: 90). Instead police actions directly affect nobody, connoting less power whilst 'not in your right place', being 'afraid' and 'flee[ing]' all suggest wrong doing and cowardliness.

Slang in each chorus is also used to suggest both negativity and authenticity. The line 'Your head is not in the right place' is slang for either 'You are high from smoking marijuana' or 'You are stupid or brainless.' In both cases, these are negative and do not represent police with power. Such negative representations help authenticate Dev as being anti-establishment, an essential part of indie authenticity. Furthermore, by Dev choosing to use slang, their 'street credibility' authenticates themselves and their fans by 'telling it like it is'. This type of first- and second-person authenticity (Moore, 2002) is notable in the use of slang by hip hop musicians which authenticates fan and musician's street credibility.

Police are also represented as blindly following orders given by the government and not working to protect the public, a popular sentiment at the time. This is evident in lines like 'Dance, hands in your pockets' and 'whose hero are you'. Lakoff and Johnson (1980) note that metaphor is 'a functional mechanism which affects the way we think, act and experience reality' (in Flowerdew and Leong, 2007: 275). In the first excerpt, police obedience to the government is recontextualized in a commonly used metaphor of not getting involved by 'keeping your hands in your pocket', simplifying what must have been a very difficult situation for many officers. The second excerpt again questions police actions and their commitment to protecting the public, though again in vague terms. During the protests, police killed and injured scores of protesters whilst obeying government orders. To do otherwise in Turkey would be instant dismissal at best, a life-changing prospect for police officers, most of whom are recruited from poor backgrounds in a country with high unemployment. Here, the situation is recontextualized through simplification to echo public opinion. As such, Dev suggests first-person authenticity within the genre of indie rock by articulating an anti-authority stance without having to deal with any of the socio-economic realities surrounding police actions.

The chorus sees Dev command the police to dance in four of the nine repeated lines sung throughout the song. These imperatives work in two ways to articulate first-person authenticity. First, to command someone to do something grants the one who commands power and legitimacy. Second, music and dance were a significant activity in the protests. This is evident by the number of music videos and dance events uploaded on to YouTube as part of the protests. Uploads include street performances by professional and university dance troops, individuals doing the Tango, the moon dance and dancing in front of police lines. Another common activity during the protests was large crowds chanting 'Jump, jump, who doesn't jump is Tayyip [Prime Minister Erdoğan]' accompanied by protesters jumping in unison in a dance of protest. By commanding the police to dance, the chorus alludes to the protest's dancing activities which authenticates Dev as 'being in the know' about the protests. This authenticates the band as being authentic and authenticates the listener for also 'being in the know' about the protests, another example of first- and second-person authenticity.

The narrator's power is also suggested in the lines 'whose nightmare are you again, I wish you could come into my dream' and 'Dance, I wish you'd take me too'. The first line indicates the police are a terror to some, while the second line challenges this negative power. The narrator wants to be involved with the police, be a part of his dream. The third line is derived from the Turkish 'içeriye aldilar' (they took him inside) meaning the person spent the night in jail. In Gezi, there were many arrests and people taken into custody. Most protesters tried their hardest to keep out of custody. Here, the narrator is showing his sympathy and alliance with those who went into custody by offering to share in their discomfort. By aligning himself with protesters, the narrator again shows his anti-establishment credentials by being part of the anti-AKP protests. This line also suggests second-person authenticity, authenticating those protesters and fans who have been 'taken in'.

Images

Images make more explicit the discourses heard in the lyrics, articulating both popular discourses of police subservience and brutality, protester power and band, protester and listener authenticity. Participants are the police and protesters who are represented as the band, a dancer and the iconic standing man, woman in red, woman in black and gas mask man. The discourse schema may be read as 'police obey orders and act violently against protesters who are strong and defiant'. Like the lyrics, these represent police and their actions negatively though not powerful because they are following orders. In contrast, protesters are represented as brave, powerful and defiant, challenging authority. As such, these authenticate protesters, listeners and the band as being anti-establishment and powerful. A closer look at the representation of actors and their actions makes this abundantly clear.

Images of protesters articulate discourses of power, opposition and defiance towards authority. These authenticate protesters as a powerful anti-establishment group. One of the protesters in the video is the dancer. She acts as a metonym for the dances of protest discussed above, activated throughout dancing energetically. In Figure 5.1, she is represented as both a protester and an indie rock fan. She wears a set of flimsy goggles on her forehead similar to the makeshift protective gear worn by protesters. Her dyed red hair, black bandana, jeans and t-shirt are similar to both the majority of young protesters on the streets and indie fans watching the video. She stares defiantly at the camera, pulling a bandana down from her face. This is an image of power and closeness. She directly addresses the viewer in a demand image, creating symbolic interaction with the viewer

Figure 5.1. Dancing protester

whilst suggesting power (Kress and van Leeuwen, 1996: 127–128). Eye contact and facial expressions connote she is challenging the viewer and/or police. At the same time, social distance is close, one of intimacy. The viewer is drawn close to her and her ideas of protest (Machin, 2007: 118–119). This works to legitimate protesters' views, another case of second-person authenticity authenticating protesters and fans alike.

Four iconic protesters from the Gezi protests are represented in the video. They became icons symbolizing bravery and defiance with their images distributed on the internet and foreign media. The woman in red (Ceyda Sungur) stands as police sprayed tear gas at her at close range. The woman in black (Kate Mullen) stands with arms spread open wide as a water cannon is aimed at her. A lone man is standing in Taksim Square staring at a statue of Atatürk and Turkish flags defying police calls to leave; a man with a gas mask stands with his arms outstretched like a conductor atop a building in Taksim Square looking over thousands of protesters. In the video their actions are recontextualized in ways which articulate power. The representation of Ceyda Sungur is one multimodal example of this.

On 28 May 2013, Ceyda Sungur was sprayed with tear gas in the face by a 23- year-old policeman on the orders of his superiors. She did not run away but stayed and suffered the discomfort. In the video, she is activated in both non-transactive (dances, poses) and material transactive (hits the spray mechanism, metaphorically attacks the police) actions, the latter connoting great power (van Leeuwen, 1995: 90). This is in contrast to the policeman who for the most part kneels as he sprays, low horizontal position connoting less power (Machin, 2007: 114). Ceyda's non-transactive actions of posing and dancing symbolize the joy of being rebellious and standing unaffected by actions of the police, legitimating protest and fans' anti-establishment sentiments. In Figure 5.2, the woman in red is represented as powerful in a material transactive activation. Both she and the policeman are in a close up, connoting social proximity. Though the side view enables less symbolic interaction than a front shot, the social distance between the viewer and the policeman is severely reduced by a dark mask and full helmet which cover his face and head (Machin, 2007: 113). In fact, most police shots are the same. This impersonal representation makes it easier to treat the police as an enemy because they are essentialized as an unchanging Other (Kress and van Leeuwen, 1996: 127–128). The woman's facial expressions, however, are dominantly sexual. Her eyes are closed, she is relaxed and in charge of the situation as she comes up close to the policeman, leaning into him almost as though ready to give him a kiss. She is activated with agency, blowing smoke into his face, metaphorically returning the tear gas and pepper spray the police used in excess when confronting the protesters. This draws upon a popular discourse at the time that the protesters were powerful. In the video, power over the police is also articulated when the masked man poses with the police, his arms spread out above them. Police kneel around him whilst heavy breathing through his mask is heard. These images and sounds not only articulate a discourse of protesters' positive power by overcoming the power of the state and police who mindlessly obey all their commands, it also legitimates protest and fans' anti-establishment views.

Figure 5.2. Iconic protester

Imagery also acts to authenticate the band as anti-establishment indie rockers. Indie rock style choices are evident in dress and visual representations of instruments. The singer's choice of a black t-shirt, longish hair and razor stubble are seen throughout indie rock from Muse to Coldplay to Arctic Monkeys. Instrumentation in the visuals include an electric guitar, an iconic instrument in indie rock, whilst excluding the drums, bass and synthesizer heard in the music. These semiotic resources help legitimize Dev as an indie rock band.

Anti-establishment legitimation is also connoted through setting, style, shot choices and activations. The band, protesters and police share the same location, a grey smoky studio. This sharing creates a type of 'integration' connoting closeness between the groups (van Leeuwen, 2005: 112). However, protesters and the band also share a similar indie rock dress code, aligning the band with protesters. In fact, the multimodal discourse also posits the band-as-protester. For the first minute of the song, the singer sings into a microphone which resembles a police car radio or one used by soldiers during war time to call in reinforcements. He holds it aggressively with the cable wrapped around his hand so it does not fall, as one would in times of crisis. Many of these shots are close-ups with the singer staring directly into the camera defiantly, suggesting he is standing strong in the face of danger. Later, he sings into a megaphone like one used by a speaker who leads a rally or gathering of large people. In the context of this video, the gathering is Gezi Park and the people Dev leads are protesters. In Figure 5.3, the singer is close to the camera connoting a close social proximity, while the police's mask and helmet contradict such closeness. He is empowered, activated verbally singing into the policeman's face, while the policeman does nothing. This articulates the popular notion of protesters' power. Facial expressions make clear he is angry and aggressive towards the policeman. He is further empowered here by demanding the police to dance in the accompanying lyrics. This first-person authenticity legitimates the band as powerful anti-establishment protesters who have significant social agency – important for indie rock authenticity. It also works as second-person authenticity, authenticating fans and protesters' feelings of frustration at police abuse of power and obeying government instructions, allowing fans to engage in a fantasy of being able to yell in the face of their abusers.

Part of being anti-establishment is to represent authority negatively. Visually, this is done by representing the police impersonally and anonymously as essentially, non-thinking abusers of power. There is one exception to this in a sequence where a policeman takes off his helmet and dances

Figure 5.3. Band and fan's anti-establishment authenticity

with the woman in black. His movements change from being robotic and abrupt to a sensual dance, acting as a metaphor for his liberation from the confinement of his hegemonic duties. This sequence offers insights into how Dev would like the police to act, being free from obedience and acting with more compassion. However, the vast majority of shots of the police represent the police dancing a very different tune. They wear full helmets and masks, dressed identically and in group shots denying viewers a point of identification and making it easy to treat them as an enemy (van Leeuwen, 1996: 48; Kress, 1989: 134). In some sequences, they are represented negatively in transactive activations, spraying the woman in red, showering the woman in black, whilst in others in non-transactive activations like standing menacingly in groups, running and stumbling. These are all negative, and some represent police using power negatively. In Figure 5.4, the dominant discourse that police unthinkingly obey commands is articulated metaphorically. Police are represented impersonally, identically dressed and helmeted. They move abruptly and robotically in unison, as though moving only when commanded. They are activated saluting, a universal sign of respect for those in authority. Although there is overwhelming proof the police were following the orders of those above them including the prime minister himself (Amnesty, 2013), to represent the police as robots is an oversimplification. However, this serves the purpose of legitimating an anti-establishment stance taken by the band. In turn, this serves to authenticate themselves as indie rockers and legitimates fans' anti-establishment ideas.

Figure 5.4. Police as unthinking robots

Music

The song is in the key of C# major. Typical rock instrumentation of a guitar and vocals are up front in the mix, bass and drums make up the rhythm section and a keyboard is used sparingly. Three sets of verses are separated by three choruses. Together, these sounds are used to articulate discourses of police obedience, danger, angst and subversion, all of which represent the band as an anti-authority indie rock band. Here we consider musical elements which articulate these discourses.

There is the meaning potential of danger from police in the use of sound effects, instrumentation, melody and tempo. These are notable at the beginning of the song. Reminiscent of Michael Jackson's 'Thriller' opening, 'Dans Et' begins with a gust of wind and an electronically generated humming sound with bass enhancement. Dogs bark in the background whilst a cracking sound intermittently occupies the foreground, suggesting a stalker in the woods. Further into the song, horror film sound effects are used again, this time heavy breathing through a mask like Jason from *Friday the 13th* films, again with bass enhanced sounds of howling wind in the background. In both cases, foregrounded sounds suggest danger and the bass-enhanced low register wind suggests dangerous power in a way a higher register would not (van Leeuwen, 2005).

After the song's initial 13 seconds of sound effects, a distorted guitar is introduced. The guitar sounds draw upon heavy metal, a genre with its own

connotations of rebelliousness, danger and menace. It is upfront in the hierarchy of sound, emphasizing its importance. A C# chord (the tonic) is strummed
quickly and regularly, followed by a pregnant pause, then a D powerchord (the
minor second). The song's guitar sounds are almost exclusively variations on
these two chords. This melody is characterized by low notes and a very narrow pitch range. Again, the low register suggests power whilst the very narrow
pitch range suggests that this power is constrained, something to be feared (van
Leeuwen, 1999: 106). Similar to the *Jaws* two-note leitmotif, this melody plays
on the song's key note and its minor second. In *Jaws*, this was used to represent
danger, evil and menace (Wingstedt, Brandström and Berg, 2010: 199). In the
films, tempo increases with perceived danger. In this song, the fast tempo of
the guitar strumming articulates imminent danger. Furthermore, van Leeuwen
notes how fast changes in notes, or 'disjunctive sound production' can come to
stand for a 'lively and energetic approach, or a bold or forceful attack' depending
on context (1999: 110). Here the articulation of the melodic phrase is fast, connoting danger is close at hand. Together, sound effects, instrumentation, melody
and tempo in the song's opening connote danger. In the context of the anti-
police lyrics and visuals, the source of this danger is obvious.

Police obedience is also connoted through instrumentation and timing. In
the first verse, the guitars and vocals are dominant. But at the beginning of the
second verse, drum sounds rise in the hierarchy of sound. The drums are sparse
with minimal reverb, sounding like the drums used in a military march. They
are very regular in timing with the meaning potential of something mechani-
cal, predictability and order (Tagg, 1990: 346). Van Leeuwen (1999: 58–63) also
notes regularity connotes rigidity, 'to stand at attention', emphasizing police
unthinking obedience. This discourse is enhanced multimodally by visuals of
the police dancing like robots in unison, suggesting police unthinkingly obey
the commands of the elite.

Instrumentation and melody also suggest angst at police and the elite. The
D power chords noted earlier and the distorted guitars throughout the song
suggest this. To this listener, guitar power chords have been used to connote
angst in The Who's 'My Generation', Nirvana's 'Nevermind' and Radiohead's
'Creep' to name but a few. Here, the D breaks up the C# strumming, adding angst to danger and obedience noted earlier. The instrumental melody
in the build up to the first chorus also connotes angst (represented in graph
form in Figure 5.5 where one and eight are a C#). Here, for the first time the
guitar strays from the C# and D melody. After spending one beat on the D,
guitar sounds drop down to the G# then rapidly climb eight steps up to a

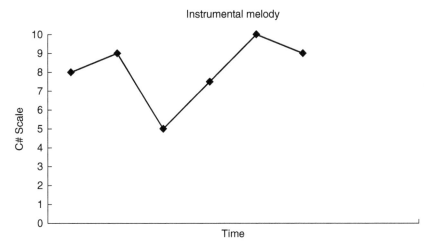

Figure 5.5. Instrumental melody

high E before going back to the C# for the chorus. The drop of three and a half notes down to the G# (the bass note of the C# chord) adds gravity to the sequence and the anger being connoted (van Leeuwen, 1999: 103). The following eight-step ascending pitch to the E suggests a 'more active and more outgoing and dynamic' movement than a descending pitch movement (van Leeuwen, 1999: 103). Ascending pitch movement can also 'energise, rally listeners together for the sake of some joint activity or cause' (van Leeuwen, 1999: 103). In this case it is anger over police actions and protesting against this. However, this is repressed somewhat by the small steps of pitch ascendancy, which 'constrains the expression of strong feelings...because we are paralysed with fear' (van Leeuwen, 1999: 106). Furthermore, this sequence ends on the third minor suggesting stability, but also sadness and pain (Machin, 2010: 218). Anger, sadness, danger and fear are connoted alongside a somewhat constrained rallying of listeners to dance the dance of protest.

Voice style and melody throughout the song are used to connote anger, this being a key emotion in this song. During the verses, the singer's voice is relaxed and in control, connoting a close social distance (van Leeuwen, 1999: 25). In the choruses voice quality changes to a gritty style of yelling suggesting anger and a lack of emotional control. Van Leeuwen (1999: 175) notes that 'naturalistic representation [in voice] requires a certain amount of "grit", or "noisiness"'. The singer's rough and gritty voice is noticeably moreso during the almost yelling of choruses symbolizing 'real' anger at police actions (van Leeuwen, 1999: 131). During these times, his voice tenses adding to a sense of urgency to his anger.

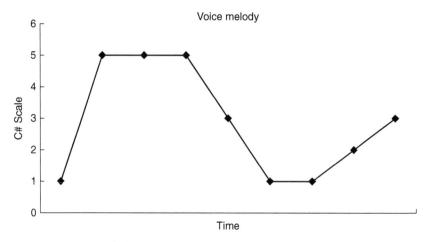

Figure 5.6. Voice melody

Furthermore, vocal pitch rises to the highest notes in the song (shown above in graph form in Figure 5.6). Rising vocal pitch is used to assert and dominate (van Leeuwen, 1999: 133), here the singer asserting his belief that police are on the wrong side of this dispute, which is collocated with the accompanying lyrics of 'tell, whose hero are you'. The melody here is dominated by the first and fifth which suggest stability, whilst the reliance on the third again connotes sadness at police actions (Machin, 2010: 218). During this line a backing vocal track further emphasizes the lyrics, as does the durational variation in vocals. Van Leeuwen (1999: 173) notes emotion is expressed by lengthening key words, as opposed to rushing words in excitement or anger, or speaking in a meas-ured style which symbolizes restrained emotions. During the chorus, emotional attachment is symbolized by elongating this line, especially the word 'tell' (van Leeuwen, 1999: 173). Together, voice style and melody articulate and emphasize anger at police wrong doing (van Leeuwen, 1999: 14–15).

Musical choices not only criticize police, but suggest subversion, key to first-person indie rock authenticity. Notions of indie rock authenticity are determined by live performance and being anti-establishment (Machin, 2010; Hibbett, 2005; Frith, 1981). Dev suggests subversiveness and authenticates itself at the same time through choosing indie rock aesthetics in instrumentation and rock guitar playing style. Electric guitars, an instrument central to indie rock, dominate the instrumental hierarchy of sound, suggesting their importance over other instrumentation such as bass, keyboards and drums. Power chords, another sound associated with rock and indie rock, authenticate Dev as being a part of this genre. A good part of the video sees the band playing 'live'. All these multimodally contribute to the idea that Dev is an authentic indie rock band with an anti-establishment subversive message.

First-person authenticity is also suggested through choices in timing. Though most of the song is characterized by a highly regular rhythm, there is a brief break from this between the third and fourth verses and a noticeable stop to the music before the final double chorus at the end. Tagg (1990: 112) notes that music can subvert 'the implacable exactitude of natural science, computers and clock time' through changes in timing such as delaying or anticipating the beat. Here the song's relentless rhythm is subverted, like the regulated movements of the police in the visuals. This subversion is short-lived but noticeable, similar to the Gezi protests themselves, before the song continues, returning obediently to its regular rhythm. Subversion is also suggested in the singing of the chorus. Here, a back-up singer is introduced into the video soundtrack. Both voices sing the same words and the same notes which has the potential 'to mean solidarity, consensus, a positive sense of joint experience and belonging to a group' (van Leeuwen, 1999: 79). While sung notes rise, suggesting a rallying call to protesters during the chorus, these voices which sing in unison, connote the togetherness and uniformity of those who join the protests and subvert police and the authorities. By musically representing subversion, Dev authenticates itself as anti-establishment indie rockers.

Conclusion

Dev imaginatively uses semiotic resources inspired by the Gezi Park protests to articulate discourses of subversion multimodally. These discourses vaguely and metaphorically articulate police as a dangerous, abusive Other who obediently follow the orders of the authorities. Likewise, protesters' anger at police and protester (and band) power, defiance and legitimacy are also connoted in lyrics, images and sounds. These subversive discourses are multimodally collocated, and simultaneously work to also articulate authenticity. First- and second-person authenticity is articulated in different multimodal ways throughout the song. Dev is represented as an authentic anti-establishment indie rock band by conveying the impression that each 'utterance is one of integrity' (Moore, 2002: 220). This is done by first establishing Dev as legitimate indie rockers, a genre with anti-establishment, countercultural connotations. The band is then represented in ways which emphasizes it as being anti-establishment in all three modes. The video also articulates second-person authenticity, validating not only listeners, but also protesters' anti-establishment sentiments, experiences and actions. This is achieved by creating a commonality between the band, indie rocker fans and protesters, and then legitimating these groups, their power and their anti-establishment stance through a number of strategies identified in lyrics, images and musical sounds.

The video was released shortly after the protests were all but done. This was not part of the protest but something made afterwards as part of the band's promotional package. Close ties between the media and the government ensured the video never received airplay on mainstream media, though the internet acted as an alternative. This worked again to authenticate the band. Dev was able to get the publicity of being banned from the airwaves other bands would not get, drawing upon anti-establishment indie rock authenticity. Furthermore, the video was accessed by a large number of fans (396,491 hits on YouTube at the time of this research). What the band has achieved is notoriety and a reputation for being an authentic anti-establishment indie band. In this sense the video is a success. Ironically, the band released a TV edit of the same song which has none of the visual references to Gezi. This has received only 40,024 views on YouTube and the author has not heard any airplay on mainstream Turkish radio or television.

Some musicians benefit from striking a subversive countercultural pose. By vaguely articulating discourses of being anti-establishment, musicians articulate authenticity for themselves and their fans. Though it is easy to be cynical about the political commitment and effectiveness of videos which use protest as part of their semiotic package, articulating discourses which are anti-establishment is important, especially in a country like Turkey. The mainstream media are all but following the party line and opposition is subdued. Though subversion can result in arrests, censorship and exile, popular music is still one of the few areas where protest can be articulated.

Appendix: lyrics

'Dans Et'

Dawn has broken, you are not in your place
It was the night, if I ask where you are
Tell, whose hero are you
Whose nightmare are you again

I wish you would come into my dream
Tell, whose hero are you
Tell, whose hero are you
You are even afraid of the darkness
Even if I asked you to save me, you'd flee
but you. . . but you
Dance, hands in your pockets
Dance, your head is not in the right place
Dance, I wish you'd take me
Whose nightmare are you again
I wish you would come into my dream
Tell, whose hero are you
Tell, whose hero are you
You are even afraid of the darkness
Even if I asked you to save me, you'd flee
but you. . . but you
Dance, hands in your pockets
Dance, your head is not in the right place
Dance, I wish you'd take me
Even if I asked you to save me, you'd flee
but you. . . but you
Dance, hands in your pockets
Dance, your head is not in the right place
Dance, I wish you'd take me

References

Amnesty International. (2013), 'Gezi Park Protests: Brutal Denial of the Right to Peaceful Assembly in Turkey', <http://www.amnesty.org.uk/news_details.asp?NewsID=20991> [accessed 12 February 2013].

Barış, Ruken. (2010), 'Media Landscape: Turkey', <http://www.ejc.net/media_landscape/article/turkey/> [accessed 19 December 2011].

Bianet. (2013), 'Dans Et'e Gezi Direnişi Sansürü', <http://bianet.org/bianet/sanat/149988-dans-et-e-gezi-direnisi-sansuru?> [accessed 26 November 2014].

Burch, B. and Ozbilgin, O. (2013), 'Turkey Seeks to Tighten Grip on Twitter After Protests', www.reuters.com/article/2013/06/26/net-us-turkey-protesters-twitter-idUSBRE95POXC20130626 [accessed 2 January 2015].

Connell, J. and Gibson, C. (2003), *Sound Tracks: Popular music, Identity and Place*. London: Routledge.

Cook, N. (1998), *Music: A Very Short Introduction*. Oxford: Oxford University Press.

Fairclough, N. (2003), *Analysing Discourse: Textual Analysis for Social Research*, London: Routledge.

Flowerdew, J. and Leong, S. (2007), 'Metaphors in the Discursive Construction of Patriotism: The Case of Hong Kong's Constitutional Reform Debate', *Discourse and Society* 18(3): 273–294.

Forman, M. (2002), *The Hood Comes First: Race, Space, and Place in Rap and Hip-Hop*. Middletown: Wesleyan University Press.

Fraley, T. (2009), 'I Got a Natural Skill: Hip-Hop, Authenticity, and Whiteness', *Howard Journal of Communications* 20(1): 37–54.

Frith, S. (1981), *Sound Effects*. New York: Pantheon books.

Frith, S. (1999), *Performing Rites: Evaluating Popular Music*. Oxford: Oxford University Press.

Gilbert, J. and Pearson, E. (1999), *Discographies: Dance Music, Culture, and the Politics of Sound*. London: Psychology Press.

Goodwin, A. (1993), *Dancing in the Distraction Factory: Music Television and Popular Culture*. London: Routledge.

Hallin, D. and Mancini, P. (2004), *Comparing Media Systems: Three Models of Media and Politics*. Cambridge: Cambridge University Press.

Hibbett, R. (2005), 'What Is Indie Rock?', *Popular Music and Society* 28(1): 55–77.

Hürriyet. (2013), 'Özgenç, Mehmet, RTÜK'ten Halk Tv ve Ulusal Kanal'a Ceza', *Hürriyet Gazetesi*. <http://www.hurriyet.com.tr/gundem/23486445.asp> [accessed 24 June 2013].

Jenkins, G. (2012), 'A House Divided Against Itself: The Deteriorating State of Media Freedom in Turkey', *Central Asia-Caucasus Institute*. <http://www.silkroadstudies.org/new/inside/turkey/2012/120206A.html> [accessed 2 February 2012].

Johansson, O. and Bell, T. (2009), 'Introduction', in Johansson and Bell (eds) *Sound, Society and the Geography of Popular Music*, pp. 1–6. Farnham: Ashgate.

Kress, G. (1989), *Linguistic Processes in Sociocultural Practices*, 2nd edition. Oxford: Oxford University Press.

Kress, G. and van Leeuwen, T. (1996), *Reading İmages: The Grammar of Visual Design*. London: Routledge.

Kress, G. and van Leeuwen, T. (2001), *Multimodal Discourse: The Modes and Media of Contemporary Communication*. London: Hodder Education.

Lakoff, George and Johnson, Mark. (1980), *Metaphors We Live By*. Chicago: University of Chicago.

Lynskey, D. (2010), *33 Revolutions Per Minute: A History of Protest Songs*. London: Faber.

Machin, D. (2007), *Introduction to Multimodal Analysis*. London: Hodder Education.

Machin, D. (2010), *Analysing Popular Music: Image, Sound, Text*. London: Sage.

Machin, D. and Richardson, J. (2012), 'Discourses of Unity and Purpose in the Sounds of Fascist Music: A Multimodal Approach', *Critical Discourse Studies* 9(4): 329–345.

Moore, A. (2002), 'Authenticity as Authentication', *Popular Music* 21(2): 209–223.

Özguneş, N. and Terzis, G. (2000), 'Constraints and Remedies for Journalists Reporting National Conflict: The Case of Greece and Turkey', *Journalism Studies* (3): 405–426.

Railton, D. and Watson, P. (2011), *Music Video and the Politics of Representation.* Edinburgh: Edinburgh University Press.

Shuker, R. (2001), *Understanding Popular Music.* London: Taylor and Francis.

Solomon, T. (2005), ' "Living Underground Is Tough": Authenticity and Locality in the Hip-Hop Community in Istanbul, Turkey', *Popular Music* 24(1): 1–20.

Sümer, Ç. and Yaşlı, F. (2010), *Hegemony'den Diktoryaya AKP ve Liberal Muhafazakar İttifak.* Ankara: Tan Kitapevi Yayınları.

Tagg, P. (1983), 'Nature as a Musical Mood Category', *Göteborg: IASPM Internal Publications.* <http://www.tagg.org/articles/xpdfs/nature.pdf> [accessed 5 January 2011].

Tagg, P. (1984), 'Understanding Musical Time Sense', in *Tvarspel – Festskrift for Jan Ling* (50 a°r), Goteborg: Skriften fran Musik veten skapliga Institutionen. <http://www.tagg.org/articles/xpdfs/timesens.pdf> [accessed 5 January 2011].

Tagg, P. (1990), 'Music in Mass Media Studies. Reading Sounds for Example', in K. Roe and U. Carlsson (eds) *Popular Music Research*, pp. 37–69. Göteborg: Nordicom-Sweden.

van Leeuwen, T. (1995), 'Representing Social Action', *Discourse and Society* 6(1): 81–106.

van Leeuwen, T. (1996), 'The Representation of Social Actors', in Carmen Caldas-Coulthard and Malcolm Coulthard (eds) *Texts and Practices – Readings in Critical Discourse Analysis*, pp. 32–70. London: Routledge.

van Leeuwen, T. (1999), *Speech, Music, Sound*, London: Macmillan Press.

van Leeuwen, T. (2005), *Introducing Social Semiotics.* London: Routledge.

van Leeuwen T. and Wodak R. (1999), 'Legitimizing Immigration Control: A Discourse-Historical Analysis', *Discourse Studies* 1(1): 83–118.

Way, L. (2016), 'Protest Music, Populism, Politics and Authenticity: The Limits and Potential of Popular Music's Articulation of Subversive Politics', *Journal of Language and Politics* 15(4).

Way, L. and Gedik, A. (2013), 'Music and Image: Popular Music's Resistance to Conservative Politics', Paper presented at Ege University 14th Cultural Studies Symposium – Confinement, Resistance, Freedom, İzmir, Turkey, 8–10 May.

Wingstedt, J., Brändstrüm, S. and Berg, J. (2010), 'Narrative Music, Visuals and Meaning in Film', *Visual Communication* 9(2): 193–210.

Wright, Will. (1975), *Six Guns and Society: A Structural Study of the Western*, California: University of California.

6

Sonic Logos

Theo van Leeuwen

Introduction

Brian Eno is often credited with the invention of ambient music.[1] When ill and in bed, so the story goes, he was listening to music at such a low volume that it was hard to disentangle from other sounds. As a result he discovered 'a new way of hearing music – as part of the ambience of the environment just as the colour of the light and the sound of the rain were parts of that ambience' (Eno, 1975). Today, ambient music has become an important part of sound design, for instance in restaurants and shopping centres (cf. Graakjær, 2012). Often it is seen as 'elemental, like atmosphere' (Kim-Cohen, 2016: 54), not meant to be consciously heard as conveying information. Yet, as Kim-Cohen also points out, ambient sound is deliberately produced and seeks to add something to the environment, to change it in some way, to infuse it with 'mood' and 'atmosphere'.

But Eno is also known for creating a piece of music that *was* meant to convey something – the startup sound of the Windows 95 operating system. As he explained in an interview in the *San Francisco Chronicle* (Selvin, 1996):

> The agency said 'We want a piece of music that is inspiring, universal, blah-blah, da-da-da, optimistic, futuristic, sentimental, emotional', this whole list of adjectives and then at the bottom it said 'and it must be 3¼ seconds long'.

Sonic logos of this kind intend to be meaningful, to convey the values and principles brands want to be seen (and heard!) to stand for. But they also have something in common with ambient music – the idea, constantly reiterated by marketing experts, that these values and principles will somehow get in by the backdoor.[2] According to Heath (2001: 44, 83):

> We rarely use 'active' processing, which makes use of our working memory to think about and interpret what we are learning [. . .instead] we use 'automatic' or 'shallow' processes which are able to penetrate at semi-conscious or even sub-conscious levels.

The same idea informs 'classic Hollywood practice': film music, too, is meant to be heard, but not listened to, to influence perception in an emotive rather than a reflective way, below the level of consciousness (Gorbman, 1987). The sonic branding industry understands this well and draws heavily on film soundtracks, acknowledging that 'almost every emotion has been tackled musically in the cinema (Jackson, 2003: 16).

Sonic branding is applied to many different 'touchpoints' – sonic logos, hold music on the telephone, mobile phone ringtones, start up and shut down sounds and even product design (for instance in the automotive industry), and it uses not only music, but also sound effects and ambient sounds, and the sound of the voice, blending these sonic elements into a multimodal whole. In this chapter, I focus especially on sonic logos of the kind Eno composed for Microsoft, as they are usually the point of departure for other applications. I will ask what it is they do and mean, and how they use music and other sounds to do so; in short, how they translate values and principles of brands into sound.

The heraldic function of sonic logos

Sonic logos have two major functions: (1) the heraldic function of drawing the listener's attention to whatever the logo is a logo for, whether a product or a service, a company or some other organization, or a radio or television programme, and (2) an identity function, expressing the values and principles which that product or service, or other entity, stands for.

Musical heralding is primarily expressed by melody and rhythm. Two aspects of melody play a particularly important role: pitch movement and pitch intervals. To begin with pitch movement, melodies can be either ascending, rising in pitch, or descending, going down in pitch. According to Cooke (1959: 102ff), ascending melodies are 'active' and 'dynamic'. This, he argues, is because in singing pitch ascending melodies relate to vocal effort. The higher the notes, the greater the effort required from the singer. Hence songs that seek to energize people, to rally people behind a cause (for instance national anthems), tend to have melodies characterized by rising pitch. A second key aspect of heraldic melodies is the size of the pitch intervals. Large, energetic steps upwards characterize strong,

Figure 6.1. The Internationale

Figure 6.2. Sung brand names

assertive, 'heroic' motifs (Marothy, 1974). In addition, heraldic melodies do not end on the tonic, and this gives them a sense of being unfinished, to be continued by something else – whether by an episode of the television series they announce or the consumer's purchase of the product they spruik. Rhythmically, dynamic melodies will be relatively up tempo and often have what is known as a 'dotted rhythm', in which each note is anticipated by a short note (de-DAA-de-DAA-de-DAA), giving a sense of exact, precisely disciplined timing. All these features can be used to different degrees and in different combinations, and while the melody may be wavy, going up and down, the upwards movement will somehow have to be its defining and most salient moment.

Heraldic melodies have a long and remarkably stable history. They are not only used in many classical compositions (e.g. Beethoven's Leonore Overture and Strauss' *Also Sprach Zarathustra*), in rousing nineteenth-century patriotic songs (cf. the 'arise' moment in 'The Internationale' in Figure 6.1) and in militaristic hymns such as Wesley's 'Soldiers of Christ Arise and Put Your Armour On', but also in the sung brand names shown in Figure 6.2: Dentaguard even jumps up by a whole octave between '-ta-' and '-guard', and the other two also end on a high note. Such logos signal energy and excitement, the melodic contour of the exclamation – Helms (1981) discusses many other examples.

The sonic expression of identity

Identity is most crucially expressed by voice quality. The sound of our voice, whether we speak, sing or produce non-linguistic vocalizations, indexes not only our unique identity, but also, and at the same time, our social identity, our age, gender, class, regional origin, and so on. Musical instruments, and the way they are played, can express identity through the same sonic qualities. Branding experts understand this. They methodically catalogue 'vocal attributes' and the way these can create 'personality profiles' (Jackson, 2003: 136) and acknowledge that musical instrumentation can become 'the very essence of the message' (Jackson, 2003: 94) – again, because of the different qualities different instruments represent and the meanings and values these qualities can express.

Below I will discuss a number of such qualities, arguing that their ability to make meaning rests on the physical, bodily experience of vocalization which we share with all human beings, and that this experience can also be brought to bear on our interpretation of musical sounds, and of sound effects and ambient sounds, including electronic ones. Take vocal tension, for example. We can recognize the sound of a tense voice, as it is higher, sharper and brighter than a lax voice. We know, again from experience, where such tension comes from – from excitement, for instance, or apprehension. We can therefore also use it to express tension when we do not actually feel tense. And we can recognize tension, that high, sharp, bright quality, also in musical instruments and the way they are played, or in other sounds. Just what tension will actually mean will of course depend on the other musical and non-musical signifiers it combines with, and on the context. Tension can express a fleeting tense moment as well as a habitually tense disposition, and it can characterize an individual's as well as a culture's style of speaking and singing. Lomax (1968: 193) has described how tensing of the voice in female singing is customary in cultures that practice sexual repression of women:

> It is as if one of the assignments of the favoured singer is to act out the level of sexual tension which the customs of the society establish as normal. The content of this message may be painful and anxiety-producing, but the effect upon the culture member may be stimulating, erotic and pleasurable, since the song reminds him of familiar sexual emotions and experiences.

Other aspects of voice quality and timbre can be understood on the basis of physical, bodily experiences and social experiences in similar ways. *Loudness*, for instance, is, as we know from experience, most crucially associated with distance (the further away we are from the listener, the louder we must speak to be heard), and therefore also with *social* distance (Hall, 1966: 184–185) – at an 'intimate range' we whisper, at 'close personal range' we speak softly, and so on, and only at 'public range' we fully project our voices. The microphone and amplification have disengaged loudness from actual social distance, so creating a flexible semiotic resource for expressing relationships: we can now whisper intimately to an audience of thousands.

Because men's voices are on average lower than those of women and children, the meaning potential of *pitch level* relates to gender and age in complex ways. Men use the higher regions of their range to assert themselves (in operas the tenors tend to be the heroes) women the lower regions. In combination with, for instance, loudness, this has created iconic and deeply influential models of female identity such as the low soft voice of Lauren Bacall in *To Have and Have Not*, at once assertive and seductive, or the higher, breathy voice of Marilyn Monroe, at once childlike, vulnerable and seductive.

Like other aspects of voice quality, *vibrato* 'means what it is'. We can recognize trembling or wavering in the sound of a voice or instrument, and we know from experience what causes it – emotion, whether it be love or fear. Vibrato is therefore equally good at pulling the heartstrings in a love song as in creating a sense of fear and foreboding in the music of a horror film. In *breathiness*, the sounds of voices or wind instruments mix with the sound of breathing. Again, we know where that comes from – exertion, or excitement. Soft breathy voices can suggest intimacy and sensuality. Advertisers use it to give their message erotic appeal, and singers and instrumentalists use it for the same reason. In *roughness* we can hear other things beside the tone of the voice itself – friction, hoarseness, harshness, rasp. A smooth voice, by contrast, is one from which all noisiness is eliminated. Again, roughness means what it is: rough. We know from experience that it may come from the wear and tear of a tough day or a hard life, and from illness or distress. On this rests it meaning potential. That meaning potential can then be activated in different ways in different contexts. It was used, for instance, in a logo produced for Castrol Oil, which had to express 'smoothness' ('liquid engineering'). The first part of the logo was 'rough': 'purposefully distorted sound with jarring timbres' and 'roughness, friction', signifying 'alarm, emergency and trouble'. This then resolved into 'gentler timbres' and a 'melodic process' (Arning and Gordon, 2006: 12).

All these qualities are, in different proportions, simultaneously present in every timbre, characterizing the habitual style of a singer or instrumentalist, the preferred speaking style of a social class or the preferred singing style of a musical genre. And they also apply to sound effects and ambient sounds, which derive their meaning not only from their source, from what they are the sound *of*, but also from their qualities. A closing door, too, can sound loud or soft, tense or lax, rough or smooth. Car manufacturers know that car doors should sound 'reassuringly solid' when they close, and buttons 'click with purpose' (Jackson, 2003: 106). In the early days of the sound film, the Hungarian film theorist Bela Balasz (1970 [1931]: 179–180) foresaw a language of sound along those lines:

> It is the business of the sound film to reveal for us. . . the speech of things and the intimate whisperings of nature. . . the meaning of a floorboard creaking in a deserted room, a bullet whistling past our ear, the deathwatch beetle ticking in old furniture and the first spring tinkling over the stones.

It is only now, in the age of sound design, with its blended sound effects and tracks that blur the distinction between music and ambient sound that this vision is beginning to be realized.

Finally, electronic sound can also realize identity meaning. Distortion is a form of roughness. Filtering, reverb and/or added hiss can suggest breathiness. Digital tremolos can be understood as a form of vibrato. Today's scores for electronic music often combine rudimentary musical scores with words evoking human experiences – words such as *squeak, scream, growl, buzzy, reedy, warm, flutey, swirly, grainy, clashing, clanking, throbbing, banging, rumbling, splashing, whooshing, ticking, clicking*, or references to musical instruments such as 'a gong-like sound', 'almost like a bowed vibraphone' (cf. Niebur, 2010). At the same time, we will recognize these sounds as technological, as displaying a clean regularity that is lacking in humanly produced speech and music, and sometimes we will recognize them as 'non-human', not possible to be produced by human articulation – sustaining for longer than the human voice can, warbling or shimmering at an impossibly fast rate. The meaning potential of such sounds can be used to contrast the 'human' and the 'technological', as we will see in the discussion of IT logos below, or to evoke other 'non-human' things, for instance 'nature', or the 'divine', or the 'alien' – and the sense of menace or mystery, of awe or dread, that can attach to such meanings.

The sonic expression of group identity

Speaking, singing and music making are by nature forms of social interaction, and the relations of power or solidarity this creates can therefore signify different kinds of group identity. Musical interaction, for instance, can blend different voices and instruments together in different ways. In *social unison* (or 'monophony', as it is called in music theory) all participants sing and/or play the same notes. This can express solidarity, a positive sense of being united by a common purpose or interest, and the voices uniting in this way may either fully blend, so that no individual voices stand out, or be 'heterophonic', with individual voices standing out to a greater or lesser extent, so that individual identity combines with group solidarity. 'Rough' choirs of this kind are often used in advertising jingles to express that the product appeals to men as well as women, the young as well as the old, and so on. In *social pluralism* (or 'polyphony') different melodies are simultaneously sung by different voices and/or played by different instruments, yet all fit harmoniously together – it is a form of interaction in which the parties that are involved are 'equal but different'. In *social domination* (the musical term is 'homophony') one voice (the melody) becomes dominant and the other voices subordinate, accompanying and supporting the dominant voice. The role of these other voices is 'harmonic' – they must 'harmonize' with the dominant voice. But this unequal relation can be subverted: with harmony comes disharmony – muffled tension and dissonance behind, or even overt clashes with, the melody, the hegemonic voice. The music must then resolve this dissonance if it is to progress towards a harmonic resolution. This too creates meaning potential. In a sonic logo for *The Times*, a clash between a minor and a major chord was used to express 'the value of different points of view and the nature of debate': 'a major chord was mingled with a minor chord and one note is always striving to be resolved into another but never quite gets there' (Arning and Gordon, 2006: 15).

Call-response patterns are common in many forms of music, and always involve interaction between a real or symbolic leader (the soloist) and his or her followers (the choir and/or the whole ensemble), whether the leader is a priest, a male singer backed up by female vocalists, or a male voice in a jingle singing the praise of a washing powder and responded to by a well-blended choir of housewives. Much can be learnt from a close study of the relationships this can create (van Leeuwen, 1999: 71–77). There can, for instance, be a respectful distance between the part of the leader and the part of the chorus, or the two an overlap and in then, in the end, join forces, as in the example below:

Leader: So listen to me baby
      Got a new plan
      Why don't we
Leader + chorus Take a shot of Comfort

And the responses may either be full responses that add new information, as in the example above, or simple affirmations such as the congregation's 'Amen' or 'Halleluiah' or the female vocalists' rapturous 'Aaah' in this example:

> *Leader:* Take me to the stars
>   And shoot me into space now
>   Move. . .
> *Chorus:* Aaah

Intertextuality

Sonic identity can also be expressed on the basis of cultural references, of intertextuality. The vocal styles developed by iconic singers and actors may eventually become a semiotic resource, understood, not on the basis of the meaning potential of their qualities, but on the basis of familiarity with the meanings and values expressed in the movie roles or songs the actors and singers are renowned for, and in their public profiles as celebrities. The instrumental styles of key instrumentalists such as Miles Davis or Bill Evans similarly can become part of the toolkit of many musicians in many genres. Sonic branding often uses existing music for their intertextual references. Michael Nyman's music for Jane Campion's film *The Piano* (1993), for instance, was used in a 2003 television commercial for Lloyds TSB Bank, so that, according to Arning and Gordon (2006: 14):

> the listener would immediately have linked the emotional resonance of the film with the brand and concluded that the brand stood for the same principles and values that the film sought to communicate (independence, passion, commitment, creativity, integrity, strength).

To give another example, after British Airways had, for 15 years, used the melody of the 'Flower Duet' from Delibes' *Lakme*, Ford used it for the launch of its people carrier Galaxy – they could do so, because the composer had been dead for more than 70 years and the music was therefore in the public domain. In this way Ford 'borrowed all the brand values that had become associated with the track through years of investment' (Jackson, 2003: 109).

Case study: news signature tunes

I have told the story of the ABC (Australian Broadcasting Corporation) news signature tune before (van Leeuwen, 1999: 60–64), but it is worth repeating, as it

(CALL)   (RESPONSE)

Figure 6.3. 'Majestic Fanfare' (ABC news signature tune)

neatly illustrates what I have said so far and shows how there is both continuity and change in heraldic music. For 32 years, the ABC, Australia's national broadcaster, had used a news signature theme called 'Majestic Fanfare'. It had a call-response structure with a typical heraldic call to action (see Figure 6.3): a rising melody, using large intervals and dotted rhythms, in a major key and a bright march tempo, was followed by a response using a range of instruments, slowing down somewhat, and rising to an unresolved high note.

What did this say about the identity of the ABC? First of all, the 'call to attention', the voice of the national broadcaster was the voice of a leader (the call-response structure). Also, it was played by trumpets (intertextually the sound of military parades and nationalistic ceremonies), disciplined (the march tempo and the dotted rhythm), unified (unison), authoritative (loud), confident (large intervals), and optimistic (major key). As Siegfried Helms commented on similar radio signature tunes: 'Despite two world wars, the march appears not to have lost any of its attraction across the world"(Helms, 1981: 81, *my translation*). The response united a large and diverse group (the whole orchestra, using different instruments and including even a harp glissando) which nevertheless was in harmony with itself (homophonic harmony). In short, the news theme was a call to action from an authoritative national broadcaster, obediently responded to by a diverse, but harmonic nation.[3]

In the late 1980s this theme was replaced with a new theme. It had three parts. The first part opened with a synthesizer drone which continued throughout the whole part – the era of the satellite and global technology had begun. Several 'call and response' phrases followed (the first of these is shown in Figure 6.4), still using a trumpet, but this time it was a single piccolo trumpet (less assertive and unified), and it played a descending melody in a minor key (more 'sentimental' and less optimistic), using jazz-like syncopation (an element of entertainment). The response was also descending (less enthusiasm) and played by a muted brass ensemble (less diversity). The middle section had a fast ostinato rhythmic pattern that could be taken as a musical imitation of, say, a teletypewriter, signifying the urgency and immediacy of the news (in many other news and current affairs tunes of the time actual sound effects were used). A newsreader read the

Figure 6.4. Call and response section of the new ABC tune

headlines over this middle section, punctuated by very short melodic phrases that alternated between a rather harsh sounding motif played by synthesized brass and a softer, more lyrical one, played by a more reedy synthesized sound (the news as varied and containing both 'hard' and 'soft' items). It was the late 1980s. Neoliberal voices questioned the value of public institutions, calling for privatization, and the ABC felt it needed to learn from the success of the commercial broadcasters, with their greater emphasis on entertainment. In short the tune represented a crisis of confidence. The old theme was soon reintroduced, but never with the same majestic aplomb.

Case study: sonic logos of IT companies

We now return to Brian Eno's sonic logo (http://www.youtube.com/watch?v=miZHa7ZC6Z0). It started on a low note that ascended glissando-like by a fourth and then jumped up an octave to four identical high notes – a static 'melody' that remained open, unresolved. Under the four high notes a synthesizer drone increased in loudness, ending abruptly. The heraldic function is therefore realized by the same attributes as the Majestic Fanfare – a steep rise up and an unresolved ending (cf. Figure 6.5). But the timbre is quite different. No trumpets here, but a soft, chime-like sound, suggesting a calm, new age mood (the tune was composed in the 1990s), as if sitting on a verandah, listening to the tinkling of a chime and contemplating the blue sky. Yet there is also an electronic edge, suggesting technological perfection. And unlike the Majestic Fanfare, no sense of group identity is invoked, reminiscent of television commercials from the period which showed people working with laptops in remote locations, amidst the grandeur of nature, with no human being in sight.

The AT&T sonic logo was designed by Joel Beckermann, CEO of the New York sonic branding agency Man Made Music. The company's website describes the brief: 'AT&T tasked us with creating a Sonic Identity System that would embody "Rethink Possible" in a more human and relatable way' (Man Made Music, 2016). This 'Identity System' included startup sounds, ringback tones, tones that reveal that security protection is engaged, and so on, all taking the company's

Figure 6.5. Brian Eno's 1995 Microsoft startup sound

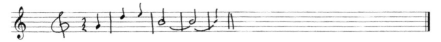

Figure 6.6. AT&T sonic logo

sonic logo as their point of departure – a four-note ascending melody remaining unresolved, a 'stair-step of crisp, bright tones' (Man Made Music, 2016) expressing a 'rally cry' (Jurgensen, 2012) – cf. Figure 6.6 and http://www.youtube.com/watch?=vaMoKo34a3bw:

In the version I analysed, the timbre mixes an old piano, a glockenspiel and a Wurlitzer with an electronic edge, thus blending sounds evoking technological perfection and innovation with the human touch of traditional instruments to make 'AT&T more human and expressive' (Kessler, 2014). Beckermann also created a longer 'Sonic Anthem' in which the logo goes through a number of repetitions with different timbres, ranging from purely electronic to synthesized strings, 'from warm to forward thinking' (Man Made Music, 2016), and with an energetic drum rhythm throughout: 'in every repetition of these four tones there is opportunity for reinvention, mirroring the brand's culture of innovation' (Ibid.).

The INTEL sonic logo, first launched in 1995, and composed by Walter Werzowa, is one of the most famous sonic logos of all (http://www.youtube.com/watch?v=OHjKDdXCR3l), hailed by the industry for having 'achieved a high level of consumer awareness and recall of its Pentium processes in excess of the tangible influence that the brand or its product have on people's lives' (Arning and Gordon, 2006: 5). It starts with a high impact 'audio sparkle' mixing 20 different sounds (Jackson, 2003: 128), including a tambourine, an anvil and an electric spark, which first becomes louder, then softer again, as if describing an orbit – the sonic equivalent of the dynamic circle that surrounds the company's name in the visual logo. This is followed by a four-note ascending staccato melody that spells 'Intel Inside' (see Figure 6.7) and blends electronic sounds with a xylophone, bells, a marimba and a 'secret recipe of instruments' (Ibid.), while we see the slogan 'leap ahead'. Again the optimism and forcefulness of the ascending

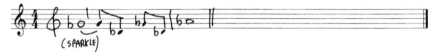

Figure 6.7. Intel logo

melody is married to a timbre that combines the sounds of technological perfection with sounds that seek to evoke affective resonance, so as to create 'a logo with emotional content, in the same way as a film score works' (Ibid).

Compared to the 'Majestic Fanfare' and other heraldic themes of the past, there is therefore both continuity and change. The assertive optimism of the rising melody continues. But the timbre has changed. Instead of the militaristic bugle call, we now have timbres that blend technological perfection with human appeal, the former through electronic sounds, the latter through a variety of approaches, from the gentle, wind-driven sound of chimes to the nostalgia of old pianos and the sweet retro sound of the Wurlitzer. As Cooke (1959) has shown, many melodic phrases have, through the centuries, been used with similar lyrics, expressing similar themes. Timbres, on the other hand, change with the times, as instrumental technologies reflect the preoccupations of the period, from the gentle harpsichord of the eighteenth century to the piano which, according to Schafer (1994: 109) 'typified the greater aggressiveness of a time in which objects were punched and beaten into existence by means of industrial processes where once they had been stroked, carved and kneaded into shape' – and to the current era of digital instruments with their focus on providing a wide array of timbres (a modern digital stage piano will offer hundreds of preset timbres). Melodic continuity and timbral change not only characterize the history of Western music, but also the history of specific logos. The Intel logo, like other sonic logos has often been updated, but 'crucially, the one thing that has not changed in the Intel sonic logo is the melody. With a consistent melody in place, sonic identities can be rearranged but still maintain their essence' (Jackson, 2003: 94).

The way I have analysed sonic logos reflects the way they are produced. Jackson describes how his company Sonicbranding (now part of CuttingEdge Commercial) set about creating a sonic logo for an IT company called Vivazzi. The process started with the identification of the values of the company. In the case of Vivazzi these were (1) 'soft technology', technology with a human touch; (2) 'modern heritage', combining the values of continuity and the trust it generates with innovation; and (3) 'human energy'. These values were then matched with musical attributes and intertextual references. 'Soft technology' was expressed by 'contemporary synthesized drum loops' as familiar from drum and bass music, but played by traditional African drums, to 'soften things up and add some humanity' (Jackson, 2003: 119). Heritage was expressed by using a string section, referencing the kind of classical music 'traditionally used in commercials for banks and insurance companies', but adding synthesized textures to give it 'an electronic edge and an unexpected bit of interest' (Ibid). Human energy was produced by a gospel choir with some vocal percussion (a la Bobby McFerrin's 'Don't Worry Be Happy') (Ibid: 120). This process created what elsewhere I have called a 'composite of connotations' (van Leeuwen, 2005: 275), expressing a composite of values. But Jackson recognizes that some composers work intuitively and holistically rather than following a rational, step-by-step process of this kind. In that case, he argues, there has to be a post hoc analysis to ensure that the intended meanings are expressed: 'Sometimes it is better to let a composer create as a whole and then analyze the branding down to its individual components rather than adopt the sonic layering process of building one layer at a time' (Jackson, 2003: 120).

Conclusion

A few conclusions can be drawn.

First of all, sonic logos, like other contemporary consumer products, combine a practical function with the expression of identity. Their functional structure is quite stable and homogeneous, calling the listener to attention through a melodic structure characterized by ascending melodies, large intervals, dotted rhythms, and a lack of resolution, so that the music has an open ending, continuing in what follows, whether it be a news bulletin or a work session of the computer user. The identity function is less stable and more varied and flexible, able to respond to new trends as they occur, and primarily carried by timbres, often created through blending sounds with specific meaning potentials or cultural references into novel 'composites of connotations'. Sonic logos therefore embody both continuity and change, both genetic homogeneity and stylistic variety.

Sonic logos also blur the distinction between the private and the public. The ringtones we choose to personalize our phones can reference musical genres, ethnic origins, and so on, but the online catalogues from which they can be downloaded also include ringtones with names like 'iPhone', 'Apple' 'Google' and so on. Like the sonic logos of IT companies these ringtones have simple ascending melodies and timbres that blend the electronic and 'metallic' with warmer edges. The 'iPhone' ringtone even has a high warbling, sometimes whistle-like drone and a three-note descending background melody sounding somewhat like strings. The meanings Eno had to express in the Microsoft startup sound ('optimistic', 'futuristic', 'emotional', 'universal', etc.) can also become individual identity markers.

Finally, we have seen that the semiotic analysis of sonic logos has much in common with the methods used to produce them. Sonic branding companies, like semioticians, methodically study the meaning potentials of vocal and musical attributes, creating systematically classified inventories of sounds. As Jackson argues (2003: 116): 'the visual branding world is very familiar with the concept of a language system' (e.g. colour palette, fonts, layouts and shapes) and so is the world of sonic branding.

In fact, marketers have often been ahead of semioticians in this regard. In our work on 'branding the self', Machin and I (2008) showed how the 1980s' cultural studies trend to see identity as fluent and flexible was preceded by at least ten years by the change, in marketing, from traditional demographics to 'lifestyle' characterizations of consumers, based on their values, leisure activities and consumer preferences. In a similar way, I have now discovered that the parametric approach to the semiotics of voice quality, which I began to develop in the 2000s (see van Leeuwen, 2008) was preceded by the work of companies such as Orange who developed 'a set of 14 attributes that they could use to describe the sound of a voice'. With these attributes Orange can describe voices as, for example, 'dynamic', as well as adjusting the definition of 'dynamic' cross-culturally (Jackson, 2003: 134ff). Semioticians would do well to pay attention to this kind of work and relate the analysis of semiotic resources and the texts in which they are used to the practices that create the texts and bring them into circulation.

Notes

1   The roots of ambient music go much further back. Telemann wrote 'table music' for his aristocratic sponsors in the eighteenth century, and in 1917 Erik Satie wrote *musique d'ameublement'* ('furniture music') for the opening of an exhibition which he deliberately intended to be background music. But as soon as the musicians started to play, people stopped talking and started listening, and Satie, apparently, walked around, waving his arms and inciting people to talk: 'Parlez! Parlez' (Murray Schafer, 1994: 90).

2 While marketers' interest in the 'shallow processing' of music is no doubt motivated by the quest for the holy grail of implanting ideas directly into the brain, there is evidence that music is somewhat of a special case. Oliver Sacks (2007), for instance, recounts the case of a man with severe amnesia, who can nevertheless remember music, which suggests that music is remembered differently from other experiences.

3 In an excellent book on advertising music, Helms (1981: 305) calls such themes 'signal music', notes the use of trumpets, broken triads, ascending melodies and 'accents on the last tone', and links it to fanfares which 'remind of heralds and kings – we involuntarily associate them with power, victory and triumph'.

References

Arning, C. and Gordon, A. (2006), *Sonic Semiotics – The Role of Music in Marketing Communication*. Amsterdam: Esomar World Research Paper.

Balasz, B. (1970 [1931]), *Theory of the Film: Character and Growth of a New Art*. New York: Dover Publications.

Cooke, D. (1959), *Language of Music*. Oxford: Clarendon.

Eno, B. (1975), Liner notes for *Discreet Music*, London: EG Records Ltd (unpaginated).

Gorbman, C. (1987), *Unheard Melodies – Narrative Film Music*. Bloomington: Indiana University Press.

Graakjær, N. (2012), 'Dance in the Store: On the Use and Production of Music in Abercrombie & Fitch', *Critical Discourse Studies* 9(4): 393–406.

Hall, E. T. (1966), *The Hidden Dimension*. New York: Doubleday.

Heath, R. (2001), *The Hidden Power of Advertising: How Low Involvement Processes Influence the Way We Choose Brands*. Henley-on-Thames: Admaps Publications.

Helms, S. (1981), *Musik in der Werbung*. Wiesbaden: Breitkopf und Hartel.

Jackson, D. M. (2003), *Sonic Branding – An Introduction*. London: Palgrave Macmillan.

Jurgensen, J. (2012), 'Making an Impression in Just Four Notes'. *Wall Street Journal*, 28 January.

Kessler, S. (2014), 'The Next (Sound) Wave in Branding: How AT&T Created Its New Sonic Identity'. <http://www.fastcodedesign.com/1671164/the-next-sound-wave-in-branding-how-att-created-its-new-sonic-identity> [accessed 26 May 2016].

Kim-Cohen, S. (2016), *Against Ambience and Other Essays*. London: Bloomsbury.

Lomax, A. (1968), *Folksong Style and Culture*. New Brunswick, NJ: Transaction Books.

Machin, D. and van Leeuwen, T. (2008), 'Branding the Self', in C. R. Caldas-Coulthard and R. Iedema (eds) *Identity Trouble – Critical Discourse and Contested Identities*, pp. 43–57. London: Palgrave Macmillan.

Man Made Music. (2016), www.manmademusic.com [accessed 26 May 2016].

Marothy, J. (1974), *Music and the Bourgeois, Music and the Proletarian.* Budapest: Akademiai Kiado.

Niebur, L. (2010), *Special Sound: The Creation and Legacy of the BBC Radiophonic Workshop.* Oxford: Oxford University Press.

Sacks, O. (2007), *Musicophilia.* New York: Vintage Books.

Schafer, R. Murray (1994), *The Soundscape: Our Sonic Environment and the Tuning of the World.* Rochester, Vermont: Destiny Books.

Selvin, J. (1996), 'Q and A with Brian Eno', *San Francisco Chronicle*, 2 June. moredarkthanshark.org/eno_int_sfc_jun96.html [accessed 13/7/16]

van Leeuwen, T. (1999), *Speech, Music, Sound.* London: Palgrave Macmillan.

van Leeuwen, T (2005), *Introducing Social Semiotics.* London: Routledge.

van Leeuwen, T. (2008), 'Parametric Systems: The Case of Voice Quality', in C. Jewitt (ed.) *The Routledge Handbook of Multimodal Analysis*, pp. 76–85. London: Routledge.

7

'If You Have Nothing To Say – Sing It!': On the Interplay of Music, Voice and Lyrics in the Advertising Jingle

Johnny Wingstedt

The Latin verb *advertere* means 'to turn toward'. From the eighteenth century, the British verb *advertise* was used with the meaning 'to call attention to something', for example goods for sale, rewards, and so on (*Oxford English Dictionary*). To 'call attention' is of course also today a basic function of advertising; not least it is an essential objective of the advertising jingle, a short song or tune used in advertising. Attracting attention by means of sound and music takes advantage of how sound is a 'wrap-around' medium, that is, the listener does not have to turn towards a sound to experience it. The sound will instead 'turn towards the listener'; it will extend and reach anyone within hearing distance (van Leeuwen, 1999). Advertising on television takes advantage of this distinctive quality. Even when the listener is away from the television set the sound will call attention to itself during commercial breaks, typically supported by an increase in loudness. But of course advertising aims to do more that just to attract attention – or rather, it attracts attention for a reason. Some important functions of the advertising jingle are to create an 'image' of a product or service, to affect and to persuade. Nicholas Cook (1998b: 3) argues that music does this very efficiently, that 'advertisers use music to communicate meanings that would take too long to put into words, or that would carry no conviction in them'. In this, the musical jingle, like all advertising, becomes a significant carrier of values, attitudes and ideologies.

The purpose of this chapter is to discuss and exemplify how discourses can be expressed by the advertising jingle through the interweaving of lyrics, music and voice. Freitas (2012) points out how advertising makes for rewarding study, due to its relevance as a continuously updated source of information as to past and present social values and beliefs – and also because of its ubiquitous presence in contemporary Western societies. This as well as its distinct purpose and compact design makes it an essential and valuable object for analytic inquiry.

Guy Cook (2001) argues that most relevant meanings in a multimodal advertising text are commonly conveyed non-linguistically, through channels such as image or sound. In examining how discourses are represented by combining modes such as lyrics, voice and music, different, or additional, *semiotic resources* and choices must be taken into consideration compared with looking at speech or writing alone. The concept of semiotic resource is used here to indicate and comprise 'the actions, materials and artefacts we use for communicative purposes, whether produced physiologically. . .or technologically' (van Leeuwen, 2005: 285). Each mode of communication, and associated semiotic resources, individually constructs meaning but above all, meaning emerges from the complex interweaving of the modes and resources involved (Kress et al, 2001; Wingstedt 2008; Wingstedt *et al.*, 2010). To examine such multimodal communication as discourse, Kress (2012) argues they need to be viewed as texts. In this sense, the concept of *text* should be understood as a *multimodal semiotic entity* in multiple dimensions.

> *Texts*, of whatever kind, are the result of the semiotic work of *design*, and of processes of *composition* and *production*. They result in *ensembles* composed of different *modes*, resting on the agentive semiotic work of the maker of such text. (Kress, 2012: 36; unless otherwise noted all emphases are in original)

The study of discursive aspects of multimodal texts, pursued by means of multimodal discourse analysis (MMDA), aims to 'elaborate tools that can provide insight into the relation of the meanings of a community and its semiotic manifestations. In MMDA, the *apt* use of modes for the realization of *discourses* in *text* in a specific situation is a central question' (Ibid., 36).

Fundamental to discourse analysis is the view that meaning always emerges in relation to different levels of context (Cook, 1998a; van Dijk, 2008; van Leeuwen, 2008; Gee, 2011). Theo van Leeuwen and Gunther Kress (2011) discuss how we must pay attention to the specific communicative potential of specific modes, and how it is important to be aware of their common properties and potentials. Semiotic resources have a *meaning potential*, a range of possible meanings, based on their past uses. Meaning potentials are 'actualized in concrete social contexts' of use (van Leeuwen, 2005: 285). A central question, as van Leeuwen and Kress (2011) point out, is to understand how semiotic resources are actually used in multimodal texts. This chapter explores how attention needs to be directed, not only towards social, cultural, situational or institutional contexts, but also to multimodal contexts; how modes constructing specific multimodal texts contextualize each other.

To illustrate and exemplify how semiotic resources and contexts come together when discourse takes the form of designed multimodal ensembles, two examples of vintage American jingles will be analysed; a jingle for the cleaning detergent *Mr Clean*', 'Mr Clean (gets rid of dirt and grime)' – and a beer commercial for *Lowenbrau*', 'Here's to good friends' (aka 'Tonight, tonight, let it be Lowenbrau').

The 'Mr Clean' jingle was composed in the late 1950s by Thomas Scott Cadden, and arranged by Bill Walker. The song is performed as a duet by singers Don Cherry and Betty Bryan. This musical theme has, in several different versions, been used by the company Procter and Gamble™ in various campaigns using the brand name of *Mr Clean*. The version analysed is the original version and is about 55 seconds long. The song is performed as an up-tempo polka. Teixeira (1974) lists typical categories of jingles, and this one could be described as being in the style of a 'hit song'. The polka was a common genre of popular, 'easy listening' melodies of the time (Greene, 1992). The strategy of using a popular style for a jingle is to blend in with the regular radio music programming, to avoid the listener 'turning off' their attention, otherwise typically an instant reaction to commercial breaks on radio or television. The 'Mr Clean' jingle is an example of a 'classic' jingle style, with a simple, rhythmic and catchy melody with frequent mentions of the brand name. The lyrics go as follows:

Male: Mister Clean gets rid of dirt and grime and grease in just a minute,
Female: Mister Clean will clean your whole house and everything that's in it.
M: Floors, doors, walls, halls, white sidewall tiles and old golf balls,
F: Sinks, stoves, bathtubs he'll do, he'll even help clean laundry too.
M: Mister Clean gets rid of dirt and grime and grease in just a minute,
F: Mister Clean will clean your whole house and everything that's in it.
M: Can he clean a kitchen sink? / *F*: Quicker that a wink.
M: Can he clean a window sash? / *F*: Faster than a flash.
M: Can he clean a dirty mirror? / *F*: He'll make it bright and clearer.
M: Can he clean a diamond ring? / *F*: Mister Clean cleans anything!
Both: Mister Clean gets rid of dirt and grime and grease in just a minute,

Mister Clean will clean you whole house and everything that's in it,
Mister Clean, Mister Clean, Mister Clean.

(Thomas Scott Cadden, 1957)

The 'Lowenbrau' jingle is from a campaign in the mid-1970s, when the brand was distributed in the United States by Miller Brewing Company™. The music is composed by William M. Backer, then an employee of the ad agency McCann Erickson, and performed by singer Arthur Prysock. The song could, just as the 'Mr Clean' commercial, be described as a hit song jingle. It is 59 seconds long and performed in a laid-back and mellow country-pop style, with a loose shuffle rhythm. At the same time it is an example of what Teixeira (1974) calls the 'standard type', which in the advertising business is also known as a 'donut' – that is, a jingle with a 'hole in the middle'. This is a formal structure that starts out with the first part of the jingle (the 'front'), where usually the main theme is sung. It is followed by an instrumental part (the 'bed', that is, the 'hole') that is used as a background for a spoken voice-over. The end of the jingle (the 'tag') is again sung. The different parts of the jingle are usually designed so that they can be played separately, truncated into so-called lifts, if shorter versions are needed. The lifts are often used at later stages in an advertising campaign, as a form of *multimodal synecdoche* (McKerrell and Way, this volume), when the audience can be expected to recognize the jingle as well as the message established by the full-length version. A shorter version of the jingle is then sufficient, just to remind the listener of the brand image established by the campaign. The advantage of the short version, besides reducing advertising costs, is also to not wear out the listener. Instead, the listener can be engaged to mentally 'fill in' what is missing from the melody and words. The full lyrics are:

LEAD: Here's to good friends, tonight is kind of special,
the beer will pour, must say something more somehow,
so tonight, tonight, let it be Lowenbrau.
It's been so long, hey, I'm glad to see ya',
raise your glass, here's to health and happiness,
so tonight, tonight, let it be all the best.
(*VOICE-OVER*:
When you're with good friends having good times,
don't just have a beer, have a Lowenbrau,
because good friends and good times deserve the taste of a great beer,

and there's really only one – Lowenbrau.)

LEAD: Tonight, let it be Lowenbrau.

(William M. Backer, 1976)

I have chosen these examples since they clearly illustrate relations of form, content and expression at the same time as they reflect certain aspects of the times and cultural contexts in which they were used. Both jingles were also relatively well known in their respective cultural settings, and are today available on the web for listening. In both songs, similar semiotic resources are employed for purposes of communication, such as pitch, tempo, rhythm, harmony, voice timbre and so on – although largely differently applied, using contrasting approaches. In this, they illustrate how different discursive choices are made depending on purpose, contexts and available resources. Cook (2001) points out the challenge of trying to describe modal expressions such as music through the mode of writing, as is done in this book. A transformation, or *transduction* (Kress, 2010), has to be made between the different modes where much is 'lost in translation'. To grasp, as fully as possible, the impact of lyrics, music and voice as a multimodal text the reader is therefore encouraged to search for and listen to the examples being discussed in the following sections. A few suggestions of sources for listening to the two jingles are available at the end of this chapter.

In order to investigate the functional organization of the multimodal texts, the following discussion will be organized according to Halliday's (1978) three metafunctions of communication, the *textual, ideational* and *interpersonal* metafunctions. Halliday describes the metafunctions as components that are present in all communication in every social context, a text is a product of all three components. The metafunctions are here taken as a starting point in exploring how discursive aspects of the two jingles are multimodally structured, how the world is represented and how persuasion is achieved.

Structural meaning potentials

Halliday (1978) describes the textual metafunction as the component of communication that provides the texture. It is the organizing of a text (in a broad sense) as a coherent message through textual resources of a mode. It expresses the relation of the communicative act with its environment, including both the 'internal' modal environment and the situational environment. The textual component has an enabling function with respect to the other two metafunctions. 'It is only in combination with textual meanings that ideational and interpersonal meanings are actualized' (Ibid: 113). Textual features of music are constituted by material aspects and the social use of musical sound. Fundamental temporal resources for music to achieve cohesive textual meaning are the use of structural features such as form, continuity and phrasing (Wingstedt, Brändström and Berg, 2010). The following section will exemplify how music structures multi-modal meaning in combination with lyrics and voice.

The favoured important word in most commercials is the product name, or sometimes a prominent word of the slogan. In the 'Mr Clean' jingle, the central word is 'clean'. In English, the word 'clean' can be used as an adjective (the table is clean) or as a verb (it is necessary to clean the bathtub). In this jingle, clean is also a noun since it is part of the product name. In combining words and music the verbal structure of the lyrics is directly affected by conventions of musical structure. The metrical regularity and cyclical form of music allows for (or even calls for) time-based constructions that make possible repetition of the phrases that are outlined by melody as well as by lyrics. As the musical structure builds on repetition, so is also repetition of words made possible. The 'Mr Clean' jingle takes advantage of this, and in the 55 seconds of the song, the word 'clean' is repeated 19 times. In common speech this would be thought of as being absurd and annoying. When certain words or synonyms are being 'over-present' in a text, it is known as *overlexicalization* (Machin and Mayr, 2012: 222). When words are set to music, excessive overlexicalization will not only be acceptable to the listener – it may even be expected, following conventions of traditional song forms and genres. The 'Mr Clean' jingle also illustrates how the exact repetition of the same word, rather than synonyms, is used and 'normalized'.

Looking closer at the combined music-lyric structure reveals that most of the repeated words appear at strategic metric positions, which occur at *stressed beats* and at *stressed bars*. The song is performed in the style of a polka, notated in 2/4 time (see Figure 7.1). This means that the basic underlying pulse of the music is organized into short repeating divisions of two beats. In music notation the divisions are indicated as the space between two bar lines – what is known as a bar or a measure. It can be thought of as a metrical 'micro cycle'. The first beat of each bar is a downbeat, which is also referred to as a stressed (or strong) beat. It doesn't matter what the time signature would be (e.g. 2/4, 3/4 or 4/4 time etc.), the downbeat of each bar is always referred to (and experienced) as a stressed beat – as opposed to an unstressed or a weak beat. This does not mean that the downbeat is necessarily played stronger or more accented. Music theorist Justin

London (2012) suggests that the experience of the downbeat as being the start of each bar results from the embodied phenomenon of *entrainment*: 'a synchronization of some aspect of our biological activity with regularly recurring events in the environment' (London, 2012: 4). However, he continues, metre is more than just a stimulus-driven form of attending; it is also culturally learnt, rehearsed and practiced. Entrainment involves the ability to predict the timing of anticipated future events. Although the experience of musical metre is grounded in the production and perception of a pulse, a metrical pattern requires coordination with at least one other level of organization. This could for example be related to rhythmical, melodic, harmonic or dynamic patterns. How this is done varies with musical style and genre.

When entrainment is in process, it 'leads us to focus our attention to the most salient temporal locations for events; attention is, by its very nature, selective' (Ibid., 12). Even though the beats of the underlying pulse may be of equal length, they will not be experienced as being equal in character or importance. When we are entrained to a regular meter, such as the 2/4 metre in 'Mr Clean', the downbeat of each bar will carry greater expectation and semiotic salience. Any lyrical text occurring on the downbeat will therefore be afforded more salience. As can be observed in Figure 7.1 the word 'clean' is almost always placed on a downbeat, and therefore is emphasized with more semiotic salience because of the multimodal interactions in the song.

In similar ways that beats in a bar are experienced differently, individual bars in a sequence will be perceived differently depending on their position in the sequence. Following conventions of traditional Western music, sequences of bars are often organized into larger cycles, 'periods' or 'parts', typically of four, eight or sixteen bars. The first bar in such a period is referred to as a stressed (or strong) bar. Just as with stressed beats, stressed bars (and associated components) achieve more importance (Huron, 2006). As can be seen in Figure 7.1, the word 'clean' most often falls on the downbeat of stressed bars, in four-bar periods. The salience of the word is thereby further emphasized by its position in the meta-structure of the song. The important word is also used to frame the entire jingle: the song starts directly with the first notes being the male voice singing 'Mr Clean'. The song's last words are performed by the male and female voices in harmony, three times hammering home the product name. This example illustrates how temporal form of speech and music come together as 'cycles in cycles', how music provides a structural framework for targeted language components to achieve salience to an extent normally not available in speech only.

The issue of repetition does not end there. A commercial jingle is part of an advertising campaign and will itself be repeated over a longer period of time, for months or sometimes even years. Furthermore it will be available across various media, for example television, radio, cinema – and in recent years on the internet. The 'Mr Clean' jingle is exceptional in this respect, as it was introduced in the late 1950s. It has since been used on and off, and in various new versions, until today. Moriarty (2015) claims it to be the longest running advertising jingle in television history. The recurrent use of a certain song is of course the basis for the listener learning to recognize the melody and words, a function of fundamental importance in advertising.

Musical salience can be achieved through a long list of factors. Machin (2010), van Leeuwen (1999, 2005) and Wingstedt, Brändström and Berg (2010) discuss several factors, such as volume, pitch, accent, repetition, timbre and potent cultural symbols, to name a few. Worth noting here is how the brand name in the example is consistently sung using an ascending interval, which can be described as going from a lower to a higher frequency and energy level (van Leeuwen, 1999; Machin, 2010). Assigning the word 'clean' to the higher note is a way to achieve salience. How pitch direction may also be associated with ideational and interpersonal meaning potentials will be discussed later in this chapter.

A different approach is taken for the jingle 'Let It Be Lowenbrau'. The lead vocal starts off directly, after a two-beat piano intro (see Figure 7.2). Again, the brand name is central, but in this song it is not heard until the eighth bar (about 17 seconds into the song), and then only once more right at the end, as the last word (at about 55 seconds). The structural strategy here is quite different compared to 'Mr Clean', and builds on principles of phrasing, and harmonic and melodic *tension-release*. Harmonically it is structured so that it starts on the *tonic* chord (the 'home chord' of the key) and then commences a harmonic progression that does not come to rest again until bar eight, coinciding with the word 'Lowenbrau'. The listener is taken on a harmonic journey building on the principle of tension-release that is not resolved until the cadence (or resolution), which is synchronous with the brand name. Bars six and seven heighten the expectations of what is to come, through a four-chord progression leading firmly towards the resolution (see Figure 7.2). The melodic structure performs a similar journey, finally landing on the 'home note' (the first scale degree of a tonal scale) on the last two syllables of 'Lowenbrau'. Here, the prominent temporal and semiotic principle is not so much periodicity but rather *connection* (Kress and van Leeuwen, 2006: 210), building on the sense of continuity and

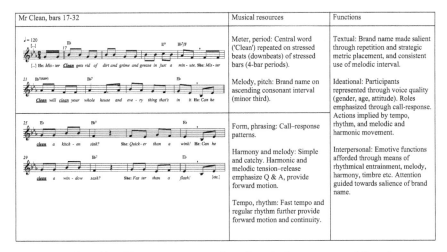

Figure 7.1. 'Mr Clean', bars 17–32, examples of musical resources and functions

Let it be Lowenbrau, bars 1-9	Musical resources	Functions
[musical notation]	Tempo, rhythm: medium slow, shuffle rhythm.	Textual: Brand name salient through melodic pitch direction and connection; harmonic/melodic tension-release with resolution at bar 8.
	Instrumentation: Beginning of song just piano and lead vocals. Strings and more instruments enter at bar 8.	
		Ideational: Participants represented through voice quality. Location, situation and activity implied through interplay with backing vocals, instrumentation, relaxed shuffle rhythm and tempo.
	Harmony, melody: Melody and chord progression lead through tension-release towards resolution at end of phrase (tonic chord at bar 8).	
		Interpersonal: Mood and emotive function through voice quality, low pitch and interaction of resources such as harmony, melody, tempo, and rhythm. From naturalistic to sensory modality through instrumentation.
	Pitch, timbre: Brand name at lowest note – affects timbre of lead vocal.	
	Form, phrasing: Brand name at end of phrase (bar 8). Call-response with lead and backing vocals at bars 6-9.	

Figure 7.2. 'Tonight, tonight, let it be Lowenbrau', bars 1–9, examples of musical resources and functions

forward motion of harmony and melody. The eight-bar phrase firmly leads the listener towards the inevitable final release, thus giving salience to the brand name. The structure is further strengthened by a backing chorus repeating the phrase 'Tonight, tonight, let it be Lowenbrau'.

A similar form and technique is also used for the spoken voice-over, layered on top of the instrumental 'bed' section. It is in the form of two extended spoken clauses, each leading up to and ending with the brand name. The jingle ends with the lead vocal finishing off with a modified version of the previous bars 5–8, condensed into two bars – now without the backing chorus. Contrary to 'Mr Clean', the 'Lowenbrau' jingle consistently synchronizes the brand name with the lowest note of the melody. Even the spoken voice-over uses a markedly lower pitch for the word 'Lowenbrau'. This recurring pitch-related device creates salience by what sometimes is referred to as a negative accent, that is, emphasizing an event by 'taking away' something (such as lowering volume, or here, pitch).

Representing the world

The ideational metafunction is about the part of communication that tells us about the world – the world we live in or fictional or 'represented' worlds. According to Halliday (1978: 112) the ideational metafunction represents the interlocutor's meaning potential as an observer. It is the content function of communication expressing phenomena of the environment, such as the creatures, objects, actions, events, qualities and states – 'of the world and of our own consciousness'. Kress et al (2001: 13) further describe ideational meaning potentials as 'who does what, with or to whom and where'. It could be added: with what and when – and how. Van Leeuwen (2008) takes the view that all representations of the world should be interpreted as *representations of social practices*. He presents a model of how elements of social practices enter into texts. Categories of elements include participants, actions, times, locations and resources. Certain elements, such as participants, locations and resources, are associated with *eligibility conditions* – that is, qualifications necessary 'in order to be eligible to play a particular role in a particular practice' (Ibid.: 10). Furthermore, *performance modes* are the manners or the pace in which actions are performed, and *presentation styles* involve dress and body grooming requirements for the participants. How are then elements of social practices represented through music, voice and lyrics in these jingles?

The participants of the two jingles are most directly represented through voice quality. On a basic level, by the sound of the voice, gender and age of the singers of 'Mr Clean' are readily recognized as two relatively young (to middle-aged) male and female Anglo-Americans. Initially, through the lyrics, they present themselves in alternating phrases as 'qualified users', having knowledge and opinions about the product by telling us about its advantages. About halfway into the jingle their roles emerge as more specialized: the man begins to ask questions such as 'can he clean a kitchen sink?' and the woman answers 'quicker than a wink' and so on. He poses four questions like this, and each time she promptly replies – answering the last question with 'Mr Clean cleans anything!' In this exchange of questions and answers the female singer assumes the role of expert authority on cleaning, in a sense fulfilling a historically normative gendered social role. After this section, the two singers repeat the beginning of the song, this time in two-part harmony. The question-answer section is musically emphasized by the use of a common musical device known as *call and response*. As the term implies it is a succession of two distinct phrases, where the second phrase is a direct response to the first. In this song the call-response structure is further accentuated by the harmonic structure. Here the chord progression plays a tension-release sequence, where the question is harmonized using a tension (*dominant*) chord pushing forward towards the answer that lands on a release (tonic) chord. A dominant chord is typically experienced as strongly pulling towards the tonal centre (the tonic), in a way demanding resolution (Goldman, 1965) – here, demanding an 'answer'. The tonic chord gives a sense of conclusiveness and decisiveness to the answer, lending it a quality of stability and self-assurance.

The voice and the music together also express aspects of the participants' mood and attitude, as the up-tempo music and simplicity of the melody may be understood as suggesting positive and enthusiastic mind-sets. As described earlier, the product name is consistently sung using an ascending interval. Furthermore, the melody is composed so that the brand name, 'Mr Clean', is always sung across the same ascending relative interval – a minor third, which is considered a *consonant* interval. A consonant interval (the opposite of a dissonant interval) is usually defined as a stable, harmonious and pleasing combination of notes (Baker, 2009). The consistent use of the same melodic interval for the brand name will provide for it to become established as a recognizable melodic shape, associated to the product name. As a consequence, the melodic sound can eventually carry the meaning of the lyrical text without the words, which is also an illustration of the concept of a multimodal synecdoche, discussed in Chapter 1 of this volume. When the word-melody connection is firmly established it may, later in the advertising campaign, be possible to play the melody without the lyrics – and the listener can mentally fill in the missing words. This is a powerful technique for persuasion, potentially making the listener 'sing' the name of the product (at least inwardly) – that is, a way to interpersonally engage the listener.

Here it should be noted that music, seen as a mode of expression, offers a wide range of meaning potentials. It is essential to bear in mind that care must be taken not to attribute specific meanings to single musical factors. As Cook (1998a: 9) puts it, 'Instead of talking about meaning as something that the music *has*, we should be talking about it as something that the music *does* (and has done to it) within a given context'. The view taken here is that meaning emerges from complex and dynamic interactions of semiotic resources and layers of contexts. According to a research overview presented by Gabrielsson and Lindström (2001), ascending and consonant intervals may potentially be associated with expressions such as happiness, serenity and pleasantness, but also with a range of other emotions depending on context. Gabrielsson and Lindström point out that interactions between melodic contour and rhythm is a factor that will affect judgements of perceived emotion, as will the complexity of the harmonic content. In the case of the 'Mr Clean' jingle, the regular rhythm and brisk tempo, and also the simple and consonant harmony potentially supports associations to happiness and gaiety. This is further strengthened by the ascending interval discussed above, which produces an extremely stable sound because of the consonance between the melody and the harmony.[1] Other contextual factors include the multimodal interactions of music with lyrics and voice quality, and the connotations of the polka as a musical genre in American culture in the 1950s. Of course, the individual use of available semiotic resources for meaning-making is also shaped by what Kress (2010: 108) describes as 'contingencies of individual experience, always in specific environments, expressed as interest'.

In the case of 'Mr Clean', there is for many potential customers also a visual image related to the name. Already during the original commercial campaign in the 1950s, a friendly looking bald and muscular character was introduced – 'Mr Clean' himself. Even when the jingle is played on radio many listeners will mentally associate the brand name and melody with the visual image of 'Mr Clean'. This is further emphasized by the lyrics consistently referring to the detergent as *he* rather that *it*, humanizing the product, such as: 'Can he clean a dirty mirror? / He'll make it bright and clearer'. This detergent is not just a resource or a tool – it is presented as a vivacious participant performing cleaning activities.

In the 'Lowenbrau' jingle, the participants represented through voice – the lead singer, backing chorus and voice-over – are all male. The lead singer's voice has a slightly rough quality and projects a laid-back relaxed attitude – suitable attributes qualifying an expert beer drinker. Here too, melody is a decisive element in the delivery of the brand name – this time however by lowering the pitch, as previously described. Lowering the pitch also dramatically affects the voice timbre, emphasizing the relaxed attitude as well as adding to the 'masculinity' factor. It is also obvious that these voices (lead singer and voice-over) have had many beers over the years. Comparing how melodic shapes are used in the 'Mr Clean' and 'Lowenbrau' jingles, illustrate how strongly pitch and melody regulate aspects of engagement and attitude. It could be described as the melody shapes the performance of the lyrics by a kind of *musical prosody*, modulating the words through affordances of melodic contour and related musical resources.

Also in the 'Lowenbrau' jingle the relationship between the singing participants is established through the previously discussed technique of call and response. In this case not as question-answer, but instead the backing chorus echoing the slogan 'Tonight, tonight, let it be Lowenbrau'. This signals agreement and closeness, suggesting friendship and male camaraderie – making the 'good friends' of the lyrics and spoken copy come to life. This discourse of 'male bonding through drinking' would be difficult to express as directly and clearly through speech alone.

The actions performed in the two examples are partly suggested by the lyrics, but more distinctly expressed through the musical sound. In 'Mr Clean' the action-words are straightforward, the main activity being to 'clean', to 'get rid of dirt and grime' and to 'make it bright' – the 'what' of the activities. The music more effectively illustrates the 'how', the performance mode, the manners and pace of cleaning. The brisk tempo and steady forward motion of the polka rhythm, combined with the simplicity of melody and chord progression makes the cleaning act appear joyful and easy. The brightness can be heard also in the instrumentation, most notably by a supplementary vibraphone part that through its clean overtones, distinct attack and long decay adds metaphorical 'shine' to the musical sound. Of course, the before-mentioned call and response pattern is a speech act – here performed as a 'singing act' where the male singer demands information (van Leeuwen, 2005: 118) and gets appropriate answers from the female singer (highlighted by the harmonic progression, as described earlier). The information provided is of course at the same time conveyed to the listener, potentially getting interpersonally engaged in the activity by means of musical entrainment and emotive expression.

In the 'Lowenbrau' jingle, similarly, the main activities are outlined by the lyrics ('having good times', 'beer will pour', 'raise your glass') but again the performance mode is more closely specified through the musical expression. The tempo is relatively slow with a relaxed shuffle bounce providing a laid-back and easy-going feeling. The activities here are obviously performed at a comfortable pace. The singing act performed by lead and backing chorus can be described as the lead offering goods ('Let It Be Lowenbrau') and the echoing/confirming reply of the backing singers shows willing acceptance. The low pitch and rough timbre of the voices (also including the voice-over) show no sign of stress or tension in the activities performed.

The location of the performers and activities of the 'Lowenbrau' jingle is in the lyrics only implicit. The musical instrumentation however, more explicitly, initially suggests a possible pub or bar setting. The song starts out with just an upright piano and lead vocals – proposing a naturalistically represented bar environment. Once established, the *naturalistic modality* (aspect and degree of 'truth') however gives way to a more *sensory modality* when backing vocals and strings enter as the lyrics approach the first mention of the product name. Van Leeuwen (2005: 170) describes sensory modality as 'a degree of articulation which is amplified beyond the point of naturalism', as 'more than real' and 'used in contexts where pleasure matters'. Here, the music, through instrumentation, arrangement, harmony, melody, rhythm, tempo and performance style, provides a lush sound and a relaxed expression that is maintained until the end of the jingle. A heightened reality is established, well suited for (interpersonal) emotive and persuasive purposes.

The 'Mr Clean' jingle is less musically descriptive or specific in relation to the imagined location. Here it is however clearly stated by the lyrics that 'Mr Clean will clean your whole house (and everything that's in it)'. Then it reels off attributes like floors, doors, walls, halls and so on, and inventory details like sinks, stoves and bathtubs. The musical expression is inexplicit about location but could be understood as a kind of music that is likely to be played on the radio in such a house in the 1950s, contributing a safe and positive atmosphere and vigorous energy to the home environment.

The two jingles appear to take place at different times of the day. The 'Lowenbrau' lyrics are specific about the time, as 'tonight' is mentioned several times, especially as part of the slogan. This is validated by the laid-back musical performance, relaxed singing style, lush sound and deep voice quality. The energetic musical expression of 'Mr Clean' instead suggests a daytime activity, even though this is not explicitly stated. In the lyrics there is however mention of another aspect of time, in that 'Mr Clean gets rid of dirt and grime and grease in just a minute'. This swiftness and efficiency is articulated by the musical performance. Yet another aspect of time is also how these jingles are time stamped by ways of style, genre and production aesthetics, telltale signs of the production period as well as of the cultural setting.

As mentioned, the 'Mr Clean' lyrics list a range of resources, mainly attributes and inventories of a household. The foremost resource however, as in most advertising, is the product to be sold. It is described above how the product name of 'Mr Clean' achieves salience by repetition and metrical position. The descriptive and metaphorical 'shine' attributed to the timbre of the supplementary vibraphone part provides qualities that are appropriate for the product. One can literally hear the whole house sparkle and gleam as a result of using the product. This is further emphasized by how the melodic vibraphone line consistently hits its highest note every time when the lyrics reach the word 'clean' on a stressed bar, as previously described. The vibraphone part is present during the whole song and is also the very last sound heard in the recording, playing the interval of an ascending and consonant perfect fifth – musically echoing the product name and at the same time leaving the listener with a lingering impression of shiny brightness. The previously mentioned ascending minor third interval for the product name not only defines the attitude of the participants, but equally the qualities to be collocated with the product.

The few resources mentioned in the 'Lowenbrau' lyrics, mainly 'glass' and 'beer', relate directly to the product. Also here, the product name achieves salience through the structural design of the music, in this case through the process of harmonic and melodic tension-release, and the hitting the low notes on the product name. Again, the musical and vocal sound and expression demonstrate eligibility by articulating the effects of using the product, connoting desirable qualities such as wellbeing, leisure and togetherness.

Engaging, convincing and seducing

Advertising is first and foremost about persuasion. It is about engaging, influencing, convincing, inspiring or seducing. In this sense advertising sets out not only to tell or show something but also to do something to the listener or viewer. Of course, it is mainly about, implicitly or explicitly, convincing the potential customer to buy something. Therefore, the most important communicative dimension in advertising is to act on others – what Halliday (1978: 112) terms the interpersonal metafunction of communication. Halliday describes the interpersonal component of communication as 'the speaker's meaning potential as an intruder. . .the speaker intrudes himself into the context of situation, both expressing his own attitudes and judgements and seeking to influence the attitudes and behaviour of others'. Wingstedt (2008) has suggested how music in film, games and advertising – in interaction with other modes – commonly contributes interpersonal meaning by *emotive* and *guiding* narrative functions.

Emotive functions have partially been discussed above, for example in how mood and attitudes of represented participants of the jingles are established through musical expression. In studies of emotions, it is often distinguished between perceived or induced emotions (e.g. Sloboda and Juslin, 2010) or similarly between *observed* or *experienced* emotions (Wingstedt, 2008). Emotions in music can be said to be observed if the listener mainly on a cognitive level will recognize a feeling, for instance will understand that a musical expression represents happiness – but not necessarily 'feel' it. If the listener however is emotionally affected by the music, for example feels happy from listening to a musical piece, then the emotion can be considered as experienced. Observed emotions can be thought of as ideational meaning-making, something is told about the world – such as expressing emotive qualities of the participants in the fictional world represented through a jingle. Communication of experienced emotions through music takes place on the interpersonal level; it does something to the listener. In a given situation there is typically a blend of experienced and observed emotions.

In the world of advertising, experienced emotions are preferred. The previous discussion of how musical semiotic resources such as tempo, rhythm, melodic contour and harmony contribute emotive qualities on the ideational level is of course also relevant for how emotive communication work musically on the interpersonal level. The positive and enthusiastic musical expression of 'Mr Clean', and relaxed and comfortable feel of the 'Lowenbrau' jingle may (and from the advertiser's point of view, should) affect and engage the listener also on the interpersonal level, as experienced emotions.

Related to this perspective on musical expression is also the notion of sensory modality discussed earlier, in connection to how strings and backing vocals contribute to a heightened reality in the 'Lowenbrau' jingle. The resulting lush sound invites emotional involvement and immersion for the listener. Similar immersive effects can be associated with the deep and resonant sound of the low-pitched voice when pronouncing the product name of Lowenbrau. In this sense, modality basically works on the interpersonal level.

Emotive involvement may also be based on functions related to remembrance and recognition. As discussed earlier, the jingles described (as any piece of music) are time stamped – or associated with certain cultures or genres. The two jingles represent popular music of different time periods, which may prompt listener reactions related to personal taste or sentiments. It could be feelings such as belonging or nostalgia – but also of indifference, dislike or ridicule. Aspects of style and genre are consequently powerful interpersonal tools of persuasion – but may also severely backfire if poorly selected by the advertiser. As mentioned in the introduction, the choice of a popular genre to 'blend in', to avoid that the listener 'turns off' his/her attention during a commercial break, is also to use genre to interpersonally address the listener.

The phenomenon of musical entrainment was discussed earlier in connection to how musical meter provides for salience of the product name in the 'Mr Clean' jingle, which also illustrates aspects of musical guiding functions. London (2012: 5) describes metric entrainment as a kind of behaviour, guiding the listener's attention as well as interacting on a pronounced physical level: 'When we are entrained our attention literally "moves with the music", and this engenders and encourages our bodily movements as well, from tapping toes and swinging arms to dancing and marching'. Entrainment being based on principles of embodiment by definition works on an interpersonal level. The brisk forward motion of the 'Mr Clean' jingle, or the laid-back shuffle of 'Lowenbrau' is set up to manifest in the listener's embodied response, discreetly or overtly. Another example of the listener's embodied response (although not directly due to entrainment) is the aforementioned 'making the customer sing the name of the product'.

Van Leeuwen (1999), Machin (2010) and McKerrell (2015) have described how social distance and address can be expressed using sound and music through for example musical arrangement, performance style, and recording and production techniques. The two jingles illustrate somewhat different approaches to this. Listening to the singing voices, they are in both cases recorded close to the microphone and mixed to the foreground of the musical arrangement. This establishes basic conditions for a close relationship to the listener. The vocal style of the two singers of the 'Mr Clean' jingle is however rather controlled, polished and formal. Diction is distinct and clear, and the presentation style has, even if positive and enthusiastic, a somewhat rigid and 'schooled' quality. The presentation is – maybe appropriately for this product – clean. At the same time, the singing performance is relatively vigorous and loud as if the singers are some distance away, suggesting remoteness to the listener. The described type of performance is at the same time fairly representative of how mainstream popular music of this time period were typically performed and produced.

The singing style of the 'Lowenbrau' jingle displays a more informal level of address. The lead singer uses a relaxed and casual singing style. The voice level is soft, as if being close to the listener. The deep, warm and slightly raspy voice quality reinforces the informal impression. Here, the listener is addressed more directly and straightforward. The lyrics support this approach by addressing the listener with 'hey, I'm glad to see ya'. The voice-over follows a similar concept, with a dark and rough voice quality. It is recorded even closer to the microphone, resulting in a heightened sense of intimacy. The two examples illustrate how the social distance of the key characters in the songs is established through recording techniques, performance style and the timbre of the voices. The differences in tempo and rhythm between the two jingles further support their respective approaches to how to establish degrees of distance, and how to address the listener on an interpersonal level.

Conclusion

The discourses apparent in the jingles discussed concern issues on different levels. On a surface level it is about the images that sell products. For Lowenbrau it is about issues such as comfort, wellbeing, friendship and togetherness. 'Mr Clean' foregrounds qualities such as efficiency, competence, happiness and wellbeing. Beneath the surface level, we find more complex issues, such as those of gender (for both jingles), alcohol and drinking ('Lowenbrau'), and social and family values ('Mr Clean').

By discussing the discursive meaning potentials of the jingles from a metafunctional perspective, the intention has been to investigate how the involved semiotic resources simultaneously communicate on the levels of structural, content and interpersonal meaning. Analysing the jingles has illuminated how overlexicalization and salience of targeted language components is constructed from the interplay of lyrics with a structural framework of musical resources such as metre, period, phrasing and pitch. Similarly, resources such as voice quality, tempo, rhythm, instrumentation, pitch and harmony work together to represent multimodal metaphors and elements of social practices (e.g. participants, actions and locations). Emotive and guiding functions, and the establishing of social distance, are accomplished through interactions of a multitude of resources including melodic contour, harmony, rhythm, metre, voice timbre and recording techniques. Many of the semiotic resources investigated work on a 'micro level', such as pitch direction or tempo. Other resources are more complex, for example musical genre that involves intricate subsets of interrelated components and dimensions. This chapter concludes with a further discussion of some of the more complex resources constructing discursive meaning of the two jingles. Besides musical genre, instrumentation, the singing voice and the 'jingle as an entity' will be given some additional thought.

The choice of musical genre for the 'Mr Clean' jingle has to some degree already been discussed above. Polka, as a genre, was in the 1950s associated with traditional and conservative American values (Greene, 1992). This can be viewed as opposed to the emerging Anglo-American youth culture that musically challenged and rebelled against the old values with rock and roll. The musical genre used for the 'Mr Clean' jingle signals a view on social values to be associated with the product. Nicholas Cook (1998a) points out how composers of advertising music not only work with notes, rhythms and timbres, but actually 'compose with styles and genres' as a basic musical technique. There are good reasons for this. Having only a few seconds to communicate a message, 'musical styles and genres offer unsurpassed opportunities for communicating complex social or attitudinal messages practically instantaneously' (Ibid.: 16). Lyrics, melodies or spoken messages take time to unfold. Just a few notes in a distinctive musical genre or style are 'sufficient to target a specific social and demographic group and associate a whole nexus of social and cultural values with a product' (Ibid.: 17).

Closely related to aspects of genre is instrumentation or orchestration, how music 'dress up' (or down). The choice of instruments is on one level directly associated to specific musical genres. But instrumentation as such also involves a complex set of interrelated dimensions concerning factors such as timbre characteristics, performance conditions, historical aspects, personal taste and cultural or subcultural associations to attitudes, values and ideologies. Instrumentation and musical genre, together with musical expression styles and production techniques, are used as powerful means for establishing a sense of personal address based on how music touch on discourses on social status and authenticity (Machin, 2010).

The basic instrumentation of the 'Mr Clean' jingle is simple (bass, piano, drums with brushes), which appears unpretentious and appropriate for the genre. The only thing that sticks out is the inclusion of a vibraphone which here, as discussed earlier, contributes mainly to the semiotics of timbre. There is however potential for attributing a certain 'jazzy elegance' to the sound, at the same time as the supplementary vibraphone part during the verses contributes additional harmonic variation and sophistication. The instrumentation of the 'Lowenbrau' jingle, as mentioned, starts out with only an upright piano accompanying the singer. The upright, slightly out of tune, piano contributes different connotations than a refined grand piano sound would do. At the first mention of the brand name, however, a larger band enters including a string section, guitar, bass, drums/brushes and also backing vocals – plus a tenor sax during the voice-over. Besides the sensory aspects discussed earlier, this orchestration also contributes a dimension of luxury and elegance, placing the intimacy of the lead vocal in a different musical context. The saxophone adds possible associations to mellow jazz. In all, this instrumentation could be said to emphasize a sense of comfort and wellbeing.

Central to the sound of the jingle is the projection of the singing voice. The listener will be inclined to direct special attention to the voice in its capacity of being 'human'. In this sense it parallels how the human face and gaze works in visual representations. The singing voice as a medium also includes and carries the dimensions of language, music and timbre-specific qualities. In this, the voice itself constitutes a multimodal ensemble, simultaneously expressing complex interrelations of verbal semantics and grammar, musical form, rhythm, pitch and genre, timbre-related content and expression, and so forth.

An important feature for building brand identity is also how music can be made highly recognizable and memorable, often by means of melody. The jingle itself (the 'work') can thus be understood as a semiotic sign, directly signifying/denoting a product – and at the same time connoting ideas and ideologies. This can be described as kind of *nominalization*, how verb processes are replaced with a noun construction 'which can obscure agency and responsibility for an action' (Machin and Mayr, 2012: 137). Machin and Mayr point out how 'nominalisations can themselves become stable entities that will enter common usage' (Ibid.: 143). An example would be recognizing the 'Mr Clean' jingle as just that, 'the Mr Clean jingle', just as the product name itself would be recognized. In contemporary societies there are numerous examples of commercial jingles that are established as entities on the level of cultural symbols.

On a fundamental level, all advertising involves discourses on commercialism. The potential buyer is today critically aware of the persuasive aims and techniques of advertisements. The soft sell technique of the 'Lowenbrau' jingle, relying on mood and the implicit promise of a better life with the product, is probably obvious to most listeners. The 'Mr Clean' jingle is maybe not a typical hard sell, but the insistent overlexicalization of repeating the brand name, and the slightly formal but direct appeal make intentions clear to most even without a close analysis. However, as customer knowledge and critical awareness grows, the classic advertising techniques of persuasion are gradually replaced with alternative strategies. Guy Cook (2001: 2) remarks that 'advertising itself has changed, becoming more subtle and more entertaining than the crude hard selling of the 1950s and 1960s'. Along with changing strategies, so are also venues and platforms for advertising changing, mostly based on emerging digital technologies. As a consequence of this the continually evolving strategies and platforms for advertising are also turning increasingly multimodal, which stresses the need for more knowledge about how discourses are multimodally mediated. Meaning is always contextually situated. Looking at the emerging commercial landscapes and keeping in mind how the modes constructing multimodal texts contextualize each other, brings perspective to advertising legend David Ogilvy's classic statement: 'If you have nothing to say – sing it!'.

Note

1   The melody starts on the third of the tonic chord (for 'Mister') and ascends a minor third to the fifth of the chord (for 'Clean'). This pattern recurs every time the melody is sung over a tonic chord. When alternately performed over a dominant chord, the same melodic interval is sung a major second lower, maintaining the ascending minor third interval relationship (this time from the fifth to the seventh of the dominant chord). In short, the product name is always sung using the same relative interval.

References

Baker, T. (ed.) (2009), *Pocket Manual of Musical Terms*, 5th edition. London: Schirmer Trade Books.

Cook, G. (2001), *The Discourse of Advertising*, 2nd edition. London and New York: Routledge.

Cook, N. (1998a), *Analysing Musical Multimedia*. Oxford: Oxford University Press.

Cook, N. (1998b), *Music: A Very Short Introduction*. Oxford: Oxford University Press.

Freitas, E. S. L. (2012), 'Advertising and Discourse Analysis', in J. P. Gee and M. Handford (eds), *The Routledge Handbook of Discourse Analysis*, pp. 427–440. Oxon and New York: Routledge.

Gabrielsson, A. and Lindström, E. (2001), 'The Influence of Musical Structure on Emotional Expression', in P. N. Juslin and J. A. Sloboda (eds), *Music and Emotion: Theory and Research* pp. 223–248. Oxford: Oxford University Press.

Gee, J. P. (2011), *An Introduction to Discourse Analysis: Theory and Method*. New York and London: Routledge.

Goldman, R. F. (1965), *Harmony in Western Music*. New York: Norton.

Greene, V. (1992), *A Passion for Polka: Old-time Ethnic Music in America*. Berkeley: University of California Press.

Halliday, M. A. K. (1978), *Language as Social Semiotic*. London: Edward Arnold.

Huron, D. (2006), *Sweet Anticipation: Music and the Psychology of Expectation*. Cambridge, MA: MIT Press.

Kress, G. (2010), *Multimodality: A Social Semiotic Approach to Contemporary Communication*. London and New York: Routledge.

Kress, G. (2012), 'Multimodal Discourse Analysis', in J. P. Gee and M. Handford (eds), *The Routledge Handbook of Discourse Analysis*, pp. 35–49. Oxon and New York: Routledge.

Kress, G. and van Leeuwen, T. (2006), *Reading Images: the Grammar of Visual Design*, 2nd edition. London: Routledge.

Kress, G., Jewitt, C., Ogborn, J. and Tsatsarelis, C. (2001), *Multimodal Teaching and Learning: The Rhetorics of the Science Classroom*. London: Continuum.

London, J. (2012), *Hearing in Time: Psychological Aspects of Musical Meter*, 2nd edition. New York: Oxford University Press.

Machin, D. (2010), *Analysing Popular Music: Image, Sound, Text*. London: Sage Publications.

Machin, D. and Mayr, A. (2012), *How to Do Critical Discourse Analysis: A Multimodal Introduction*. London: Sage.

McKerrell, S. (2015), 'Social Distance and the Multimodal Construction of the Other in Sectarian Song', *Social Semiotics* 25(5): 614–632.

Moriarty, S. E. (2015), *Advertising and IMC*, 9th edition. Eurasburg: Cram101.

Sloboda, J. A. and Juslin, P. N. (2010), 'At the Interface Between the Inner and Outer World: Psychological Perspectives', in P. N. Juslin and J. A. Sloboda (eds), *Handbook of Music and Emotion: Theory, Research, Applications*, pp. 73–98. Oxford and New York: Oxford University Press.

Teixeira, A. Jr (1974), *Music To Sell By: The Craft of Jingle Writing*. Boston: Berklee Press Publications.

van Dijk, T. A. (2008), *Discourse and Context: A Sociocognitive Approach*. Cambridge: Cambridge University Press.

van Leeuwen, T. (1999), *Speech, Music, Sound*. London: Macmillan press.

van Leeuwen, T. (2005), *Introducing Social Semiotics*. Oxon: Routledge.

van Leeuwen, T. (2008), *Discourse and Practice: New Tools for Critical Discourse Analysis*. Oxford: Oxford University Press.

van Leeuwen, T. and Kress, G. (2011), 'Discourse Semiotics', in T. A. van Dijk (ed.) *Discourse Studies: A Multidisciplinary Introduction*, 2nd edition. pp. 107–25. London: Sage.

Wingstedt, J. (2008), 'Making Music Mean: On Functions of, and Knowledge about, Narrative Music in Multimedia', Doctoral diss., Luleå University of Technology, Dept. of music and media, <http://epubl.ltu.se/1402–1544/2008/43/>.

Wingstedt, J., Brändström, S. and Berg, J. (2010), 'Narrative Music, Visuals and Meaning in Film', *Visual Communication* 9(2): 193–210.

Discography

The recordings of the discussed jingles can be found at several locations on the internet. Here are a few suggestions for listening:

Hark (n.d.), *Mr Clean 60s Jingle* [audio]. <http://www.hark.com/clips/myvvmlbfpw-mr-clean-60s-jingle> [accessed 28 September 2015].

Scupper77 (2 July 2013), *Lowenbrau Beer Commercial: So Tonight Let It Be Lowenbrau Christmas* [video]. <https://www.youtube.com/watch?v=nQuwg8wWNm4> [accessed 28 September 2015].

TvAdSongs (n.d.), *Lowenbrau – Heres to Good Friends Commercial* [audio]. <http://www.tvadsongs.com/Lowenbrau_-_Heres_To_Good_Friends.html> [accessed 28 September 2015].

TvAdSongs (n.d.), *Mr Clean – 1950s Commercial* [audio]. <http://www.tvadsongs.com/Mr_Clean_-_1950s.html> [accessed 28 September 2015].

8

When the Fairy Tale Is Over: An Analysis of Songs and Institutional Discourse against Domestic Violence in Spain

Laura Filardo-Llamas

Introduction[1]

Following recent trends in Critical Discourse Analysis (CDA) (Machin, 2010; Machin and Mayr, 2012; van Leeuwen, 2012), it can be argued that songs may spread ideological beliefs in such a way that they may reach a wide audience thanks to the combination of different semiotic resources – including text, music and image. The cognitive effect of listening to a song is certainly not the same as the one of reading or listening to a speech, for example, as we approach different communicative genres in different ways (Machin, 2010: 22). In songs, the text-determined meaning potential of the lyrics is widened because it is often integrated with two other modes of communication: music and images. It can be thus argued that the combination of meanings stemming from these three semiotic resources results in a new blended discourse space (Fauconnier and Turner, 2002; Filardo-Llamas, 2015) which is more communicatively effective than other type of monomodal discourses.

With this in mind, in this chapter, I analyse two songs which were produced in Spain in 2004 and 2005 to react against domestic violence, which is understood here as referring to one of the three contexts in which violence against women is exercised (United Nations, 1993: Article 2.a). This type of violence is not the consequence of biological differences, but of a cultural conception of genders and the roles and identities that are usually associated with them (Maqueda, 2006: 2). Given the cultural origin of some of the beliefs underlying episodes of domestic violence, songs are arguably an interesting and fruitful area of research, not only because they offer us the possibility of identifying those originating cultural beliefs, but also because through songs we can also oppose them. This has been the case in Spain, where we can see an increasingly growing interest on the elaboration of lists including songs which either promote gender stereotypes or can be used to fight against domestic violence (cf. Peña Palacios, 2009; Llorens Mellado, 2013). However, hardly any research has been done on the semiotic resources which characterize these songs and why this combination of different modes of communication is effective.

While trying to fill that gap, this chapter builds bridges between cognitive linguistics and multimodality. I hypothesize that the emotional impact – or cognitive effect (Steen and Gavins, 2003: 6) – of songs about domestic violence is partly caused by the mental representation triggered by these songs, and partly by the relationship established between such mental representations and those experiences of the world that are socially shared by the audience.

The hypothesis that in songs we construct multimodally given mental representations – or worldviews – will be tested by analysing two songs according to the postulates of Text-World Theory (TWT) (Werth, 1999; Gavins, 2007). This theory proves to be particularly interesting for this objective, as it aims at uncovering the mental representations (or 'text-worlds') that can be evoked by particular instances of discourse. This approach is useful for describing the linguistic cues which help the audience trigger those text-worlds. To prove that the discourse (Gee, 1999) transmitted through these songs resembles other public examples of discourse aimed at fighting domestic violence, reference will be made to some cases of institutional discourse as seen in awareness campaigns produced in the same years as the analysed songs.

Given that songs are multimodal discourses, not only the lyrics of the songs will be analysed, but the textual findings will be backed by an analysis of music and image. The emphasis will be particularly placed on how the combination of modes results in the creation of a blended mental space (Fauconnier and Turner, 2002) in the song. I will prove that these multiple semiotic resources increase the emotional impact of songs, thus making them very powerful in the fight against domestic violence.

Domestic violence in Spain

Domestic violence is understood in Spain as violence against women which happens in the domestic context (United Nations, 1993: Article 2.a). This includes physical violence and emotional abuse exercised by one person in a relationship to control the other. The origin of this type of violence is frequently presented as a consequence of discriminatory, unequal and subordinated situations which arise from the normative social roles found in patriarchal society (Puleo, 2005; Maqueda, 2006). Therefore, this type of violence does not stem from biological factors, but emerges from specific socio-cultural notions of gender. This implies that social expectations about what can be considered male or female may change throughout time, and may vary across regional contexts.[2]

Even if gender-based discrimination and violence have been suffered by women throughout history, the existence of this problem was not acknowledged until the 1990s when after a World Conference on Human Rights, the United Nations issued a Declaration on the Elimination of Violence against Women (20 December 1993) (Maqueda, 2006: 2). In Spain, legal responses can be found with Organic Law 14/1999 (9 June) and Organic Law 27/2003. Both of these modify the criminal code with the aim of protecting victims of domestic violence.

Particularly important is 2004, when Organic Law 1/2004 was passed, offering measures to protect victims of gender-based violence.[3] In the preamble to the law, this type of violence is identified as the one that is exercised against women just because they are women (Maqueda, 2006: 4). This new law tries to eradicate domestic violence by taking measures aimed at lengthening prison sentences for the aggressors, creating specialized courts, or producing awareness campaigns.

Awareness campaigns are particularly important for this chapter as they exemplify institutional discourse and the official posture about this problem. Currently available at the website of the Ministry of Health and Social Policy,[4] official awareness campaigns produced between 2006 and 2010 have been considered, as it is in them that we can more easily see official and institutional discourse on domestic violence. The choice of 2010 shows the year when the Ministry of Equality is disbanded. This ministry had been created in 2008 to promote the legal measures included in the above-mentioned Law against gender-based violence (2004) and the Law for Equality (2007). No campaigns for the years 2004 and 2005 have been found. All the awareness campaigns were communicated across television, radio and posters.

A number of recurrent features can be seen in the studied awareness campaigns:[5] Violence is delegitimized by removing the 'male's' distinguishing feature ('you stop being a man' (2008)), and this type of behaviour is socially condemned (2006 and 2010). There is a focus on the role of the victims, particularly on the psychological process followed by the woman (2009, 2010) and on how the new law – or other institutional measures – can help her overcome this problem (2006, 2007). Although they are not explicitly recognized as victims in the law, the role of children as victims is also acknowledged in two campaigns (2008, 2010). Finally, we also see attempts to create a strong woman who can handle situations of domestic violence and discursively oppose her aggressor (2008). Two other significant aspects are the reference to the role of the victim's inner circle in helping her solve the problem (2006, 2010), and the acknowledgement of different types of abuse, both physical and verbal. All these aspects construct a unitary social and institutional discourse which, as we will see below, can also be observed in songs aimed at fighting domestic violence.

Methodological approach

Departing from a CDA approach to the study of discourse, the objective of this chapter is to understand how episodes of domestic violence are constructed in two songs and how these discursive constructions result in a delegitimation of those episodes.[6] This emphasis on the notion of discursive constructions justifies in itself the adoption of a cognitive (linguistics) approach to multimodality, as it is through it that we can explain the mediating role that discourse plays between language (or images and music) and the social effect they have (Filardo-Llamas, Hart and Kaal, 2015). TWT (Werth, 1999; Gavins, 2007) proves to be useful for this as it has not only been widely applied to the stylistic analysis of literary and filmic discourses (see Gavins, 2007 for example), but also to the study of ideologically motivated discourse (Filardo-Llamas, 2013, 2015). This evaluative discourse can be explained by doing a text-world analysis in which we identify those entities which are represented in discourse while establishing the speaker's point of view about those identities (Werth, 1999: 52). By identifying text-worlds we can, thus, identify how discursive constructions explain and justify given views of the world.

Worldviews, I argue, are the outcome of the combination of given text and discourse worlds. Text-worlds are the mental representations that can be triggered from a particular instance of discourse, and discourse worlds refer to the construal of those text-worlds in context (Gavins, 2007: 9–10, 18–31). Two main elements determine the existence of these worlds: world-building elements (including participants, locations, and times), and function-advancing propositions (or the actions done by participants). This is why a textual analysis based on cognitive linguistics helps in identifying the referential entities that are constructed through discourse. Text-worlds acquire new meanings in collocation with music-worlds and video-worlds, and when the three of them together are used in context they become a discourse world. It is when text-worlds become discourse worlds that they are related to spreading ideological beliefs.

Chilton's (2004, 2005) Discourse Space Theory (DST) proves to be a fruitful complement to TWT in order to explain that ideological meaning, which stems from the proximal-distal relationship that is established between the different entities that are discursively presented and the deictic centre. By relying on DST, we can recast mental representations and place them 'across spaces as coordinate correspondences on three fundamental dimensions' (Chilton, 2005: 81): Space, Time and Axiology (Cap, 2010). Point of view, as the defining concept to explain ideological meaning, is thus related to the position which the speaker adopts in terms of space, time, and axiological space. Emotions arise from the relationship between the (ideally ego-centric) deictic centre and the other entities present in the discourse world: the closer entities are located in terms of space, time and axiology to the speaker – and those who share knowledge and beliefs with him/ her – the more effective discourse is in creating a shared identity, characterized by a shared notion of space, time, values and beliefs. Although DST has mainly focused on the study of textuallydetermined meaning, the notion of social proximity can be also applied to the study of images and music (Moore, Schmidt and Dockwray, 2009), and it is particularly useful to understand how intimacy or otherness are discursively constructed.

As theories of discourse, both DST and TWT stress the importance of uncovering linguistic features, which are considered cues to (multiple) contextual interpretation(s). The meaning of an instance of discourse can be described by relying on the notion of a 'mental space', that is 'a construct distinct from linguistic structures but built up in any discourse according to guidelines provided by the linguistic expressions' (Fauconnier, 1994: 16). It can be argued that both text and discourse worlds are contextually determined mental spaces. Thus, given that the emphasis of this chapter is to identify some mechanisms through which ideological meaning is constructed, all the analysed linguistic features share an indexicality trait, that is they can be explained by relying on a proximity relationship established within a particular space (regardless of whether this points at space, time or axiology). In the same way that linguistic categories have to be acknowledged when looking at the construction of text-worlds, certain multimodal features have to be considered. As noted by Sweetser (2012: 3), viewpoint is built as a consequence of linguistic and multimodal stimuli, and the Mental Spaces framework proves to be a useful tool to represent that. Following this, I argue that TWT and DST can be equally useful to explain the conceptual structure that underlies the two music videos analysed in this chapter. If we consider that a discourse world is accessed not only by relying on linguistic cues, but also on any other element which can be sensorially perceived, the analysis of multimodal features becomes significant. The three communication modes are thus of key importance, and it is their combination that increases the impact of the two analysed music videos.

In 2004, Spanish pop-rock singer María Nieves Rebolledo Vila, Bebe, releases what is probably still today the best-known song against domestic violence in Spain, entitled 'Malo' (Bad). This song is part of the album *Pa'fueratelarañas* (EMI Music), of which around five million copies were sold only in Spain. The album was so popular that it occupies number 14 in the list of the 50 most important albums of 2004 in Spain (Promusicae, 2013). The album also had an important international success, and since then, Bebe has been frequently considered a symbol of the fight against domestic violence and female empowerment. One year later, in 2005, Domingo Antonio Edjang Moreno, El Chojin – one of the most famous rappers in Spain –, releases 'El final del cuento de hadas' (The end of the fairy tale) as part of the album *8jin* (Bombo Records). Although he is well-known among hip hop fans, no official figures about the number of sales of this album have been found and it does not appear either in any of the lists of popular songs or albums of 2005. However, this song was chosen by Amnesty International to fight against domestic violence. Both songs have been chosen because they were produced at a time when there was an increasing social awareness about domestic violence in Spain, and their release coincides with the beginning of the introduction of new legal and institutional measures aimed at fighting this problem. As we will see in the analysis, the discourse worlds that are constructed through them reflect very well given aspects of what later became salient features of institutional Discourse (Gee, 1999) on domestic violence.

Analysis

1. Bebe's 'Malo'

A close look at the basic song structure (Machin, 2010: 78) shows that two parts can be clearly identified in the lyrics and the music of this song. In both cases, we have a female voice telling her story from her own perspective – that is with a first-person singular pronoun. In the main stanzas an account of domestic violence from the point of view of the female victim is presented, whereas in the chorus the singer addresses the physical abuser. The activity schema (Ibid.: 80) of the song, which is repeated twice, can be thus summarized as follows:

Woman suffers physical abuse

⇩

Woman reacts to violent episode

⇩

Woman addresses physical abuser

It is interesting to note that this activity schema is not only found in the lyrics, but it is also present in the music and the video. In the description of the violent episodes we hear Bebe's husky voice in a very low tone which rises in pitch at the same time as the story progresses. This ascending melody reaches its peak at the chorus, where we can also see the use of more instruments. It is significant to note how the first time the chorus is used, Bebe plays the guitar herself in such a way that a quicker rhythm is emphasized. As we can see, the gradual female awakening that can be inferred from the activity schema in the lyrics is also matched by the use of an ascending melody accompanied by a short burst of attacks in phrasing. These musical features show the dynamic and energetic role that is acquired by the woman (van Leeuwen, 2012: 321; Machin, 2010: 112), and it could be argued that the combination of vocals with drums and the guitar in this particular song acquire the metaphorical meaning of moving forward (Machin, 2010: 128) and rejecting a violence-dominated relationship.

The same active role of women is transmitted through the images in the video. Shot in black and white, in the video we only have the image of Bebe singing. The 'size of frame' (Machin and Mayr, 2012: 97) changes throughout the video (see Table 8.1) and it gradually moves from a long shot to a close one. This has ideological implications, as the distance between the singer – Bebe – and the audience – in this case symbolized by the physical abuser she's directly addressing – is minimized. In this way, the relationship established between the victim – represented by Bebe – and her physical abuser is presented as a close one; something which is already implicit in the definition of domestic violence. Likewise, the humanity and emotion of the victims are highlighted, thus stressing the negative evaluation evoked by the word 'malo' (bad (guy)) which gives title to the song and with which the chorus begins (cf. Kress and van Leeuwen, 1996: 133).

Gaze and pose are also important in understanding the attitude of Bebe (and the woman victim in the activity schema above) towards the physical abuser. In the closer shots, and particularly in the chorus of the song, we can see that Bebe

Table 8.1 Activity, visual and musical schemas for Bebe's 'Malo'

Activity schema	Visual schema	Musical schema
Woman suffers physical abuse	Long shot of singer, contextualized, unclear gaze and more relaxed pose	Husky voice, low tone, long decay in phrasing, background instruments
⇩	⇩	⇩
Woman reacts to violent episode	Medium shot, decontextualized, gaze addressed at viewer, change in pose	Rising tone, percussion indicates end of each line
⇩	⇩	⇩
Woman addresses physical abuser	Short shot, decontextualized, gaze clearly addressed at the viewer, aggressive pose	Higher voice, short burst of attack and decay in phrasing, guitar and percussion together. Quicker rhythm.

is directly looking at the viewer's eyes, as if she was trying to establish some kind of contact with him[7] (Kress and van Leeuwen, 1996: 122). This implies that Bebe is both textually and visually addressing the physical abuser, while at the same time demanding some answer from him (Machin and Mayr, 2012: 71). How the viewer shall respond is partly determined by the 'aggressive' attitude – or pose (Machin and Mayr, 2012: 75) – of the singer, through which the intensity of her feelings is emphasized.

The discourse strategies used to construct participants in this song are particularly interesting. The song is uttered by a female voice who tells the story in the first-person singular pronoun and who addresses a male participant with the second-person singular pronoun. The use of pronouns, as person deictics, without any other textual mark allows the audience to interpret them in such a way that any person could occupy those discursive positions. In this way, it can be argued that participants, as one of the key aspects helping to construe a discourse world (Werth, 1999: 167; Gavins, 2007: 36), do not acquire meaning textually but discursively, thus allowing for an empathy/hostility relation to be established with different members of the audience. Likewise, the use of the first-person singular pronoun is important because of its musical and intertextual connotations that link this song back to other songs related to women empowerment that were produced in the United States between the 1940s and the 1990s where the same first-person-singular strategy is used (Bruno, 2011: 7–9).

The textual representation of discourse participants has been analysed by looking at the attributive processes found in the lyrics (Gavins, 2007: 43). These are mainly of two types: nouns and adjectives which are used to describe the physical appearance, and words that are either actively or passively related to the participant's action. Thus, the woman is described as a beautiful girl ('niña linda') who is tired ('cansada') and growing old ('envejeciendo'). The outcome of her being physically abused can be seen in her tears ('lagrimitas'), the purple in her cheeks ('el morao de mis mejillas') or the sadness in her heart ('la penita de mi corazón'). These latter nominalizations deprive the woman of any active role while suffering the episodes of physical domestic violence. The woman only occupies a domestic space, which is presented as the deictic centre – the one in which she's standing – and which is symbolized in the reference to the stove in the kitchen ('el fogón'). The main attribute associated to the man is not a physical feature, but an evaluation of his behaviour as seen in the words bad ('malo') and stupid ('tonto'). Even if a reference to beauty can be found, particularly interesting is the fact that the man's steel fists are mentioned as the ones causing the harm to the woman. Unlike in the case of the woman, the man does not occupy clearly defined spaces. However, the use of verbs indicating movement towards the deictic centre stresses the proximity of the male threat (Cap, 2010). This happens at the beginning of the song, where the man is presented as turning up in the house on a cold night ('apareciste una noche fría').

All of these strategies together allow for an individualization of the participants who are at the same time anonymized. This discursive construal of an anonymous female victim of domestic violence – a strategy which can be also frequently found in the instances of institutional discourse studied – makes it possible for different members of the audience to identify with the content of the song. As a consequence its marketing and influence potential are increased (Bruno, 2011: 11). This is partly the consequence of a blend (Fauconnier and Turner, 2002) between the textual world in the lyrics, the visual world evoked by the images in the video, and the use of both of them in context (Figure 8.1). It is this deictically centred blend that is of key importance in order to explain the social effectiveness of this song.

The negative evaluation of domestic violence can also be explained by looking at how modality is used. This results on the axiological characterization of the violent action (Cap, 2010; Hart, 2014), that is on the creation of two opposed text-worlds, one for each of the discursively, and visually, represented genders. On the one hand, the use of metaphorical expressions shall be noted. On the second step of the activity schema identified above, the female reaction against

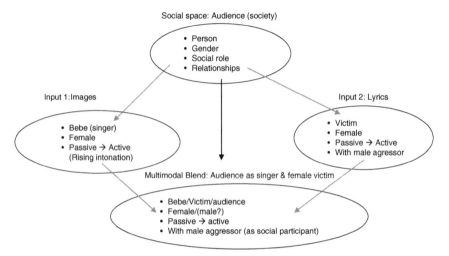

Figure 8.1. Multimodal blend in Bebe's 'Malo'

domestic violence is presented via the metaphor ANGER IS FIRE (Kövecses, 2003: 21), as seen in the verse 'voy a volverme como el fuego, voy a quemar tu puño de acero' (I'm going to become like fire, I'm going to burn your steel fist). By relying on a natural force to represent the woman's reaction, and focusing on the destructive power of fire – whose object is in this case a negative entity – some emphasis is placed on the role of (female) emotions and their importance in order to react against domestic violence. This type of strategy can also be observed in some of the institutional campaigns study. The ascending music that accompanies this part of the song also helps in emphasizing this as it shows the active role of the singer (van Leeuwen, 2012: 321), and of female victims, in reacting to this social problem.

On the other hand, the use of negation in the chorus is equally significant (Hidalgo Downing, 2000). As it has been mentioned above, it is in the chorus that the male participant is directly addressed and negatively characterized as a 'bad', 'stupid' and 'weak' person. The factual tone associated to the present simple in which the verb to be is employed ('malo eres' – you are a bad person) stresses the certainty of the beliefs held by the woman about the male behaviour. The same present simple appears in the following verses, where the singer tells the male addressee what should not be done: 'no se daña a quien se quiere' (one does not hurt the loved person), 'no te pienses mejor que las mujeres' (don't you think you're better than women). There is a clear reference to the audience in the use of the pronoun 'you', and the action is evaluated by the blended singer-victim self that occupies the deictic centre position (Nuyts, 2000). By doing this, the male abuser is axiologically distanced from the speaker, as shown in Figure 8.1. Besides, the use of the negative rechannels the actions and beliefs held by the man, hence delegitimizing them (Hidalgo Downing, 2000: 149). This results in a discursive construal of two social groups – victims and abusers – with whom the two discourse participants can feel aligned. This is particularly interesting as it is not only one of the strategies that is used in institutional discourse (as it happens in the 2008, 2009, 2010 campaigns), but it also explains why some of the men convicted of domestic violence who have been interviewed for another part of this study point at this song as one they do not like (interview T07)

2. El Chojín's 'El final del cuento de hadas'

Two aspects shall be mentioned about the basic song structure (Machin, 2010: 78) of this song. On the one hand, a clear narrative schema can be identified in which a love fairy tale seems to be told. This fairy tale, which can be found in the first stanzas of the song, reproduces commonly held beliefs which are related to the myth of romantic love and the process of wooing. On the other hand, this pseudo fairy tale is part of a broader discourse schema in which the violent episode(s) recalled in the song are included. Both schemas are mixed throughout the song, with the chorus – and the title 'The end of the fairy tale' – stressing the intertextual relation between the lyrics of the song and traditional fairy tales. This results in an activity schema (Ibid.: 80) which can be summarized as follows:

Woman falls in love with man

⇩

The love relationship becomes violent

⇩

Man kills woman

This activity schema, which seems to reflect the way in which domestic violence evolves and which stresses the process through which a love relationship may become violent, has also been found in some public accounts of episodes of domestic violence.[8] The reproduction of gender stereotypes in fairy tales is identified by some authors as one of the causes of domestic violence (Duque Sánchez et al, 2015). El Chojin tries to oppose this view of fairy tales as presenting prototypical love relationships by creating a discursive blend of fairy tales and domestic violence episodes. Likewise, the activity schema shown above stresses the inextricable link between being in love (or loving someone) and having to cope with absolutely everything, which are at times identified as key beliefs that explain why some people justify given episodes of abuse in love relationships (Ruiz Arias et al, 2010: 297).

By departing from this schema, El Chojin tries to oppose the fairy tale narrative, whereby a princess meets a prince, they get married and they live happily ever after.[9] To do this, certain episodes of psychological or physical abuse are inserted within the fairy tale. These episodes of domestic violence are multimodally marked in the visual and musical schemas, which also stress the shift from 'love' to violence, as we can see in Table 8.2. First, we can observe a change in the lyrics' narrative technique, which shifts from a third-person narrative in which the story of a woman is told to a first- and second-person dialogue between a man and a woman, thus exemplifying 'real' conversations. The music changes and the repetitive instrumental beat that underlies the rap stops for a second before each beating, which is also indicated with 'real' sounds that could be heard in those situations.

The video, which was not officially commissioned by El Chojin even if it is accepted by him, is equally effective and each violent episode is visually marked. The video begins with a black screen, and it later shows a woman who gradually advances towards the audience. The proximizing effect that can be associated to changes in size of frame (Machin and Mayr, 2012: 97) – from long to short shot – are thus stressed, and the empathy that can be felt between the audience and the visually depicted woman is strengthened (cf. Kress and van Leeuwen, 1996: 133). Given that the woman is physically in the visual deictic centre, which is occupied both by her and the audience, when she is beaten, it is easier for the audience to feel as if they were also beaten themselves, particularly given our physical and spatial understanding of reality (Hart, 2015). Multimodal metaphors also help in stressing this meaning, and the movement of the woman towards the deictic centre could be understood as a visual representation of the metaphor LIFE IS A JOURNEY (Kövecses, 2002; Forceville, 2009). The lack of female movement, usually during the beating episodes, becomes equivalent to a lack of life. It can thus be argued that the multimodal combination of the features summarized in Table 8.2 contributes to delegitimizing domestic violence.

The title and chorus are highly meaningful as they both indicate that the fairy tale has ended. The linguistic context, or co-text (Benke and Wodak, 2003: 225), in which the word 'the end' can be found does not only imply a rejection of the fairy tale narrative, but it also stresses the fact that this type of narrative does not necessarily work in real life. This can be seen in phrases such as 'quién

Table 8.2 Visual and musical schemas for El Chojin's 'El final del cuento de hadas'

Stanza's main activity	Visual schema	Musical schema
	Long shot of woman decontextualized, gaze addressed at viewer	Rapped stanza. Male voice. Instrumental beating. No rising or lowering pitch
	⇩ Movement	⇩
One episode of domestic violence	Short shot of woman, decontextualized, gaze addressed at viewer	Dialogue. Male and female voices in conversation. Instrumental beating
	⇩	⇩
	Black screen	Melodic chorus. Male voice with female choir singing title of song. Rising pitch and decay in phrasing

le iba a decir que sería así' (who would have told her it would be like that) or 'nunca pensó que podría pasar' (she never thought this could happen). The chorus appears only twice: once after the first beating and another time at the end of the song. It could be argued that this has a double function. On the one hand, it stresses the need to react to domestic violence from the beginning; something which is frequently repeated in institutional discourse. On the other hand, it stresses the fact that a significant number of women are dying at the hands of their partners. The lack of images (a black screen) while the chorus is sung also stresses the invalidity of the fairy tale narrative. Based on the metaphor 'KNOW-ING IS SEEING' (Kövecses, 2002: 218), and mappings triggered by it, the visual use of black arguably signifies the lack of knowledge of those who believe in the fairy tale narrative. The rising pitch and female voice which musically accompany the 'end of the fairy tale' verse in a chorus which is not as clearly rapped as the rest of the song also confirm this meaning. The rising pitch can be also explained by relying on the same 'KNOWING IS SEEING' metaphor, as the association of brightness and truth it evokes stresses the idea that fairy tales are not necessarily real (cf. Machin, 2010: 100). We can clearly see how the combination of the three communication modes emphasizes the invalidity of the fairy tale narrative.

This song is also significant in as much as it reproduces some of the features of domestic violence that have been identified by the experts (Ruiz Arias et al, 2010). First of all, we can observe how several types of domestic abuse (cf. Monereo and Triguero, 2012: 45) can be found: psychological abuse is implicit in phrases like 'estás gorda' (you are fat) o 'todo el día en casa acumulando grasas' (you spend your day at home gaining weight), verbal abuse is observed in the shouting done by the man in the dialogued sections of the song, and physical abuse is clearly indicated through the actual beatings. This attempt to show that domestic violence is not only equivalent to physical abuse can also be seen in some of the institutional campaigns studied, for example focusing on verbal abuse in 2010.[10] In the song, however, the sequence in which these three types of violence generally evolve – from psychological to physical – can be observed.

Equally important is the reproduction of the discourse of the aggressors, in which some commonly held beliefs and stereotypes can be identified (Ruiz Arias et al, 2010). Particularly interesting for this is the reference to the myth of romantic love (Sampedro, 2004; Ruiz Arias et al, 2010) and its associated beliefs. In 'sé que eres mía. Estabas destinada a mí, lo supe desde el primer día' (I know you're mine. You were destined for me. I know it from day one), we can observe the ideas of love happening at first sight, the influence of fate and the existence a Mr Right, and the fact that men possess women. In 'te he demostrado que te quiero' (I've proved I love you), the idea that love has to be constantly proved is stressed, and in 'se que no le gusto a tus padres . . . lo que opinen los demás no vale nada (I know your parents don't like me . . . Other people's opinions are not worth it), the opinion of others is downplayed while at the same time stressing the omnipotence of love, which can always overcome external obstacles. All of these beliefs reproduce a discourse which does not only construct an unreal view of love but which contributes to objectifying and passivizing the role of women. The fact that these beliefs are recontextualized in a song aimed at delegitimizing domestic violence subverts their meaning.

Those beliefs are held by the male participant in the text-world, who is mainly characterized by his relationship with alcohol ('estaba un poco borracho' (I was a bit drunk)). The male participant occupies two spaces: the house and the outside world, and his actions are mainly violent: courtship, insulting, shouting, beating and killing the woman. The use of verbs of knowledge ('sé que' (I know)), which trigger mental processes (Halliday, 2004), to characterize the man is likewise important as he is presented as the source of knowledge. Although the male participant is not visually acknowledged, a proximizing relationship (Cap, 2010) is both textually and visually established between this negatively evaluated man and the (victim) woman, thus resulting in the song stressing the threat posed by this type of behaviour. The female character is mainly presented through the male gaze, and her role in the narrative changes from that of a (fairy tale) queen to her degradation as being a big mouth, fat and being in charge of household chores. A clearly sexist stereotypical description of the role of men and women can be thus seen in the song.

The fact that these two participants are only indexed through the pronouns 'he' and 'she' allows their story to be generalized as it only acquires meaning contextually. Time and space deictics are also universal, which allows the delegitimized domestic violence situation to be presented as a global problem. A strategy of individualization and anonymization (Machin, 2010: 88) similar to the one found in Bebe's 'Malo' can be also observed here. The blended discourse world created in the song, particularly prominent in the conversations and the visual proximity moments, allows for the audience to identify with the main participants textually involved in the recalled situations. Generalization and repetition are also musically indicated throughout the song which is rapped over a constantly repeated instrumental beat with a falling pitch that could also indicate the falling, mourning, mood of the song (Machin, 2010: 104). The falling tone is particularly prominent at the end of the song where El Chojin refers to this 'fairy tale' as a fairy tale that is told every week in every city. All of these aspects together serve to reject once again the fairy tale narrative schema and present it as one of the possible causes of some of the commonly held beliefs that are recalled when explaining why domestic violence happens.

Conclusion

The analysis presented here shows the importance of multimodality for the construction of effective communication. The effectiveness of the two songs studied in this chapter stems not only from the text-world constructed in the lyrics, but also from the combination of those text-worlds with music and images. As discussed in the analysis, these three worlds combined together result in a new blended mental representation, or discourse world, in which a particular point of view about society is presented. Therefore, it can be argued that in the case of songs the world is understood by constructing working models of it in our mind which are multimodally evoked and contextually meaningful.

The two songs try to delegitimize or subvert narratives of domestic violence. Even if they are sung by different gender artists who have different musical styles, similar strategies can still be identified. Both songs rely on a process of individualization and anonymization which makes it easier for their message to become global, thus reaching a wider audience. This is the consequence of a vague textual construction of participants that relies on the use of pronouns, the present tense, and unspecified spaces. These together result in decontextual-ized accounts of domestic violence which are only meaningful when the audi-ence interprets them. Visual strategies also have a similar effect in both songs, as they both rely on the visual proximization of the abusing threat. Because this happens in a decontextualized setting, the audience can establish an empathic relationship with the visually represented female victim. Although with a similar effect, this visual strategy differs slightly in the case of the two singers. Given that Bebe is a female singer, she's the one that metaphorically represents the (female) victim while visually, textually and musically addressing the physical abuser. However, in the case of El Chojin, there is a clear visual addressing of the audience from the point of view of the female victim. This is neither textually matched, because there are no second-person pronouns, nor musically matched, given the male voice singing the song.

Certain similarities can be found between the discursive delegitimization of domestic violence in the analysed songs and that of institutional discourses. This results in a unitary Discourse on domestic violence. If we compare the songs with the awareness campaigns broadcasted in similar years, we can see that they all rely on similar discursive strategies. In the songs, the lyrics activity schema mainly includes at least two discourse participants: the female victim and the male physical abuser although this is slightly widened in the case of El Chojin who also acknowledges the importance of the victim's inner circle, including friends and family, and the judiciary. Similar accounts of participants can be seen in the public awareness campaigns. Likewise, both songs and awareness campaigns negatively evaluate the behaviour of the aggressor, be it explicitly in the case of Bebe and the 2008 and second 2010 awareness campaigns, or implic-itly in the case of El Chojin and the 2006, 2007, 2009 and the first 2010 cam-paigns. Stereotypical gendered roles are opposed either by seeking to activate the woman and make her react to domestic violence in the case of Bebe, or by recontextualizing these and implicitly identifying them as the cause of domestic violence. Both aspects are also evident in the awareness campaigns. Finally, a textual and musical reference to the different types of domestic violence can be found both in 'El final del cuento de hadas' and some of the studied campaigns. This is important in as much as it contributes to rejecting the belief that domes-tic violence is only physical. If we compare the analysed campaigns and songs, it can be seen how in all of them a unitary Discourse against domestic violence can be found. However, even if all of them spread similar views, songs can reach a wider audience, and this can be partly explained because their effectiveness stems from the combination of three communication modes: text, music and images. This is particularly the case of Bebe's 'Malo', a song which has almost become a socio-cultural symbol of the fight against domestic violence, and whose impact can only be understood by studying the discursive combination of different semiotic resources.

The bigger socio-cultural impact of songs can help us argue in favour of studying them as effective socio-cultural discourses which may be useful to react to different social (and political) events. Using cognitive linguistics to do this, and pairing it with tools taken from multimodality, particularly musical analysis and visual communication, has proved to be useful to understand how given points of view are transmitted. Understanding the construal of different mental representations or discourse worlds that songs may trigger is thus of key importance if we want to explain the socio-political effect, be it in terms of sales, marketing, or social action, of such musical responses.

Notes

1 Research funded by the Instituto de la Mujer (Ministerio de Sanidad, Servicios Sociales e Igualdad) under the National Programme of R+D+I, in the framework of the Project entitled 'La transmisión de estereotipos de género a través de la canción y su relación con la violencia de género' (039/12).

2 A much more complex debate underlies how the terms gender and sex have been used in the case of the Spanish legislation about domestic violence (Coll-Planas, Moreno and Rodríguez, 2008).

3 It is important to note that a distinction can be found in Spain between domestic violence and gender-based violence. After a debate, it was the latter term that was chosen to define the content of the 2004 law (Coll-Planas, Moreno and Rodríguez, 2008: 189–190). Given the content of the analysed songs, I have decided to use the term domestic violence.

4 These campaigns can still be consulted at the following webpage: <http://www. msssi.gob.es/campannas/portada/home.htm>

5 This chapter focuses on the multimodal strategies that are used in songs. This is why no thorough description is made of the discursive strategies used in these awareness campaigns. However, their content is significant in order to understand how both songs and awareness campaigns are parts of a unitary Discourse aimed at opposing domestic violence.

6 We follow in this Berger and Luckmann's (1966: 110–146) idea of the construction of social reality, and their identification of legitimation. This process implies the objectivation of meaning. This can be done through explaining – or ascribing

cognitive validity to the said meaning – or justifying – or giving normative dignity to related actions. Given the negativity of the actions portrayed in the analysed songs and that they show an against-domestic-violence discourse, we talk about delegitimation.

7 The masculine pronoun has been chosen to reflect the use of masculine adjective 'malo' in Spanish. Also important for this is the setting in which the video is shot, which we only see at the beginning and end: Bebe appears singing in a theatre, and there are only two persons – whose shades resemble those of male persons – in the audience.

8 See, for example, some of the stories compiled in the website 'Amores que matan' that is hosted by the TV station Telecinco <http://www.telecinco.es/amoresqueduelen/>.

9 This type of strategy can be also found in books, such as the ones written by Marcia Grad (2008) or López Salamero (2009), and it was also used by Maria Tardon (a judge expert on domestic violence) in an interview broadcasted in COPE radio station in March 2015 <http://www.cope.es/detalle/No-hay-reinas-ni-princesas-ni-cuentos-de-hadas.html>

10 Although not acknowledged in the analysis in this chapter, it shall be noted that in recent years (2014 and 2015) the focus of awareness campaigns has shifted towards psychological violence, particularly in the case of young people.

References

Analysed data

Bebe. (2004), 'Malo', *Pa'fueratelarañas*. EMI Music. <https://www.youtube.com/watch?v=D0y87BGWtzg> [accessed 15 September 2015].

El Chojin. (2005), 'El final del cuento de hadas', *8jin*. Boa Music, Bombo Records. <https://www.youtube.com/watch?v=XYltop9ju8Y> [accessed 15 September 2015].

Books cited

Benke, G. and Wodak, R. (2003), 'Remembering and Forgetting: The Discursive Construction of Generational Memories', in M. Dédaic and N. Nelson (eds) *At War with Words*, pp. 215–244. Berlin: Mouton de Gruyter.

Berger, P. L. and Luckmann, T. (1966), *The Social Construction of Reality: A Treatise in the Sociology of Knowledge*. New York: Penguin.

Bruno, F. (2011), '"Stone Cold Dead in the Market": Domestic Violence and Americanized Calypso', *Popular Music and Society* 34(1): 7–21.

Cap, P. (2010), 'Proximizing Objects, Proximizing Values: Towards an Axiological Contribution to the Discourse of Legitimization', in U. Okulska and P. Cap (eds) *Perspectives in Politics and Discourse*, pp. 119–142. Amsterdam: John Benjamins.

Chilton, P. (2004), *Analysing Political Discourse: Theory and Practice*. London: Routledge.

Chilton, P. (2005), 'Vectors, Viewpoint and Viewpoint Shift: Toward a Discourse Space Theory', *Annual Review of Cognitive Linguistics* 3: 78–116.

Coll-Planas, G., García-Romeral Moreno, G., Mañas Rodríguez, C. and Navarro-Baras, L. (2008), 'Cuestiones sin resolver en la Ley integral de medidas contra la violencia de género: las distinciones entre sexo y género, y entre violencia y agresión', *Papers Revista de Sociología* 87: 187–204.

Duque Sánchez, E.(coord.), (2015), *IDEALOVE&NAM: Socialización preventiva de la violencia de género*. Madrid: Ministerio de Educación, cultura y deporte.

Fauconnier, G. (1994), *Mental Spaces. Aspects of Meaning Construction in Natural Language*. Cambridge: Cambridge University Press.

Fauconnier, G. and Turner, M. (2002), *The Way We Think. Conceptual Blending and the Mind's Hidden Complexities*. New York: Basic Books.

Filardo-Llamas, L. (2013), ' "Committed to the Ideals of 1916": The Language of Paramilitary Groups: The Case of the Irish Republican Army', *Critical Discourse Studies* 10(1): 1–17.

Filardo-Llamas, L. (2015), 'Re-contextualizing Political Discourse: An Analysis of Shifting Spaces in Songs Used as a Political Too', *Critical Discourse Studies* 12(3): 279–296.

Filardo-Llamas, L., Hart, C. and Kaal, B. (2015), 'Introduction for the Special Issue on Space, Time and Evaluation in Ideological Discourse', *Critical Discourse Studies* 12(3): 235–237.

Forceville, C. (2009), 'The Role of Non-Verbal Sound and Music in Multimodal Metaphor', in C. Forceville and E. Urios-Aparisi (eds) *Multimodal Metaphor*, pp. 383–400. Berlin: Mouton de Gruyter.

Gavins, J. (2007), *Text-world Theory: An Introduction*. Edinburgh: Edinburgh University Press.

Gee, J. P. (1999), *An Introduction to Discourse Analysis: Theory and Method*. New York: Routledge.

Grad, M. (2008), *La princesa que creía en cuentos de hadas*. Barcelona: Obelisco.

Halliday, M. A. K. (2004), *An Introduction to Functional Grammar*, 3rd edition. (Rev. Christian M. I. M. Matthiessen). London: Edward Arnold.

Hart, C. (2014), *Discourse, Grammar and Ideology: Functional and Cognitive Perspectives*. London: Bloomsbury.

Hart, C. (2015), 'Viewpoint in Linguistic Discourse', *Critical Discourse Studies* 12(3): 238–260.

Hidalgo Downing, L. (2000), *Negation, Text Worlds and Discourse: The Pragmatics of Fiction*. Stamford: Ablex.

Kövecses, Z. (2002), *Metaphor: A Practical Introduction*. Oxford: Oxford University Press.

Kövecses, Z. (2003), *Metaphor and Emotion. Language, Culture and Body in Human Feeling*. Cambridge: Cambridge University Press.

Kress, G. and van Leeuwen, T. (1996), *Reading Images: The Grammar of Visual Design*. London: Routledge.

Llorens Mellado, A. (2013), *150 canciones para trabajar la prevención de la violencia de género en el marco educativo*. Valencia: Ayuntamiento de Valencia.

López Salamero, N. (2009), *La cenicienta que no quería comer perdices*. Barcelona: Planeta.

Machin, D. (2010), *Analysing Popular Music: Image, Sound and Text*. London: Sage.

Machin, D. and Mayr, A. (2012), *How to Do Critical Discourse Analysis. A Multimodal Introduction*. London: Sage.

Maqueda Abreu, M. L. (2006), 'La violencia de género. Entre el concepto jurídico y la realidad social', *Revista Electrónica de Ciencia Penal y Criminología* 8: 1–13, <http://criminet.ugr.es/recpc/08/recpc08-02.pdf> [accessed 15 September 2015].

Monereo, J. L. and Triguero, L. A. (2012), 'El derecho social del trabajo y los derechos sociales ante la violencia de género en el ámbito laboral', *Anales de derecho* 30: 42–89.

Moore, A. F., Schmidt, P. and Dockwray, R. (2009), 'A Hermeneutics of Spatialization for Recorded Song', *Twentieth-Century Music* 6(1): 83–114.

Nuyts, J. (2000), *Epistemic Modality, Language, and Conceptualization*. Amsterdam: John Benjamins.

Peña Palacios, E. M. (2009), *MP3. MP4. ¿Reproduces sexismo?* Canarias: Instituto Canario de la Mujer. Fundación mujeres.

Promusicae. (2013), *Listas anuales*, <http://www.promusicae.es/estaticos/view/21-listas-anuales> [accessed 15 September 2015].

Puleo, A. (2005), 'El patriarcado, ¿una organización social superada?' *Temas para el Debate* 133: 39–42.

Ruiz Arias, S., L. Negredo López, A. Ruiz Alvarado, C. García-Moreno Bascones, O. Herrero Mejías, M. Yela García, and M. Pérez Ramírez (2010), *Violencia de género. Programa de intervención para agresores (PRIA)*. Madrid: Ministerio del Interior.

Sampedro, P. (2004), 'El mito del amor y sus consecuencias en los vínculos de pareja'. *Revista página abierta* 150. <http://centropilarsampedro.es/pages/index/publicaciones> [accessed 14 July 2016].

Steen, G. and Gavins, J. (2003), 'Contextualizing Cognitive Poetics', in J. Gavins and G. Steen (eds) *Cognitive Poetics in Practice*, pp. 1–12. London: Routledge.

Sweetser, E. (2012), 'Introduction: Viewpoint and Perspective in Language and Gesture, From the Ground Down', in B. Dancygier and E. Sweetser (eds) *Viewpoint in Language: A Multimodal Perspective*, pp. 1–22. Cambridge: Cambridge University Press.

United Nations. (1993), *Declaration on the Elimination of Violence against Women*, <http://www.un.org/documents/ga/res/48/a48r104.htm> [accessed 15 September 2015].

van Leeuwen, T. (2012), 'The Critical Analysis of Musical Discourse', *Critical Discourse Studies* 9(4): 319–328.

Werth, P. (1999), *Text Worlds. Representing Conceptual Space in Discourse*. New York: Longman.

9

Indigenous Hip Hop as Anti-colonial Discourse in Guatemala

Rusty Barrett

Introduction

Guatemala has a long history of racial discrimination against indigenous peoples. Although the population is roughly evenly divided between indigenous (primarily Maya) and non-indigenous, there is a long history of Maya oppression. The ethnic divide in Guatemala reached a tipping point during the height of the civil war (1960–1996) in which the Guatemalan government committed genocide against the Maya (Perera, 1995). The end of the civil war saw the rise of the Maya Movement, a political movement promoting Maya culture and human rights. This movement encouraged the use of Mayan languages in new contexts, such as in popular music. Although most music in Mayan languages has been pop or soft rock music, in the last decade, hip hop in Mayan languages has begun to gain popularity.

This chapter examines the emergence of Mayan-language hip hop, focusing on the music of the group Balam Ajpu who rap in Spanish and a combination of Mayan languages. The chapter follows the methodology of scholars like van Leeuwen (1999, 2012) and Machin and Richardson (2012) in analysing the meaning potential of sounds as part of multimodal discourse. Following van Leeuwen (1999), the chapter examines the ways in which various elements of Balam Ajpu's music (rhythm, timbre, the relationship between voices, and so on) work together to produce music that challenges the colonial discourse associated with the historical domination of the Maya.

Colonial discourse and ethnicity in Guatemala

The period of Spanish colonial rule in Guatemala (1524–1821) saw the formation of an elite indigenous class known as ladinos, who became fluent in Spanish and interacted primarily with colonial rulers. In most of Latin America, this ladino identity evolved into *mestizo* identity (or *mestizaje*) in the period following Spanish colonial rule (see Frye, 1996: 37). This new *mestizo* identity recognized a multicultural heritage including both European and indigenous traditions. In practice, however, *mestizo* identity typically involved only symbolic appropriation of elements of indigenous culture as part of the creation of a nationalist identity that perpetuated the colonial denigration of indigenous peoples. In contrast to other parts of Latin America, Guatemala has maintained ladino as the primary identity category for those who do not identify as indigenous. The persistence of ladino as a Guatemalan identity category in Guatemala is part of a broader maintenance of colonial discourse involving the simultaneous appropriation and denigration of indigenous people and their cultures.

Colonial discourse in Guatemala is founded upon a presumed disconnect between the contemporary Maya and their pre-Columbian ancestors (Montejo, 2005; Hale, 2006). Because of the supposed 'collapse' of pre-Columbian Maya civilization and the 'disappearance' of the Maya, the dominant ideology in Guatemala has held that today's Maya have no authentic connection to the pre-Columbian Maya. The 'collapse' of Maya civilization did not mean that the Maya ceased to exist or disappeared. There is ample genetic, linguistic and cultural evidence to demonstrate that today's Maya are without question the same Maya that existed before the conquest (see Fischer and Brown, 1996; Montejo, 2005). Even so, the dominant view holds that the 'true' Maya had disappeared before Columbus and that the 'Indians' that the Spanish encountered in Guatemala were a mix of groups from Mexico who were not Maya.

The denial of Maya cultural continuity allows for disparate attitudes towards pre-Columbian and modern Maya. Contemporary Maya have been depicted as backward and primitive people who 'have been rejected as active participants in the social, political, or economic life of the country' (Montejo, 2005: 4). Mayan languages, historically viewed as *dialectos* (dialects), rather than *idiomas* (languages), are seen as having only local relevance and being generally incompatible with modern society. While the contemporary Maya have been denigrated as primitive Indians, the pre-Columbian Maya have been celebrated as a classical civilization that symbolizes Guatemalan national heritage (see Otzoy, 1996;

Montejo, 2005; del Valle Escalante, 2009). Thus, elements of Maya culture have been appropriated for use as symbols of a Guatemalan nationalist identity, even as the Maya themselves have been denigrated and excluded from Guatemalan society.

The combination of appropriation and denigration in Guatemalan colonial discourse can be seen in analyses of non-musical modes of discourse. In particular, scholars have examined visual images of traditional Maya clothing and narrative and visual depictions of Tecún Umán [Tekum Umam], the K'iche' Maya king believed to be killed by Pedro Alvarado during the Spanish invasion of Guatemala (see Hendrickson, 1991; Otzoy, 1992, 1996, 1999; Montejo, 2005).

Maya women in highland Guatemala typically wear traditional indigenous clothing or *traje* as it is commonly called in Guatemala. The designs of *traje* are specific to individual towns, but generally involve a *huipil* (a hand-woven blouse) worn with a skirt folded from a large piece of fabric. Guatemalan national discourse often exploits this national dress as a marker of national identity (Hendrickson, 1991; Otzoy, 1992, 1996). For example, the 'national costume' of Guatemala always involves the use of a *traje*. Ladino beauty pageant contestants wear *traje* as a national costume, although it is always styled in a way that is marked as clearly inauthentic (see Hendrickson, 1991). Images of women wearing *traje* can be seen on Guatemalan currency and are commonly used in materials marketed to tourists (Hendrickson, 1991). In contrast, materials aimed at local Guatemalan audiences depict the use of *traje* as backward and primitive. Even though the Maya *huipil* serves as a symbol of Guatemalan banal nationalism (Billig, 1995), discrimination against women who wear *traje* is still common. In 2002, for example, anthropologist and journalist Irma Alicia Velásquez Nimatuj was denied entrance into a Guatemalan city restaurant explicitly because she was wearing *traje* that conveyed her Maya identity (Velásquez Nimatuj, 2005).

The narrative of Tecún Umán also shows the combination of appropriation and denigration typical of Guatemalan colonial discourse (see Otzoy, 1999; Montejo, 2005). According to legend, Tecún Umán was the K'iche' king who fought against Pedro de Alvarado during the Spanish invasion of Guatemala. Tecún Umán dies in the battle and a quetzal bird (the national symbol of Guatemala) falls and dies beside him. As with indigenous dress, the story of Tecún Umán has been appropriated as a symbol of Guatemalan nationalism. Tecún Umán is a national hero, recognized with his own holiday when children enact his story in local school pageants. Statues of Tecún Umán are common throughout Guatemala and potraits of him are common in schools, government offices and on currency. In these representations, Tecún Umán is depicted as the ideal hero who sacrificed his life for the freedom of his people. Montejo analyses the traditional version of the Tecún Umán legend as presented in a social studies textbook used in Guatemalan elementary schools (2005: 54–59). Although Tecún Umán is depicted as a brave warrior, the Spanish invaders are represented as inherently superior throughout the text. As with most public images of the battle, Tecún Umán is portrayed as wearing a loincloth and holding a spear while fighting armed men on horseback. The textbook depicts Tecún Umán as not being smart enough to distinguish between Alvarado and his horse while the Spaniards are represented as trying to save and 'civilize' the primitive 'Indians' that Tecún Umán represents (Montejo, 2005: 58).

Colonial discourse in Guatemala thus appropriates elements of Maya culture as symbols of nationalism while denigrating the actual Maya as primitive and unable to function in modern society. Colonial discourse is multimodal, involving visual modes such as images of indigenous dress and textual modes as in the depictions of Tecún Umán. The following section examines the ways in which colonial discourse is reproduced through musical culture in Guatemala.

Musical manifestations of colonial discourse in Guatemala

Classic Maya art and literature clearly demonstrate that musical performances such as processions and dances were central components of pre-Columbian Maya culture (see Grube, 1992; Sanchez, 2007; Looper, 2010). The murals at the archaeological site of Bonampak, for example, depicts an elaborate musical performance. In addition to artistic representations, archaeologists have described a wide variety of musical instruments used by the Maya before the conquest (Hammond, 1972a, 1972b; Bourg, 2005). These instruments include a variety of drums and other percussion instruments, wind instruments such as flutes and trumpets, and instruments taken from nature like conch horns and turtle shell drums. In addition to the archaeological records, there are Maya musical traditions that have survived to the present day. For example, the dance-drama *Rab'inal Achi*, which is still performed today, includes instruments and performance features that match those in the archaeological records (Tedlock, 2003; Breton, 2007; Howell, 2007). The *Rab'inal Achi* is a play infused with dance numbers that tells the story of a war between the K'iche' Maya and the Achi Maya. Such war dance-dramas are common throughout the highlands of Guatemala, though most have shifted to focus on the Spanish conquest rather than pre-Columbian conflicts such as the one depicted in *Rab'inal Achi*.

Comparing the musical structure or *Rab'inal Achi* with another dance-drama about the Spanish conquest, Howell (2007) concludes that the instruments of *Rab'inal Achi* are likely a reflection of pre-Columbian musical traditions. In *Rab'inal Achi*, music is performed on slit drums and trumpets like those reflected in Classic Maya art. Howell finds that *Rab'inal Achi* contains a number of possible musical features with probable pre-Hispanic origins. For example, the structure of *Rab'inal Achi* is built around sacred Maya numbers (particularly 13). The numbers 13 and 20 are sacred in Maya culture as they serve as the basis for the 260-day lunar calendar (consisting of 20 days each repeating 13 times). Indeed, Howell suggests that pre-Columbian Maya music may have been constructed around sacred geography (such as cardinal directions) as well as being constructed around the Maya calendar.

Another distinctive characteristic of *Rab'inal Achi* is that although rhythmic patterns regularly repeat, the repeated pairs do not share a unifying metre. While Howell notes that while it would be possible to divide the music of *Rab'inal Achi* according to metre, doing so would be pointless as the metre changes regularly throughout any given song. In contrast, other Maya dance-dramas are more closely tied to metrical organization. These shifting rhythmic patterns without a unified metre are a feature that O'Brien-Rothe (1975, 2010, 2015) has described for traditional folk songs of the Tz'utujil Maya. These songs mix traditional Maya and Western musical elements and contain a mix of Spanish and Mayan-language lyrics. The variable rhythmic structure of Tz'utujil folk songs is associated with the poetic structure of the lyrics of the songs, which follows the traditional couplet structure found in Mayan verbal art (see Barrett, forthcoming). Mayan verbal art involves widespread use of syntactic parallelism and couplets in which a clause is repeated with one constituent replaced. An example can be seen in the opening of the *Popol Wuj*, an extensive K'iche' Maya text transcribed in the seventeenth century:

(1)	Waral xchiqatz'ib'aj wi	Here we shall inscribe,
	xchiqatikib'al wi ojer tzij.	we shall implant the Ancient Word.

In this example (Tedlock, 2010: 310–311), the structure of the verbs in the two lines is exactly the same ('we shall X it') but the two verbs have different roots. The object of both verbs (*ojer tzij* or Ancient Word) only occurs after the repeated verb. The poetic character of the couplet (and what makes it an artistic use of language from a Maya perspective) is the repetition of an identical verb structure. This form of poetic parallelism contrasts sharply with Western views of poetry that emphasize phonological parallelism (through unified metrical and rhyming structures). Although the lines in Maya poetry show parallel morphological and syntactic structures, they do not display parallel rhythms or rhymes. When this poetic structure is used to form musical lyrics, the varying length and rhythmic structure of (syntactically parallel) lines results in regular rhythmic alternations. In the Example (1), the rhythm of the verbs within each line would be identical, but the larger rhythm of each line would be different. This corresponds to the description of rhythmic structure described for both *Rab'inal Achi* and Tz'utujil folk songs (Howell, 2007; O'Brien-Rothe, 2010). There are internal elements that repeat specific rhythmic structures, but there is not a larger unifying metrical structure like that found in Western musical or poetic traditions.

The poetic parallelism in Maya verbal art reflects another broad pattern in Maya music involving pairings between related but oppositional signs. Maya music is constructed in a similar way as Maya poetry involving pairings between syntactic structures or related words (mother/father, sky/earth, wind/rain, etc). Navarrete Pellicer notes that Maya music builds on created balances between complementary pairs, such as high/low, left/right, or *q'ojom* (percussion instruments)/*su'* (wind instruments) (2005: 54). Music is arranged so that members of a pair are in dialogue with one another. Thus, high-pitched trumpets will be in dialogue with low-pitched trumpets, flutes will be in dialogue with drums, and so forth. This creation of balance in Maya music corresponds to similar pairings throughout Maya culture. For example, Maya prayers often involve pairings between complementary spirits, opposing cardinal directions (east-west, south-north), or opposing ends of the *axis mundi* (the sky, the earth). Thus, Maya music is constructed in ways that reflect broader Maya cultural patterns and beliefs.

It is clear that there is a diverse Maya musical tradition that extends back before the Spanish conquest. Even so, with music one finds the same pattern of denigration with appropriation that one finds in other aspects of colonial discourse. As with Maya *traje*, the Maya use of the marimba has been appropriated as a symbol of Maya nationalism. Apart from marimba music, Maya music is typically represented as restricted to the pre-Columbian period. Maxwell (2009) reports that even after efforts to develop a multicultural educational curriculum, depictions of Maya music were restricted to the pre-Columbian period. Indeed, public imagery of Maya music typically involves representations of loincloth-wearing men blowing on conch shells or beating a drum. Representations of contemporary Maya music are almost entirely limited to marimba players.

The marimba is without question the Guatemalan national instrument and is often portrayed as 'a symbol of Guatemalan national unity' (Taracena Arriola, 2011: 150). Similar to Piotrowska's (2013) discussion of the appropriation of Gypsy music in Hungaian nationalist discourse, the Guatemalan national 'unity' associated with the marimba emerges only through ladino appropriation of the Maya marimba tradition. Although there have been suggestions that the marimba has African origins, Guatemalans generally believe that marimbas have been used by the pre-Columbian Maya (O'Brien-Rothe, 1982). Guatemalan marimba music has traditionally involved two distinct musical genres, the *son* and the *pieza* (see Navarette Pellicer, 2005). The *son* is defined by 'homophonic texture, major tonality, diatonic melody, triadic harmony, a moderate to rapid tempo, and a combination of simple triple and compound duple meters' (Navarrete Pellicer, 2005: 98). Although *sons* may be of either ladino or Maya origin, the *son* is the defining genre for indigenous music. For example, *Rab'inal Achi* involves sets of *sons* that may be combined in unique ways in each performance. In contrast to the *son*, the *pieza* is not a traditional Maya genre and involves popular music of other genres (waltzes, foxtrots, cumbias, merengues, etc.) adopted for the marimba (Navarrete Pellicer, 2005: 58). While *sons* show characteristics of Maya music (such as the combination of multiple metres), *piezas* adhere to the Western musical traditions of their origins (such as a uniform 3/4 metre for a waltz).

The use of 'Indian' marimba groups as entertainment for ladinos and foreign tourists has a long tradition in Guatemala. The *pieza* emerges from this context, in which Maya musicians perform for ladino audiences wishing to hear popular Western music. Because of this history, the distinction between *son* and *pieza* symbolically maps onto the ethnic division between the Maya and ladinos (Navarrete Pellicer, 2005: 163). This does not mean, however, that Maya audiences are not fond of *piezas*. In his study of Achi Maya marimba music, Navarrete Pellicer found that *piezas* are being incorporated into ritual contexts traditionally reserved for *sons* (2005: 211). The broadened use of *piezas* leads to a further loss of Maya musical tradition as *sons* contain uniquely Maya musical elements absent in *piezas*.

There is a long history of mixing ladino and Maya musical elements in *sons*, so that Maya folk music is often performed in Spanish rather than in Mayan languages. However, marimba music is almost always purely instrumental. Popular representations of Maya music are typically reduced to marimba groups, so that

Maya music is often thought of as not having lyrics at all. Although folk songs with lyrics certainly persist (O'Brien-Rothe, 2010, 2015), they are not widely heard through the media and they are rare even in purely Maya social settings. In local Maya contexts (such as festivals, parties, wedding receptions and so on), the music is almost always instrumental marimba music. The form of dancing associated with marimba music in Maya communities is quite specific. The dance partners do not touch; the male partner must keep his hands behind his back and the female partner must keep her hands on her skirt (which she lifts up from the ground in order to move more freely). Both partners hop from side to side in rhythm with the music, with the arms remaining still.

Maya hip hop artists use their multimodal performances to challenge the symbolic colonialism prevelant in these discourses of traditional Maya folk music. For example, Tz'utujil rapper Tz'utu Baktun Kan notes, 'What they call *traditional* is really just *colonial*. They have made music another form of oppression.' The popular representation of 'traditional' Maya music in Guatemala involves a group of marimba players (often wearing elements of *traje*) playing popular *pieza* songs as the Maya dance without moving their arms. In colonial discourse, the full range of Maya musical traditions is reduced to a single form (instrumental marimba music). With the increased use of *piezas*, marimba music contains fewer and fewer distinctive Maya elements despite being portrayed as 'traditional' Maya music. The only genre of widely recognized Maya music is purely instrumental, with the Maya voice being completely erased. Tz'utu sees the restricted movement of the dance associated with the marimba as another form of colonial oppression, saying 'they expect us to dance as if we were tied up like slaves'.

Marimba music is a central component of colonial discourse in Guatemala. On the one hand, the marimba is a symbol of Maya culture believed to have pre-Columbian roots. Indeed, even contemporary Maya rock bands always include a marimba player to index their Maya ethnic identity. As an appropriated symbol of national unity, however, the marimba presents a reductive and false view of Maya music and culture. The music itself is increasingly devoid of traditional Maya elements and is often geared to non-Maya audiences. For younger activist audiences like Tz'utu, the absence of lyrics and the restrictive dance associated with the marimba produces semiotic associations with the colonial history of silencing, slavery and genocide. Thus, while Maya activist musicians may include marimba in their music, it is always combined with vocals and elements of rock or hip hop that do not lend themselves to the restrictive dance typically associated with marimba performance. Rock bands like Kab'awil, for example, combine marimba with electric guitars and rock percussion. Similarly, in Maya hip hop, marimba is mixed with other sampled music and electronic drum beats. Before discussing contemporary Maya hip hop in more detail, it is important to understand the context of its emergence (and its anti-colonial stance) as part of a larger Maya cultural revitalization movement in Guatemala.

The Maya movement and anti-colonial discourse in Guatemala

Since the late-1990s, there has been a rise in popular music performed in Mayan languages in Guatemala. The first Maya rock group to gain popularity was Sobrevivencia, a Mam Maya group that sang in a variety of Mayan languages (in addition to Mam). Following the success of Sobrevivencia, other rock bands began to perform in their local languages, such as the K'iche' group, Kab'awil, and the Sakapulteko group, Tujal Rock. Hip hop gained popularity in Guatemala in the early twentieth century, particularly through Reggeatón music in Spanish. There are now rappers who perform in a variety of Mayan languages across Belize, Mexico and Guatemala. The rise of popular music in Mayan languages is part of a broader Maya cultural revitalization movement that gained ground following the civil war in Guatemala (and the Zapatista rebellion in Mexico).

There has, of course, been continual Maya resistance to Spanish and ladino domination since the arrival of Spanish invaders. However, a concerted pan-Maya political movement emerged in the wake of the violence of the Guatemalan Civil War (1960–1996). The violence (*la violencia*) peaked in the early 1980s with a genocide in which over 200,000 Maya were killed (see Carmack, 1988; Perera, 1995). During *la violencia*, Maya often tried to hide their indigenous identity from ladinos and government officials through abandoning *traje* or refusing to speak Mayan languages in public. Traditional Maya religious ceremonies, such as burning rituals, were also banned during this period.

During the years following the worst of the violence, the Maya Movement emerged as a cultural revitalization and human rights movement focused on preserving and promoting Maya culture and Mayan languages (see Fischer and Brown, 1996; Cojti Cuxil, 1997; Gálvez Borrell and Esquit Choy, 1997; Warren, 1998; Montejo, 2005). The Maya Movement challenges the colonial assumption of a cultural disconnect between the pre-Columbian and modern Maya. Drawing on research in historical linguistics, activists emphasized the fact that contemporary Mayan languages are clearly related to the language found in pre-Columbian hieroglyphic writing. The linguistic view of a unified genetic family of Mayan languages supported a broader political goal of pan-Maya unity. Maya linguists and activists worked to develop reference and educational materials related to their languages (see England, 2003; Barrett, 2005; French, 2010). Much of this work aimed at increasing communication across different Mayan languages. The Unified Mayan Alphabet was introduced so that all of the Mayan languages would share the same writing system. Similarly, uniform neologisms (to replace Spanish loanwords) were introduced into related languages to increase shared vocabulary.

The Maya Movement also challenged the assumption that Mayan languages (and the Maya more generally) were inherently primitive and unsuited for participation in modern, global society. To demonstrate the utility of Mayan languages for modern society, activists sought to change the strict compartmentalization (Kroskrity, 2000: 337) in which Mayan languages and Spanish were relegated to separate social domains. Although there has certainly been variation, many towns in Maya regions of Guatemala have a pattern of bilingualism with diglossia (Fishman, 1967) such that Spanish is used in public and official domains (education, religion, media, literature) and Mayan languages are restricted to local or private/domestic domains. Language activists involved with the Maya Movement worked to change this, developing materials for bilingual education (see Maxwell, 2009) and promoting local literacy in Mayan languages. Maya began to use their native languages in a wide range of new contexts, including literature, technology, law, journalism and healthcare. The emergence of popular music in native languages is part of this larger trend.

Efforts to standardize Maya languages for use in public contexts led to the adoption of Western language ideologies associated with a single language for a single nation (Reynolds, 2009; French, 2010; Fox Tree, 2011). This resulted in a shift in dominant understandings of Maya identity from a local village-based identity (e.g. 'a person from Sololá') to a language-based ethnic identity (e.g. 'a Kaqchikel Maya'). Thus, despite efforts to promote pan-Mayanism, the categorization of Maya along linguistic lines introduced new divisions between Maya communities (see England, 2003; French, 2010). The Maya Movement has introduced a new discourse of multiculturalism into Guatemalan politics (del Valle Escalante, 2009; Maxwell, 2009). The use of Mayan languages in education and government in now more common and there is more public acceptance of displays of Maya identity. However, as del Valle Escalante (2009) notes, this multiculturalism is one-sided so that while displays of Maya identity are more tolerated, Maya are still expected to assimilate to ladino society and ladinos typically have minimal interest in learning about Maya culture (see Barrett, 2016).

While the Maya Movement has challenged colonial discourse, prejudice and ethnic discrimination are still common in Guatemala. Many ladinos still adhere to the assumptions underlying colonial discourse; Maya are still denigrated and they must still justify their relationship to their pre-Columbian ancestors. Although del Valle Escalante (2009) has held that ladinos take no interest in Maya culture, they have shown increased interest in learning Mayan languages (Maxwell, 2009). Hip hop music is one social domain where Maya and non-Maya have found common ground and challenged assumptions regarding ethnic identity (Barret, 2016). The hip hop group Balam Ajpu includes both Maya and non-Maya, but promotes a overtly Maya-centric form of hip hop that is both highly political and grounded in traditional Maya spirituality. The following sections will discuss the work of Balam Ajpu examining the ways in which their music performs an anti-colonial stance across multiple modes.

Maya hip hop and Balam Ajpu

The early part of the twenty-first century saw the sudden popularity of hip hop in Guatemala. Although Guatemalan hip hop has been primarily in Spanish, artists who perform in Mayan languages have been part of the hip hop scene in Guatemala for some time. Some Maya rappers perform in both Maya and Spanish, while others (like Tz'utu Baktun Kan) rap only in Maya. Maya hip hop simultaneously gained popularity in the Maya regions of Mexico, with artists such as Pat Boy (Yukatek Maya) and Slaje'm K'op (Tzotzil Maya). Maya hip hop groups have not had major rivalries or conflicts and tend to promote an ideology of pan-Mayanism. For example, Tz'utu Baktun Kan has performed duets with the members of Slaje'm K'op in Mexico. As with the promotion of pan-Mayanism, Maya hip hop tends to follow the ideologies associated with the Maya Movement. Indeed, rapping in a Mayan language is itself a subversive act that challenges the view of Mayan languages as unfit for modern society.

Tz'utu Baktun Kan formed the group Balam Ajpu with two other musicians, MChe and Dr. Nativo. While Tz'utu is Tz'utujil Maya, MChe and Nativo do not identify as Maya, but identify as *mestizo* unlike most other non-indigenous Guatemalans who identify as ladino. Nativo is the musical director of the group and typically composes and performs instrumentals and back-up vocals. MChe raps in Spanish in bilingual songs, but also beatboxes to accompany Tz'utu in songs that are entirely in Maya. Although Tz'utu is the only Maya member of the group, Balam Ajpu's music focuses entirely on promoting Maya culture. Thus,

Balam Ajpu is a clear counter example to the view that non-Maya have no inter-est in learning about Maya culture (see Barrett, 2016). Balam Ajpu promotes an ideology of Hip Hop Cosmovision in which hip hop and Maya culture are intrin-sically linked. For members of Balam Ajpu, the emergence of hip hop in Mayan languages is understood as part of a larger new era for Maya culture that began in 2012 with the ending of the thirteenth baktun. A baktun is a cycle of 144,000 years in the Mayan calendar. The end of the thirteenth baktun was also the end of a smaller 52- year cycle known as a *calendar round*. A *calendar round* marks the period between days in which the 365.25-day solar calendar and the 260-day lunar calendar coincide. According to the members of Balam Ajpu, this last calendar round began with the earliest emergence of hip hop in the United States and cul-minated with the emergence of Maya hip hop at the end of the thirteenth baktun.

The name Balam Ajpu conveys the centrality of Maya culture to the group's musical image. The name is taken from the two 'hero twins' in the *Popol Wuj*, the sacred Maya book that describes the creation of the earth (Tedlock, 1996). The twins, XBalamke (Deer Jaguar) and Jun Ajpu (One Hunter), represent the pairing of complementary elements found throughout Maya culture. In combin-ing the names of the two twins, Balam Ajpu follows a Maya rhetorical tradition of creating new compound words through the pairing of related words. Balam Ajpu also links hip hop and Maya worldviews in their understanding of the basic elements of hip hop. Following K.R.S. One, hip hop is often said to contain four basic elements: rapping, break dancing, graffiti art, and DJ-ing (or scratching). Balam Ajpu teaches three basic elements (without DJ-ing which is difficult in contexts without electricity). For Balam Ajpu, these three elements correspond to the three stones that form a traditional Maya hearth (or *xkub'*). The three stones of the *xkub'* are said to have been laid in place at the beginning of the world, with the world tree (*axis mundi)* growing out of the hearth's centre. The placement of the *xkub'* marks the centre of a Maya home in addition to symboli-cally marking the axis between the underworld and the centre of the sky.

The lyrics to Balam Ajpu's music are written in collaboration with local spiritual guides, traditional Maya priests who provide guidance based on the Maya calendar and communication with the Maya ancestors or with local nat-ural spirits known as nawals. Each of the 20 days in the Maya (260-day) cal-endar is associated with a nawal. For their first CD, a tribute to the 20 nawals, Balam Ajpu asked their spiritual guides to help prepare hip hop lyrics related to each of the 20 nawals. In each case, the spiritual guide would perform a burning ceremony (the ritual that had been prohibited during the civil war). These burning ceremonies involve arranging a large circle of various elements, including candles, copal incense, ocote pine chips (which are highly flammable), flowers, sugar and other elements such as fruit or candy. The elements included in the circle are meant to please the ancestors and nawals as they burn. The collection of these elements is burned and the burning is accompanied by a long prayer that moves through all 260 days of the lunar calendar. After asking the nawals to transmit hip hop lyrics, the spiritual guide closes his eyes and goes into a trance-like state where he rapidly utters the lyrics sent by the nawals. As the spiritual guide produces lyrics, Tz'utu rapidly transcribes them into Maya. Once the ceremony is complete, Tz'utu arranges the transcriptions into rap lyrics and works with the other members of Balam Ajpu to develop songs from them and write corresponding Spanish lyrics.

In addition to their music, the members of Balam Ajpu run a hip hop school for local children in the town of San Pedro la Laguna. The *Casa Ahau Escuela de Hip Hop* teaches painting, rapping and break dancing in addition to teaching lessons about Maya culture and promoting the use of Mayan languages. Although the school has had sporadic funding, it typically operates on a minimal budget. Even so, the school has developed a number of projects for children in the area, including a hip hop dance performance of the *Popol Wuj* and painting a series of political murals in the town of San Pedro. The murals focus on themes related to the preservation of Maya culture, historical memory regarding the genocide of the civil war or environmental messages protesting the mining of Maya lands. The school thus combines hip hop and Maya culture along the lines promoted by Balam Ajpu's ideology of Hip Hop Cosmovision.

In bringing Maya culture and hip hop together, Balam Ajpu challenges the view that Maya culture is a relic of a primitive past. Balam Ajpu's Maya-centric understanding of hip hop, the political messages of their art and philosophy, and the critical pedagogy of the Casa Ahau school all contribute to anti-colonial discourse. However, the heart of Balam Ajpu's subversion of colonial discourse is their music, which constructs related but distinct anti-colonial stances across a range of modes.

Maya hip hop as anti-colonial discourse

The music of Balam Ajpu articulates anti-colonial discourse across a range of distinct modes. This is true not simply of visual and linguistic modes, but also through the musical elements included in their music and the ways in which these elements are combined. This section lays out the various articulations of anti-colonial discourse within Balam Ajpu's music and musical performances.

In the visual mode, Balam Ajpu draws heavily on highly traditional and pre-Columbian sources. At their concerts, the members of Balam Ajpu wear long white hand-woven robes. The robes are not typical forms of *traje*, but are more reminiscent of ceremonial clothing in pre-Columbian Maya art. The members of the group also paint their faces in black, white and red paint. The face paint styles are taken directly from depictions of musicians in pre-Columbian art. Thus, the clothing worn by Balam Ajpu indexes their cultural heritage as descendants of the pre-Columbian Maya. At their performances, Balam Ajpu builds a ceremonial fire similar to the one used by spiritual guides (although often contained inside a ceramic bowl). Balam Ajpu concerts open with the lighting of the fire and a prayer for blessings from the ancestors and the nawals. The fire reproduces and celebrates the rituals banned during the civil war period. Before music has even begun, the members of the group have articulated anti-colonial discourse through their appearance and through the lighting of the fire.

The cover of Balam Ajpu's CD also articulates anti-colonial discourse in multiple ways. The CD has hieroglyphs for each of the 20 nawals arranged in a circle with the glyphs that fall in the cardinal directions painted in the color associated with that direction. Inside the circle are two heads, a jaguar (Balam) facing left and a hunter (Ajpu) facing right. Beneath the two heads, the words *hip hop* are written in hieroglyphic Maya. All of the visual imagery in the CD cover reflects central elements of Maya culture that are also tied to the philosophy of Hip Hop Cosmovision.

Another mode for articulating anti-colonial discourse can be found in the internal structure of Balam Ajpu's music. As Howell (2007) notes, traditional Maya music may be organized around sacred numbers. Balam Ajpu's music is structured around the Maya calendar and sacred geography. The CD *Jun Winaq Rajawal Q'ij* (Tribute to the 20 Nawals) is constructed around the 260-calendar, with one song for each of the 20 days in the calendar. The cycle of the 20 days repeats continuously so that there is no 'first' day in the calendar. Balam Ajpu's cycle of songs follows the progression of days in the calendar and the musicians recommend that when one listens to the CD they should always begin with the song associated with the day on which they are listening. Thus, like the calendar, the CD has no inherent beginning or ending but follows a regular repeating pattern.

As van Leeuwen (1999: 2) notes, modern recording technologies and forms like the spoken songs of rap music blur the boundaries between music and the sounds of everyday life. The hip hop music of Balam Ajpu juxtaposes sounds associated with contemporary Maya life against those associated with everyday life of the pre-Columbian Maya. The musical instruments used (and sampled) by Balam Ajpu include a number of pre-Columbian instruments such as drums, flutes, conch shells and turtle shells. The use of such instruments in contemporary hip hop music visually and sonically challenges the colonial representation of Maya music as limited to the pre-Columbian era. Balam Ajpu regularly include sampled sounds from nature in their music such as bird calls, jaguar howls, rain or thunder. The inclusion of natural sounds indexes a view of ladino culture as overly detached from the natural world and the central place of natural sounds in Maya verbal art (see Barrett, 2014). The animal and bird sounds are those of species found specifically in the Maya region, creating a locally specific soundscape that links the pre-Columbian instrumental sounds with the modern sounds of hip hop. Several songs on *Jun Winaq Rajawal Q'ij* begin with sampled sounds from nature (such as bird calls) playing alone for several seconds before being joined by an accompaniment on pre-Columbian flutes or drums. This is followed by the incorporation of hip hop beats and rapping so that the natural sounds continue through a soundscape that moves from the pre-Columbian to the modern. This parallels anti-colonial political discourse which emphasizes the cultural continuity between the pre-Columbian and contemporary Maya (Montejo, 2005).

The alternation between Spanish and Maya in Balam Ajpu's music places the two languages on equal footing, challenging the colonial discourse that denigrates Maya languages as inferior. The alternation between langauges also reflects the use of complementary pairings found in traditional Maya poetry and music (Howell, 2007; O'Brien-Rothe, 2015). Similarly, the rhythmic structure of Balam Ajpu's music also follows the broader pattern of complementary pairings found in Maya verbal art and music. Musical samples are often combined in ways that create alternations between different metres. Thus, the sampled elements produce the structure pattern of shifting metres that Howell (2007) describes for *Rab'inal Achi*. Similarly, the alternating raps in Maya and Spanish often produce similar shifts in metre so that the pairing of languages often corresponds to the pairing of rhythmic patterns. In terms of rhythmic structure, the music of Balam Ajpu is also anti-colonial, refusing to assimilate to the unified metrical pattern found in Western music.

The anti-colonial semiotics of Balam Ajpu's music can be illustrated by the song 'Ajmak' from *Jun Winaq Rajawal Q'ij*. Within Maya cosmology, the nawal Ajmak (Sinner) is associated with asking for forgiveness from the ancestors. In particular, Ajmak is associated with sins against one's own family or community (see Tedlock, 1992: 121–122). Because these sorts of sins require asking the ancestors for forgiveness, the day of Ajmak is one for reflecting on the ancestors, not only praying to them for forgiveness but also giving them thanks for providing life. The lyrics of the song 'Ajmak' revolve around this theme, conveying the importance of the ancestors associated with this specific nawal. Praying to the ancestors is done through the traditional burning ceremonies that were banned during the civil war. The theme of the lyrics is itself anti-colonial, celebrating aspects of Maya religion that defy colonialist efforts to eradicate Maya culture.

These burning rituals begin by partitioning the world into the four cardinal directions associated with sacred Maya geography. 'Ajmak' is structured around groupings of four, some directly refering to the four cardinal directions. The song opens with samples of *a capella* fragments from four different singers. Although none of the singers actually produces recognizable lyrics, each has a unique voice quality and timbre (van Leeuwen, 1999: 9) associated with a particular ethnic musical style. The four singers are (in order) a European woman, an African man, an Asian woman and a Native American man. The harmonic relations within the melodies each sings is also indicative of a particular regional/ethnic musical style. Within Maya cosmology, each of the four cardinal directions is associated with a specific color (north/white, west/black, south/yellow, and east/red). The four colors are associated with the four colors of corn (the Maya refer to 'blue corn' as 'black'). Humans were created from corn (Tedlock, 1996), so that the four colours of corn also represent four 'races' of humanity (which are white, black, yellow and red like the corn). The order of the cardinal directions associated with the singers in 'Ajmak' moves counterclockwise (North-West-South-East), following the counter-clockwise direction used in prayers to the nawals and to the ancestors (Hanks, 1992).

As with other forms of Maya music and poetry, the complementary pairings found in these four samples extend beyond marking the four cardinal directions. In Maya poetry, traditional quatrains are structured so that there are specific relationships between alternating lines as well as between inner and outer pairs of lines (Barrett, forthcoming). Thus, one structure will mark a relationship between lines one and three and between lines two and four while some other structure marks a relationship between lines one and four and between lines two and three. The four sampled voices that open 'Ajmak' reflect this poetic structure in the musical mode (indeed, without words at all). The voices also alternate between male and female singers, so that voices one and three are female and voices two and four are male. However, the melodies sung by each voice mark opposing directions in terms of tonal gravity (McKerrell, 2015). In each of the fragments, the melody includes unidirectional movement from the starting note, to the same note an octave higher or lower. Although the melodies contain distinct harmonic relationships, the pitch range and tonal associations are the same. The direction in which the pitch moves across the octave, however, differs from line to line. The melodies of the first and fourth voices both involve movement to an octave higher while the melodies of the second and third voices involvement movement to an octave lower. Thus, through different modalities, the music produces distinct relationships between the four sampled voices. These relationships reflect both traditional Maya poetics and the sacred geography associated with Maya religious beliefs and practices that the dominant culture has tried to eradicate for centuries.

This pattern of complementary pairings continues through the song with alternations between quatrains in Maya and in Spanish. The Maya lyrics play on the phonological similarity between the name of the day (*Ajmak* or *Ajmaq*), the K'ichean word for 'nation' or 'tribe' (*ajmaq'*), and the word for sin (*mak* or *majk*). The Maya lines open with the primary elements of the prayers associated with the day Ajmak, namely giving thanks and askng for forgiveness. The following Spanish quatrain repeats the pairing of giving thanks and asking forgiveness raised in the Maya quatrain, but also involves a secondary set of complementary pairings (between air and water and between fire and earth):

(2) Ajmak (Balam Ajpu, 2015)

Ajmaq' kinmaltyoxij chawe	Great nation of the ancestors, I thank you
Ajmaq' tasacha k'a li numajk	Great nation of the ancestors, forgive me for my sins
Ajmaq' kinmaltyoxij chawe	Great nation of the ancestors, I thank you
Ajmaq' tasacha k'a li numajk	Great nation of the ancestors, forgive me for my sins
GRACIAS por el AIRE por el AGUA	Thank you for the air, for water
GRACIAS porque alimento nos DAS	Thank you for the food that you give us
GRACIAS por el FUEGO por la TIERRA	Thank you for the fire and the earth
PERDON por nuestras Faltas AJ MAK	Forgive us for our sins, Ajmak

The two verses complement one another in that they each contain four lines and convey the same basic meanings (giving thanks and asking for forgiveness). The internal structures of the verses, however, are not the same. Although not involving perfect rhyme, the Spanish quatrain has end rhyme, a pattern typical of Spanish-language hip hop (including all of the Spanish lyrics of Balam Ajpu).

In contrast, the Maya lyrics show syntactic parallelism without the use of rhyme. The pairing of these two quatrains is not simply a pairing of two languages, but also a pairing of contrasting poetic styles. Of course, the pairing also indexes the opposition between Maya and ladinos. However, the Maya quatrain precedes the Spanish one (an ordering that is clearly anti-colonial). The ordered alternation between the two languages (which pairs them as equals) also challenges articulations of colonial discourse that claim the inherent superiority of Spanish. This pair of quatrains serves as the chorus for the song. In addition to this chorus, there are two verses to the song, one in Spanish and one in Maya. The Spanish lyrics reaffirm the meaning of the Ajmak nawal, repeating the themes of giving thanks and the healing power of performing the burning ceremony to ask for forgiveness:

(3) Ajmak (Balam Ajpu, 2015)

Que es el Amor sin sentir DOLOR	What is love without pain
AJMAQ es el Pecado también es el PERDON	Ajmak is sin but also forgiveness
Un pecador con buen manejo de PALABRA	A sinner skilled with words
El humo es Abuelo sanador cuando HABLAS	The smoke is the ancestor, the healer when you speak

As with the two quatrains in the chorus, the Spanish lyrics are not a direct translation from the Maya lyrics. The Mayan-language verse in 'Ajmak' is taken directly from the words channeled by the group's spiritual guide and contain more symbolic and esoteric lyrics:

(4) Ajmak (Balam Ajpu, 2015)

Ojer taq Te' Ta', saq kePAS	Our ancestors, with white belts
Saq kijolom, saq keMETZ'	with white hair, with white eyelids,
Q'en taq alanxax, Saq taq ALANXAX	Yellow citrus fruits, White citrus fruits,
Rex taq kotz'i'j, tikil pa li ULEW.	Blue flowers planted in the earth

The lyrics again build on the pattern of complementary pairs (white hair/ white eyelids, yellow fruit/white fruit), even though the symbolism involved would not be immediately apparent to most listeners. The more symbolic character of the lyrics indexes the origins of the verse as channeled words received from the ancestors themselves and marks the lyrics as inherently spiritual. This contrasts sharply to the Spanish verse in which comparatively obvious meanings are paired with Western rhythmic and rhyming structure.

It might be argued that a song like 'Ajmak' fails to serve as anti-colonialist discourse because the symbolism in the lyrics is so symbolic and abstract that it is devoid of any clear political meaning. As Way (2013: 18) suggests for Turkish protest music, such abstraction may be an inherent part of popular music. Even so, an analysis based solely on the content of Balam Ajpu's lyrics would fail to recognize the ways in which anti-colonial discourse is articulated across modes. In addition to visual imagery, combinations of sampled elements and choice of musical instruments, the modes involved include the basic internal structure of songs and the rhythmic patterns found within the music. By rejecting Western musical traditions and incorporating pre-Columbian elements into contemporary hip hop, Balam Ajpu challenges dominant discourses that attempt to erase Maya musical traditions (and Maya culture more generally) from contemporary Guatemalan society.

Conclusion

The music of Balam Ajpu illustrates the ways in which music operates as multimodal discourse. The content of lyrics and the purpose of their songs are directly linked to their political activism and efforts to promote Maya culture. The instruments used and the sounds sampled in their music connect the musicians both to the pre-Columbian Maya and to the natural environment of the Guatemalan highlands. The musical structure of Balam Ajpu's songs builds on traditional Maya understandings of mathematics, geography and time. Alternations in metre reflect pre-Columbian musical patterns while creating complementary pairings between different rhythmic patterns.

Hegemonic discourse in Guatemala has long held that Mayan languages and Maya culture have no place in the modern world. While the Ancient Maya have been celebrated, the contemporary Maya have been repeatedly denigrated as having no connection to their pre-Columbian ancestors. In their music, Balam Ajpu challenges this colonial discourse through demonstrating that Maya culture (and Maya music in particular) has not only survived 500 years of oppression but is likely to flourish as we enter into the new baktun.

References

Balam Ajpu. (2015), *Ajmak. Jun Winaq Rajawal Q'ij/Tributo a los 20 Nawales* (musical CD). Los Gemelos and Venancio Morales: spritual guide, Tz'utu Baktun

Kan: executive producer and Tz'utujil lyrics, MChe and Mc P.A.N.A: Spanish lyrics, Dr. Nativo: musical producer and Danilo Rodríguez: co-producers.

Barrett, Rusty. (2005), 'Five Oxlajuuj Keej Maya Ajtz'iib' Reference Grammars', *International Journal of American Linguistics* 71(2): 215–221.

Barrett, Rusty. (2014), 'Ideophones and (non-)arbitrariness in the K'iche' Poetry of Humberto Ak'abal', *Pragmatics and society* 5(3): 406–418.

Barrett, Rusty. (2016), 'Mayan Language Revitalization, Hip Hop, and Ethnic Identity in Guatemala', *Language & Communication* 47: 144–153. <http://dx.doi.org/10.1016/j.langcom.2015.08.005> [accessed 13 July 2016]

Barrett, Rusty. (forthcoming), 'Poetics', in Judith Aissen, Nora England and Roberto Zavala (eds) *The Mayan Languages*. Routledge Language Family Series. New York: Routledge.

Billig, Michael. (1995), *Banal Nationalism*. London: Sage.

Bourg, Cameron Hideo. (2005), 'Ancient Maya Music Now with Sound', MA thesis, *Department of Foreign Languages and Literatures*, Louisiana State University, Baton Rouge.

Breton, Alain (ed.). (2007), *Rabinal Achi: A Fifteenth-century Maya Dynastic Drama*. Translated by Teresa Lavender Fagan and Robert Schneider. Boulder: University of Colorado Press.

Carmack, Robert M. (ed.). (1988), *Harvest of Violence: Maya Indians and the Guatemalan Crisis*. Norman: University of Oklahoma Press.

Cojti Cuxil, Demetrio. (1997), *Ri Maya' Moloj pa Iximulew: El Movimiento Maya en Guatemala*. [The Maya movement in Guatemala]. Guatemala City: Cholsamaj.

Del Valle Escalante, Emilio. (2009), *Maya Nationalisms and Postcolonial Challenges in Guatemala: Coloniality, Modernity, and Identity Politics*. Santa Fe, NM: School for Advanced Research.

England, Nora. (2003), 'Mayan Language Revival and Revitalization Politics: Linguists and Linguistic Ideologies', *American Anthropologist* 105(4): 733–743.

Fischer, Edward F. and McKenna Brown, R. (eds). (1996), *Maya Cultural Activism in Guatemala*. Austin: University of Texas Press.

Fishman, Joshua A. (1967), 'Bilingualism With and Without Diglossia; Diglossia with and without Bilingualism', *Journal of Social Issues* 23(2): 29–38.

Fox Tree, Erich. (2011), 'Global Linguistics, Mayan Languages, and the Cultivation of Autonomy', inMario Blaser, Ravi De Costa, Deborah McGregor, William D. Coleman (eds) *Indigenous Peoples and Autonomy: Insights for a Global Age*, pp. 80–106. Vancouver: University of British Columbia Press.

French, Brigittine. (2010), *Maya Ethnolinguistic Identity: Violence, Cultural Rights, and Modernity in Highland Guatemala*. Tucson: University of Arizona Press.

Frye, David. (1996), *Indians into Mexicans: History and Identity in a Mexican Town*. Austin: University of Texas Press.

Gálvez Borrell, Víctor and Esquit Choy, Alberto. (1997), *The Mayan Movement Today: Issues of Indigenous Culture and Development in Guatemala*. Guatemala: FLASCO.

Grube, Nikolai. (1992), 'Classic Maya Dance: Evidence from Hieroglyphs and Iconography', *Ancient Mesoamerica* 3(2): 201–218.

Hale, Charles R. (2006), *Mas que un indio: Racial Ambivalence and the Paradox of Neoliberal Multiculturalism in Guatemala*. Santa Fe, NM: School of American Research Press.

Hammond, Norman. (1972a), 'Classic Maya Music: Part I: Maya Drums', *Archaeology* 25(2): 124–131.

Hammond, Norman. (1972b), 'Classic Maya Music: Part II: Rattles, Shakers, Raspers, Wind, and String Instruments', *Archaeology* 25(3): 222–228.

Hanks, William. (1992), 'Santification, Structure, and Experience in a Yucatec Ritual Event', *The Journal of American Folklore* 97: 131–166.

Hendrickson, Carol. (1991), 'Images of the Indian in Guatemala: The Role of Indigenous Dress in Indian and Ladino Constructions', in Greg Urban and Joel Sherzer (eds) *Nation-states and Indians in Latin America*, pp. 286-306. Austin: University of Texas Press.

Howell, Mark. (2007), 'Possible Prehispanic Music Survivals in the "Rab'inal Achi"', *The World of Music* 49(2): 105–138.

Kroskrity, Paul V. (2000), 'Language Ideologies in the Expression and Representation of Arizona Tewa Ethnic Identity', in Paul V. Kroskrity (ed.) *Regimes of Language: Ideologies, Polities, and Identities*, pp. 329–359. Santa Fe: School of American Research Press.

Looper, Matthew G. (2010), *To be Like Gods: Dance in Ancient Maya Civilization*. Austin: University of Texas Press.

Machin, David, and Richardson, John E. (2012), 'Discourses of Unity and Purpose in the Sounds of Fascist Music: A Multimodal Approach', *Critical Discourse Studies* 9(4): 329–345. http://dx.doi.org/10.1080/17405904.2012.713203 [accessed 13 July 2016]

Maxwell, Judith M. (2009), 'Bilingual Bicultural Education: Best Intentions Across a Cultural Divide', in Walter E. Little and Timothy J. Smith (eds) *Mayas in Postwar Guatemala: Harvest of Violence Revisited*, pp. 84–95. Tuscaloosa, AL: University of Alabama Press.

McKerrell, Simon. (2015), 'Social Distance and the Multimodal Construction of the Other in Sectarian Song', *Social Semiotics* 0(0): 1–19. <http://dx.doi.org/10.1080/10350330.2015.1046216> [accessed 13 July 2016]

Montejo, Victor. (2005), *Maya Intellectual Renaissance: Identity, Representation and Leadership*. Austin: University of Texas Press.

Navarrete Pellicer, Sergio. (2005), *Maya Achi Marimba Music in Guatemala*. Philadelphia: Temple University Press.

O'Brien-Rothe, Linda. (1975), 'Songs of the Face of the Earth: Ancestor Songs of the Tzutuhil-Maya of Santiago Atitlan, Guatemala', PhD dissertation, University of California – Los Angeles.

O'Brien-Rothe, Linda. (1982), 'Marimbas of Guatemala: The African Connection', *The World of Music* 24(2): 99–104.

O'Brien-Rothe, Linda. (2010) 'The Poetics of the Ancestor Songs of the Tz'utujil Maya of Guatemala', *Journal of International and Global Studies* 1: 74–99.

O'Brien-Rothe, Linda. (2015), *Songs That Make the Road Dance: Courtship and Fertility Music of the Tz'utujil Maya*. Austin: University of Texas Press.

Otzoy, Irma. (1992), 'Identidad y trajes mayas', *Mésoameria* 23: 95–112.

Otzoy, Irma. (1996), 'Maya Clothing and Identity', in Edward F. Fischer and R. McKenna Brown (eds) *Maya Cultural Activism in Guatemala*, pp. 141-155. Austin: University of Texas Press.

Otzoy, Irma. (1999), 'Tekum Umam: From Nationalism to Maya Resistance', PhD dissertation, Department of Anthropology, University of California, Davis.

Perera, Victor. (1995), *Unfinished Conquest: The Guatemalan Tragedy*. Berkeley and Los Angeles: University of California Press.

Piotrowska, Anna G. (2013), '"Gypsy Music" as Music of the Other in European Culture', *Patterns of Prejudice* 47(4–5): 395–408. <http://dx.doi.org/10.1080/0031322X.2013.846615> [accessed 13 July 2016]

Reynolds, Jennifer F. (2009), 'Shaming the Shift Generation: Intersecting Ideologies of Family and Linguistic Revitalization in Guatemala', in Paul V. Kroskrity and Margaret C. Field (eds) *Native American Language Ideologies: Beliefs, Practices, and Struggles in Indian Country*, pp. 213–237. Tucson, AZ: University of Arizona Press.

Sanchez, Julia L. J. (2007), 'Procession and Performance: Recreating Ritual Soundscapes Among the Ancient Maya', *The World of Music* 49(2): 35–44.

Taracena Arriola, Arturo. (2011), 'Marimba', in Greg Grandin, Deborah T. Levenson, and Elizabeth Oglesby (eds) *The Guatemala Reader: History, Culture, Politics*, pp. 150–156. Durham, NC: Duke University Press.

Tedlock, Barbara. (1992), *Time and the Highland Maya*. Albuquerque, NM: University of New Mexico Press.

Tedlock, Dennis. (1996), *Popol Vuh: The Definitive Edition of The Mayan Book of The Dawn of Life and The Glories of Gods and Kings*. New York: Touchstone.

Tedlock, Dennis. (2003), *Abinal Achi: A Mayan Drama of War and Sacrifice*. New York: Oxford University Press.

Tedlock, Dennis. (2010), *2000 Years of Mayan Literatura*. Berkeley and Los Angeles: University of California Press.

van Leeuwen, Theo. (1999), *Speech, Music, Sound*. Basingstoke, London: Macmillan.

van Leeuwen, Theo. (2012), 'The Critical Analysis of Musical Discourse', *Critical Discourse Studies* 9(4): 319–328.

Velásquez Nimatuj, Irma Alicia. (2005), *Pueblos indígenas, estado y lucha por tierra en Guatemala: Estrategias de sobrevivencia y negociación ante la desigualdad globalizada*. PhD dissertation. Department of Anthropology, University of Texas at Austin.

Warren, Kay. (1998), *Indigenous Movements and their Critics: Pan-Maya Activism in Guatemala* (Princeton: Princeton University Press).

Way, Lyndon C. S. (2013), 'Discourses of Popular Politics, War and Authenticity in Turkish Pop Music', *Social Semiotics*. <http://dx.doi.org/10.1080/10350330.2013.819723> [accessed 13 July 2016]

10

Song, Sonic Metaphor, and Countercultural Discourse in British Folk-Rock Recordings

Matthew Ord

Introduction

This chapter explores the contribution of sound recording techniques to the communication of countercultural meanings in the British folk-rock movement of the late 1960s and early 1970s. While discourse analysts have tended to concentrate on verbal/textual communication and official forms of discourse, the recent turn to multimodal approaches has meant a greater attention to entertainment media and the role of non-verbal modes, including music, in the communication of cultural values (Way, 2015: 181). Discourses, Way notes, 'project certain values and ideas which contribute to the (re)production of social life', and music 'can be shown to communicate ideas, attitudes and identities, through cultural references and through specific meaning potentials' (2015: 184). In this chapter I consider recorded songs as multimodal blends which generate complex meanings through the interplay of textual, musical and production elements and suggest that record production, the creative manipulation of recorded musical sounds, can be considered an active component of discourses in which the values of groups are communicated, explored and celebrated.

Recent work in critical discourse analysis (CDA) and musicology suggests that sound recording can transform the semiotic potential of multimodal texts by shaping the material properties of sounds and constructing multimodal metaphors (van Leeuwen, 1999, 2012; Zbikowski, 2002, 2009; Forceville, 2009; Machin, 2010). This chapter considers sound recording as a mode of discourse,[1] combining techniques from CDA, conceptual metaphor theory (CMT) and blending theory (BT) to explore the link between sound production and countercultural values in the context of British folk-rock. The folk-rock movement emerged at a transitional point in the performance of folk music in Britain in which, I suggest, an anti-commercial recording aesthetic associated with the post-war folk revival was challenged by musicians seeking to draw on the semiotic resources of the studio in their interpretations of traditional song and align themselves with the oppositional discourse of progressive rock. This chapter thus explores the uses of recording at a specific moment in its evolution as a semiotic mode, by a particular community of practice, and for the expression of extra-musical values linked to countercultural discourse.

The controversial evolution of the recording mode

Van Leeuwen (2004: 26–27) notes that semiotic innovation often involves controversy over the legitimacy of new practices, pointing out that the evolution of the 'self-effacing art' of typography into a semiotic mode was initially resisted by some practitioners as 'anathema' to the craft's 'true calling' (Ibid.: 27). Similarly, as sound recording developed beyond the mimetic into a powerful set of semiotic resources, its creative use gave rise to controversies related to discourses of musical authenticity and critique of industrial mass-culture.

With the explosive development of recording technology and the record industry after 1945, techniques such as multi-tracking, echo and reverb began to open up rich seams of creative possibility for musicians, and allowed the record producer to emerge as 'an indispensable interpreter between the technical and artistic aspects of making records' (Moorefield, 2005: 41). 'Serious' music critics, however, often equated the use of new studio techniques such as echo with commercial gimmickry and cultural homogenization (Zak, 2012). Technical innovation did not guarantee musically interesting results: Middleton (1990: 85) argues that the experimentation of the late 1940s and early 1950s was followed by the reestablishment of a 'new symbiosis, recognisably related to the old dominant model', while Zak (2010) notes that studio production was closely associated with a new generation of recording stars, often perceived as the puppets of Svengali-type producers adept at using technology to mask a basic lack of substance. Perceptions of production as a commercially motivated talent compensator fuelled fierce debates over the legitimacy of approaches which moved beyond the mimetic representation of live performance.

Folk into Folk-Rock

The folk revival's valorization of unadorned performance and acoustic instrumentation has been seen as a reaction against the mass-produced sounds emanating from major labels (MacKinnon, 1993), and revivalist folk recordings of the early 1960s typically downplayed evidence of technological mediation. By endeavouring to keep the art of traditional performance separate from the supplementary craft of recording, revivalist producers asserted a vision of authenticity and creative autonomy deliberately opposed to industrial mass-culture.

A tangential offshoot of the revival, folk-rock began to emerge from independent rock labels such as Island and Chrysalis at the end of the 1960s. Rock music had by this time attained a countercultural status which was increasingly associated with innovative approaches to studio sound production. Whiteley (1990: 37) argues that countercultural discourse constructed music as 'a symbolic act of self-liberation and self-realisation in which reality and musical experience were fused', and rock musicians were routinely treated as generational spokespersons despite the comparative lack of political content in their lyrics. Instead, the oppositional status of musical texts was located in sounds themselves, from Hendrix's fuzz-laden guitar to the echoic spatiality of Pink Floyd. 'Such was the power of rock music', Bennett observes, 'that it came to bespeak notions of an alternative community that hippies believed could be experienced and realized through the music itself' (2014: 18). Rock records were thought to bear witness to and even to manifest an alternative community in sound, indicating a shift in the perceived significance of music and sound in political life.

In their adoption of rock instrumentation and studio techniques, bands such as Pentangle, Fairport Convention and Steeleye Span brought a countercultural aesthetic to bear on the interpretation of traditional material. Excoriated by traditionalists for abandoning the naturalist aesthetic of the early revival and embracing what were seen as commercial production techniques,[2] folk-rock reflected the shift towards a countercultural politics of sound; its departure from the revival's aesthetic values was an indicator not so much of commercial intent but of musicians' desire to incorporate the new sonic palette into folk performance practice. As fiddler Dave Swarbrick of leading folk-rock act Fairport Convention put it:

> You know, if you're singing about a bloke having his head chopped off, a girl
> fucking her brother and having a baby and the brother getting pissed off and
> cutting her guts open and stamping on the baby and killing his sister . . .having

to work with a storyline like that with acoustic instruments wouldn't be half as powerful or potent, dramatically, as saying the same things electrically. Because when you deal with violence. . .someone slashing with a sword, say, there are sounds that exist electrically – with electric bass, say – that can very explicitly suggest what the words are saying. (Swarbrick in Denselow, 1975: 140)

Music and metaphor theory

Swarbrick's vivid evocation of the capacity of electronic sound to convey the actions, events and images in traditional texts hints at the explanatory potential of metaphor theory for understanding how recording can intervene in the construction of song narratives. In the sonic analogies that Swarbrick describes, metaphors such as 'volume is physical force' are used to structure interpretations of musical sounds and extend the power of textual images. Lakoff and Johnson's (1980) CMT argues that abstract domains of experience such as music rely on processes of cross-domain mapping, in which structure from a basic-level source domain is mapped across onto a more abstract target domain. One example is the use of spatial concepts to understand musical pitch, where an 'up/down' schema drawn from the spatial domain is used to think and talk about musical notes as if they occupied a position in physical space (Zbikowski, 2002). Cognitive metaphors thus allow us to understand relatively abstract experiences in terms of more basic ones. As Johnson and Larson (2003) argue, the conceptual structures that allow us to understand the domain of music have embodied experience at their core.

Going further, recent work on musical metaphor suggests that musical sounds not only enter into homologous relationships with other modes, but do so in principled and culturally mediated ways. CMT is concerned with the kind of stable, entrenched metaphorical relationships that support more abstract cognition: the conceptualization of time in spatial terms, for example, is a very basic mapping which supports a vast number of conceptual and linguistic activities, as indicated by expressions such as 'facing the future' or 'Christmas is coming up fast'. Although these examples are based in universal cognitive processes, the content of conceptual mappings is culturally specific. In English, Lakoff and Johnson (1980: 4) note, it is conventional to use the domain of war to talk about verbal debate, for example, 'There's a breach in your argument' or 'his position was attacked and undermined' (Figure 10.1).

Zbikowski notes that understanding musical pitch in terms of verticality is a European phenomenon; other cultures use metaphors of size, age, or the

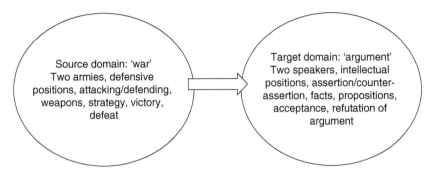

Figure 10.1. Cross-domain mapping for the metaphor 'argument is war'

physical structure of natural phenomena (like waterfalls) to conceptualize tonal relationships in spatial terms (2002: 67–68). Although these mappings all share a basic underlying schema ('notes are points along a continuum') their articulation is informed by the shared experiences and values of cultural groups.

Identifying the cognitive metaphors that underlie discourses can reveal the values and assumptions of their producers, and indicate how metaphors are used strategically to shape others' perceptions of social reality. Hart (2010: 153) for example, shows how flood metaphors can be used to manipulate immigration discourse in the interests of powerful groups. Zbikowski (2009) and Forceville (2009) have argued that music and non-verbal sound can supply source domains for multimodal metaphors involving music, image and/or text. Their work raises new possibilities for understanding how recorded songs communicate social meanings; if underlying cognitive metaphors can be identified in musical compositions, then perhaps record production can also be used to construct meanings in a cohesive and observable way, reflecting producers' values and shaping perceptions of social reality.

Fauconnier and Turner's (1998) conceptual blending theory (BT) allows analysis of metaphorical constructions at a more local and specific level. While it acknowledges the existence of CMT's domains, BT is more concerned with the temporary and novel conceptualizations that occur in ongoing processes of representation and interpretation (Grady, Oakley and Coulson, 1999: 101). BT posits the existence of 'mental spaces', 'partial and temporary representational structures which speakers construct when thinking or talking about a perceived, imagined, past, present, or future situation' (Ibid.: 102). These temporary spaces build upon the basic cognitive metaphors identified by CMT, but map only selected structure across in the course of an ongoing, pragmatic process.

Zbikowski (2002) shows how conceptual blending underpins the technique of word-painting in music. In his example from a mass by Palestrina, the text 'descendit de caelis' is illustrated by a descending scalar passage in the music, creating the blended entity of a physical descent that has the qualities of stately, stepwise motion mapped across from the musical articulation (Ibid.: 63). The entrenched metaphor 'pitch is position in space' supports a temporary meaning which emerges in the blend of text, music and articulation.

The key aspect of conceptual blends is that they produce new emergent meanings in a blended space; they are more than the sum of their parts. A melodic descent can be conceived as motion in space because of the shared structure of the two 'input spaces' (the content of the 'generic space') but its meaning in the local interpretive context is the product of a blend which incorporates the textual and musical inputs and the spatial, textural or timbral qualities of the performance, generating new meanings which exceed those already present in the input spaces.

Where CMT deals with a relatively stable system of underlying cultural metaphors, conceptual blending describes an ongoing process of interpretation in which concepts are articulated into 'short-term [constructs] informed by the more general and more stable knowledge structures associated with a particular domain' (Grady, Oakley and Coulson, 1999: 102). It thus allows for more detailed discussion of the live processes of sense-making that we engage in when composing, playing or listening to music. The following example uses blending theory to consider recording's contribution to emergent meanings in the multimodal context of recorded song.

Recording, meaning and metaphor

Patti Page's 'Confess' (1947) has become a classic example of how recording began to transform popular song after 1945.[3] The song had already been recorded as an upbeat duet by Buddy Clark and Doris Day.[4] As the recording budget could not stretch to a second vocalist, however, Page used the relatively new technique of overdubbing to add the second part herself (Lacasse, 2000: 128). In her slow, introspective reading the languid vocal is framed by a sparse piano, guitar and bass accompaniment, as she plaintively urges her lover to admit his true feelings:

Confess,
(Confess, confess)

Why don't you confess?
(Say yes, say yes)
I wish you'd reveal to me,
(Reveal to me)
The way that you feel.
(I wish you'd tell me the way that you feel)

In Page's version, aspects of the recording process contribute significantly to the meaning potential of the total recorded performance. The main vocal is recorded dry and frontally positioned, while the second is positioned back in the mix, as if it were an echo of the lead part, and is noticeably reverberant. Although echo-chambers and reverb units were initially developed to mimic the reflective properties of real spaces, Lacasse (2000) notes that the semiotic potential of reverb was recognized by film-makers and recordists as early as the 1930s. Van Leeuwen (1999: 167) observes that reverberation can be used 'to make some sounds appear subjective and "interior", almost as though heard from inside the body', and the relationship between the reverberant quality of the vocal and the song's textual structure supports such an interpretation here. The lines given to the second, reverberant voice (shown in brackets) are shorter and more urgent ('say yes, say yes') compared to those in the lead voice (which might be interpreted as representing Page's outward social persona) which is more wistful, less direct ('I wish you'd reveal to me/ the way that you feel'). This, combined with the fact that the second voice is clearly Page herself, and the lyrical concern with feelings that remain unvoiced encourages the notion, as Lacasse (2000: 128) and Doyle (2005: 145) both suggest, that the second part is Page's inner voice, rising to the surface with 'an aching need to be heard'.

Where Clark and Day's realist recording evoked an image of two lovers poised together on the brink of a deeper intimacy, Page's version uses echo and overdubbing to suggest a lonelier and more introspective experience. We are less sure of the reality of the feelings that Page demands that the other confess – is she imagining them? The recording affords the listener an emotional intimacy with the singer that is lacking from other versions (we seem to hear her innermost thoughts) while it denies her the kind of interpersonal intimacy that Clark and Day's duet version vividly portrays. In Page's 'Confess', the production provides crucial material for aesthetic interpretation; the potential interpretation of Page struggling with her own unexpressed feelings emerges multimodally in the imaginative space conjured between the recording and the listener by the combination of text, music and studio sound.

BT can help describe this as an emergent meaning resulting from a blend of two input spaces. When we listen to Page's 'Confess' and hear her overdubbed second vocal, we can make sense of the experience because of our capacity to construct imaginative blends of structure from two or more spaces. Our interpretations can also draw on existing cultural tropes (such as the notion of an interior monologue, common, for example, in cinema) to construct a blended mental space in which the second voice we hear on the recording is Page's inner voice, her conscience or soul. This emergent meaning feeds into how we interpret the song as a whole. Page's reading becomes a study of anxiety, introspection and possibly unrequited love, rather than a celebration of shared intimacy.

'Confess' drew on a preexisting cultural link between the echoic space of recordings and the mind. This convention acquired new countercultural significance in the 1960s with psychedelia. Where Page's 'Confess' used overdubbing and echo to suggest the voice of unconscious desire, the countercultural preoccupation with consciousness led to the use of studio techniques to represent the experiential quality of altered states (whether the result of psychedelic drug use or of spiritual awakening) sonically. As Whiteley (1990: 38) notes, these techniques quickly became indexical of countercultural identity through what she calls 'psychedelic coding'; in adopting sound as a means for exploring the psychology of song characters, folk-rock musicians tacitly aligned themselves with countercultural aesthetics and values.

The uses of production in folk-rock: 'Boys of Bedlam'

When folk singer and guitarist Martin Carthy joined folk-rock outfit Steeleye Span in 1971, he had already recorded a string of albums featuring his solo voice and acoustic guitar, sometimes with fiddle accompaniment. In this new context, he was able to draw upon the semiotic resources of a rock band line up and the contemporary studio in his interpretations of traditional material. Whilst recording the song 'Boys of Bedlam' (1971),[5] he and joint lead-vocalist Maddy Prior experimented with an unusual approach to recording their vocals:

> [T]he idea was to make the voices sound odd. Well, nowadays you'd just put a lot of nonsense and that bought stuff, but then we hadn't that kind of thing you see. So we sang in the back of a banjo. That's why it's got this strange vocal sound. Martin said, 'oh yes, this sounds great! Sounds like crazy lunatics' (Prior quoted in Sweers, 2005: 180).

In the song's eighteenth-century text, a sequence of absurd yet ominous images conveys a sense of lunacy and vague threat.[6] The lyric is set to a recently composed tune in a seventeenth-century style by revivalist band The Halliard which strongly suggests an unspecified and exoticized past. The unorthodox mic positioning lends the vocals a highly unusual timbre, as if the singers' voices were distorted by an impure or obstructed signal. In the context of the lyric, this technique, by changing the frequency profile of the singers' voices and altering and obscuring their natural tone with a rough sonic patina, is able to stand for the altered mental state of the song's protagonists; it is, as Prior remarks, an audible representation of lunacy.

Van Leeuwen (1999: 205) argues that the semiotic affordances of timbre are rooted in what he calls 'experiential meaning potential', which arises from 'our experience of what we physically have to do to produce a particular sound'. Thus perceived articulatory qualities of smoothness, roughness, laxness or tension invoke interpretations based in our own experiences of our physical state when producing these sounds: 'The sound that results from tensing' van Leeuwen suggests, 'not only *is* tense, it also *means* tense – and makes tense'; and these meaning potentials can be extended to other sources, machines, instruments, and so on, which share the same timbral properties (1999: 131). Sound recordings can evoke experiential meaning by manipulating the perceived articulatory characteristics of sounds. The treatment given to the vocals in this track accentuates qualities of nasality and roughness, creating a sense of tension and rigidity which is further emphasized by the relatively small space assigned to the two vocals within the stereo array. In the musical-textual space of the song, these generalized embodied meanings of tension, rigidity, and roughness are inflected by the lyrical references to madness to construct a sense of otherness and threat.

Applying a CMT approach can add a further layer to this analysis by revealing the underlying conceptual metaphors which might structure such uses of the medium. The implied proposition made in the song's production could be expressed verbally as 'madness is obstructed signal', framing 'understanding' in terms of point-to-point communication. The basic conceptual metaphor at play here – 'understanding is hearing' – underlies linguistic constructions such as 'I hear you loud and clear', or 'you're not hearing me'. As CMT requires that we identify a source domain and a target domain, it could be argued that the domain of communication, as cued by the unusual sound of the vocals, which evoke the common cultural experience of a poor signal hampering understanding (on the telephone or radio, perhaps) is used to construct madness in terms

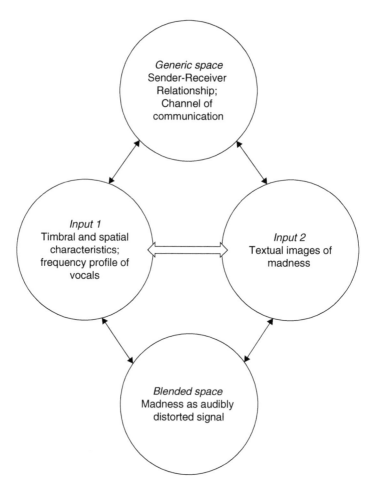

Figure 10.2. Conceptual integration network showing the blend of production and musical-textual elements in 'Boys of Bedlam'

of this metaphor of an obstructed or altered signal. This would constitute a multimodal metaphor whose source domain is primarily cued by the sonic medium, and whose target domain is located in the textual mode.

Using blending theory, we could argue that the mental spaces set up by the textual and production aspects combine in a blended space in which emergent meanings are produced. This relationship can be expressed as a 'conceptual integration network' (Figure 10.2) which has at least four spaces (Fauconnier and Turner, 1998; Zbikowski, 2002).[7] The input spaces feed into the blended space, but there is also a fourth 'generic' space which contains the shared invariant structure recruited from the input spaces, in this case, a sender and receiver and a signal passing between them. The salient aspects of each input space (the sound of the vocals, the image of madness in the text) create a temporary blend in which madness has an audible (vocal) aspect (Figure 10.2).

CMT and BT both hold that identifying underlying metaphors in representations can reveal tacit values. What then does this example tell us about the song's underlying values or cultural assumptions? The effect of this treatment of the vocal has implications for how the relationship between the song's persona and the listener is constructed: the effect of the vocal sound in the introduction is 'othering', distancing us from the singers by virtue of their vocal strangeness and the notion that this reflects an altered mental state. We do not identify directly with the singers, but are threatened by their essential difference from us. In the lyrical context suggested by the title's reference to Bedlam, we are placed in a voyeuristic relationship to the song's mad protagonists. The song's production helps establish a subject-position in which we see the Bedlamites as other.

Later in the song, the mix changes, and the vocal sound becomes much clearer, with Prior dropping out and Carthy taking the lead vocal. The vocal sound image is larger and more prominent in the mix, and articulated more clearly. It is a mix that, aside from the slightly unusual instrumentation, is much closer to a conventional rock configuration, with a centrally positioned vocal and other instruments balanced across the stereo array – the arrangement that Dockwray and Moore (2010) call the 'diagonal mix'.[8] If a sound, van Leeuwen (1999: 23) argues, 'is positioned as Figure, it is thereby treated as the most important sound, the sound which the listener must identify with, and /or react to and/or act upon'. The positioning of Carthy's vocal as figure in the second mix enacts a more intimate social distance, suggesting that we identify with the song persona more closely, that we are less estranged from it. The song's production thus constructs two distinct social distances, suggesting that madness whether experienced as sense or nonsense is a function of perspective. Structural aspects of the mix create the outline of a narrative, an audible shift in perspective that feeds into the text and allows new potential meanings to emerge.

Here, as in 'Confess', production is used to tell us about the inner state of the song's personae and how we should respond to them, managing the perceived social distance between protagonist and listener. The production choices not only reflect entrenched cultural metaphors that organize a range of verbal, textual and sonic practices, but speak to cultural values, desires and assumptions; in 'Confess', these have to do not only with conventional ways of mapping the mind and the internal structures of thought, but with the social implications of the relationship between inner desire and outward behaviour; in 'Bedlam Boys', they relate to the nature of madness as a cultural construct. In both cases a meaning not present in the lyric is constructed multimodally, using production techniques to elaborate on the textual images.

Recorded space as psychic space: 'Pentangling'

Other examples can be found of aspects of recording technique helping fill out a subject's inner life. In Pentangle's track 'Pentangling' a widening of the stereo field using panning and echo is used to suggest a corresponding broadening of the subject's mental horizons.[9] At the beginning of the track, the stereo space of the recording is comparatively narrow, dry and depthless, an effect achieved by close mic positioning, a centrally clustered mix and avoidance of echo. At the point of transition to the next section of the piece (0.32s), however, the stereo field suddenly becomes wider and deeper, creating an aural effect which is the equivalent of an adjustment of a camera lens' aperture. This is produced by using panning to increase the width of the stereo image while a simultaneous increase in the level of echo applied to the track creates a sense of enhanced depth. As a result, the three-dimensional space of the recording suddenly seems to 'open up'.

Applying a CMT/blending approach, I suggest that production techniques are used here to construct a multimodal metaphor in which space (specifically, the stereo field) acts as source domain for understanding the evolving mental state of the song's subject. There are three main elements in the construction of this metaphor: First, and most importantly, the use of panning and echo allows the space of the recording to supply the source domain for the metaphor. Second, the text establishes an introspective orientation and specifies the subject of the song through a series of impressionistic images. Third, stylistic changes in the musical domain further elaborate the nature of the transition in the subjective state of the song's protagonist (specifically, a transition from introspection and stiffness to a more relaxed outward orientation); this is done through a stylistic shift from a relatively tensely articulated folk-baroque style to a lighter, looser, jazz-inflected feel in the song's second section.

In the first section of the lyric, passive verb processes suggest a trance-like state, with verbs like 'slip' and 'float' evoking smooth, gentle movement, and the casting off of a familiar viewpoint for a transformed perceptual orientation:

The swimmer slips below the surface
Floating slowly in clear water

Drinking sunlight through the fisheye
See the moon broken

A subject for the song ('the swimmer') is identified, described in the third person before the final line of the verse shifts grammatically from third- to second-person imperative, with the phrase 'see the moon broken'. This line immediately precedes the transition to the song's second section and the shift from a flat, anechoic mix to a more spacious configuration. This section's lyric invokes a more complex field of interaction for the song's subject, one far richer in interactional possibility:

Moonflowers bright with people walking
Drinking wine and eating fruit and laughing
Heart and soul life passes one to another
Death alone walks with no one to converse with

Grammatical aspects of the lyric, and the stylistic contrast between the sections of the song, outline a narrative of perceptual change, but production also plays a crucial role; it is primarily through the use of stereo panning that the metaphor of an 'expanded' consciousness comes to frame the meaning, elaborating on and clarifying the shift from stiffness and constraint to relaxation, as one that results from a change in mental orientation on the part of the subject (Figure 10.3).

Image schemata

The condition of possibility for the 'stereo space = mind' metaphor is the shared structure that underlies conventional thinking about both stereo recordings and the mind as physical containers. Lakoff and Johnson (1999) posit the existence of preconceptual 'image schemata', which are rooted in primary experience and link the sensorimotor level to abstract thought and language. The 'container' schema allows us to cognize relationships such as 'inside/outside' and to make inferences such as 'If 'A is in B, and X is in A, then X is in B' (Ibid.: 31). The minimal structure of the container schema includes 'an inside, an outside and a boundary' (Ibid.: 32). Image schemata, Lakoff and Jonson argue, are cross-modal: they can be imposed upon a visual or an auditory scene (marking out a sub-field within it), 'as when we conceptually separate out one part of a piece of music from another' (Ibid.: 32).

In recorded song, use of the container schema is observable in the way the stereo field is conceived as a four-dimensional space with lateral, vertical,

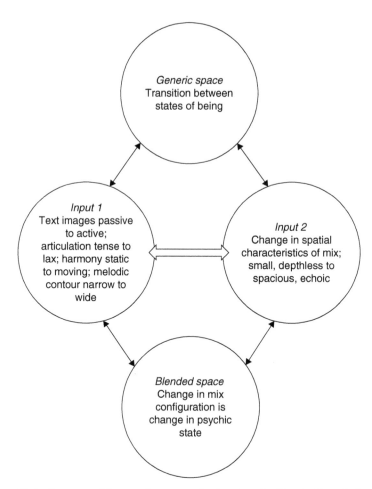

Figure 10.3. Conceptual integration network showing the blend of musical-textual elements and production techniques in 'Pentangling'

temporal and axial dimensions and an audible boundary (the space between the speakers) (Dockwray and Moore, 2010; Moylan, 2012).[10] This space can be mentally divided into smaller sub-fields, with sound sources distributed across them. The shared structure of a container schema is what allows for the tempo-rary mapping of stereo space onto psychic space in the previous example, sug-gesting a broadening of the perceptual field of the song's subject. The notion of the mind as a container for thoughts, concepts, impressions and experiences is one which underlies many linguistic expressions relating to thought. The song's use of panning thus relates to popular ways of thinking and talking about men-tal states as qualities of spaces, or objects within spaces, in phrases like 'keeping an open mind', 'in the back of my mind' or a 'head full of ideas'. The underlying preconceptual framework of the container schema underpins the suggestion that in the transition between musical sections, we should hear an expansion of the subject's field of consciousness.

Similar approaches can be observed in other countercultural song-texts such as The Small Faces' 'Itchycoo Park' (1967) and The Beatles' 'Strawberry Fields Forever' (1967) which use changes in the spatial or timbral characteristics of the recorded space to signal altered perception. Moreover, through the textual imagery and the stylistic shift in the music, in this track, psychic exploration and consciousness expansion are represented as desirable. Again, metaphor theory grounds the uses of production in shared, cross-modal conceptual structures, linking the aesthetics of production to group ideologies.

Production and subject-position: 'The Murder of Maria Marten'

The Albion Country Band's 'The Murder of Maria Marten' (1971)[11] also uses multimodal metaphor to elaborate the inner experience of the song's persona. Like the previous examples, it makes use of tape editing to splice together different mix configurations and atmospheres. Here, however, this technique is used to set up the metaphor 'different mixes are points in narrative time'. The filmic quality of the piece, with its audible 'scene changes' reflected a conscious strategy on the part of the band's bassist, Ashley Hutchings:

> It was my idea to cut it up, to cut up the song so that it doesn't start at the beginning and end with him being hung, it takes the action from the middle – it's like a movie. That song at the time was unique because it treated the song like a film with flashbacks. (Ashley Hutchings, fieldwork interview by the author, Newcastle, July 2014)

The track is based on a nineteenth-century broadside in the form of a last confession by the murderer William Corder who was executed for the murder in 1828.[12] Hutchings reordered the ballad's original verse sequence for the recording, beginning the song at the moment when Corder arranges to meet Marten at the Red Barn, the scene of the killing. At this point, the protagonist is speaking to his prospective victim in the future conditional tense, the murder of the title has yet to take place and we are in the middle of a story already unfolding:

If you meet me at the Red Barn
As sure as I have life

> I will take you to Ipswich town
> And there make you my wife

In order to convey this sense of our entering at a crucial moment in the narra-tive, the track fades in to reveal a temporal sequence already in motion; the song, effectively, has no beginning. The first section recounts Corder's preparation for the murder itself before a cross-fade into the second mix takes us straight to the execution scene and the killer's warning from the gallows. With this dra-matic change in the instrumentation and the vocal quality, which becomes highly echoic, the recording effects a quasi-cinematic scene change allowing us to switch between two different points in narrative time. After two verses, we are returned to the unfolding present of the ballad and Corder's first-person narrative:

> I went unto her father's house
> The 18th day of May
> And said 'my dear Maria
> We will fix our wedding day'

The narrative continues for several verses, recounting the murder itself, the appearance of Maria's ghost to her mother in a dream, the discovery of the girl's body by her father and his confrontation of Corder with the corpse at the trial. The song then ends up once more at the gallows, and Corder's appeal to the crowd:

> So all young men that do pass by
> With pity look on me
> For murdering of that young girl
> I was hung upon a tree

The recording then concludes with the sound of a horse-drawn wagon (intended, Hutchings says, to represent the executioner's cart) crossing the stereo field from left to right, before a final fade out (fieldwork interview by the author, July 2014).

The track uses instrumentation and mix characteristics to locate the action at different points in time. The unfolding present of the main action of the ballad is denoted by full rock-band instrumentation (two vocals, two electric guitars, electric bass, kit and violin) and an overall mix which is comparatively dry and present and uses a conventional 'diagonal' configuration. The second point in narrative time is represented by a mix in which a highly echoic female vocal is accompanied by a droning hurdy-gurdy, also treated with reverb. This section is harmonically and rhythmically static and characterized by a sense of stasis and entropy, contrasting with the 'staggering' irregular metre of the previous section.

In the context of the narrative, this sparse, echoic mix accompanies the verses in which the song's main character stands awaiting execution and issuing a warning from the gallows to the gathered spectators. Machin (2010: 125) refers to the cultural-historical connotations of reverb, linking it to spaces of authority, even the 'voice of God', and to isolation and loneliness. In this case, I argue, the use of reverb accomplishes a number of discursive effects; first, it evokes cultural references signalling, as Machin suggests, a sense of loneliness and exposure, and encouraging us to identify with the emotional trajectory of the song's anti-hero; second, it augments the song's narrative rhythm by its difference from the song's other mix configuration; and third, it smooths the vocal timbre, contributing to its lax and breathy quality, and the low-affect, entropic mood of the performance.

The music/sound discourse in the Albion Band's reading of 'Maria Marten' (1971) both amplifies and exceeds aspects of the textual structure. The characteristic switching between tenses, times, and from first to third person in the ballad text itself provides a frame for interpreting certain musical and textural features of the recording, and the two contrasting mixes allow us to move between two different times within the narrative. But the blend of textual and musical/textural spaces allows for significant elaboration on the text-image, and meanings are produced multimodally that cannot be reduced to meanings inherent in any of the modes taken individually.

Conceptual blending can again help to explain how these meanings emerge through the interaction of music, text and sound. A blend (Figure 10.4) between aspects of the textual structure – its switching between different tenses, viewpoints and times – and the musical structure constructs a sense of the music's representing different times and places. The music exemplifies a meaning that seems to reside in the text itself; but there is also a remainder that allows further elaborated meanings to emerge in the song's blended space. The repetitive rhythmic character of the arrangement in mix 1 could be heard as mechanistic; one verse follows the next in quick succession, the vocal seeming to be pushed forward by the ensemble, which could suggest a determinist reading of the song's narrative. Coupled with singer Shirley Collins's delivery (breathy, low-affect), a sense of passivity or even automatism could be read into the song at this point, a sense that Corder, rather than an autonomous actor, is caught up in events that are unfolding outside of his control. In mix 2, which accompanies the song's 'gallows scene', the slower tempo (combined with a more rubato feel),

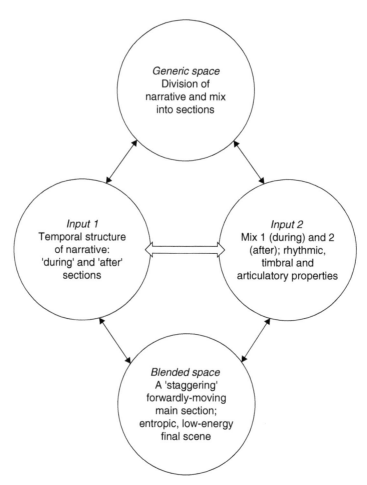

Figure 10.4. Conceptual integration network showing the blend of musical-textual and production elements in 'The Murder of Maria Marten'

the static harmony, the smoothing out of articulation with echo, and the low-energy of Collins's vocal combine to create a sense of entropy, as if the narrator has reached a point of termination, no longer driven along by the force of events and lacking the energy to continue.

Hutchings points out that in its broadside form, 'The Murder of Maria Marten' was sensationalist tabloid fodder, 'the equivalent of a whole month of front page stories in The Sun' (fieldwork interview by author, July 2014). Where previous readings of the tale (such as Tod Slaughter's portrayal of Corder in the somewhat overheated film version of 1935) revel in its lurid aspects,[13] the Albion Country Band's recording, while retaining the language of the original ballad text, adds a layer of interpretation that moves the piece beyond pure melodrama and affords a more nuanced perspective, one which identifies more strongly, if not sympathetically with the killer, rather than with the victim.

Conclusion

In this chapter I have argued that within the multimodal context of recorded song, recording constitutes a powerful set of resources for the construction of textual and social meanings. The example of folk-rock in the late 1960s and early 1970s demonstrates how studio techniques such as echo, reverb and multi-tracking were used to reinterpret traditional ballad texts and to construct countercultural values and identities. Studio recording was exploited as a semiotic mode, generating interpretive affordances that exceeded the textual or musical components of traditional song-texts.

The work of multimodal discourse analysts such as van Leeuwen, Machin, and Forceville provides a theoretical toolkit which can be usefully augmented by theories of conceptual metaphor and cross-domain mapping as advanced by Lakoff and Johnson. By grounding the meaning potential of the sonic aspects of production in embodied and cultural experience, metaphor theory helps to clarify how recorded songs establish countercultural subject-positions and afford experiences of group identity and shared values. Analysing the way recordings are made to sound as well as their musical and textual elements, I suggest, can offer an insight into historical values and attitudes, as well as the felt resonances between sound and political meaning in contemporary musical practice.

Notes

1   A mode is considered here as 'a set of socially and culturally shaped resources for making meaning' (Mavers and Gibson, 2012).

2   For discussions of the negative response to folk-rock among traditionalists on the folk scene see Watson (1983), Sweers (2005) and Burns (2012).

3   See references to the record in Lacasse (2000: 127), Doyle (2005: 30, 144) and Moore (2012: 130).

4   YouTube version available at <https://www.youtube.com/watch?v=QC_X9lYfXjo> [accessed 7 April 2016].

5   YouTube version available at <https://youtu.be/o8VD8tx3l_w?list=RDo8VD8tx3l_w> [accessed 15 March 2016].

6 The song, also known as 'Mad Maudlin' (Roud No. V16366) certainly predates Thomas D'Urfey's *Pills to Purge Melancholy* (1728), its earliest appearance in a printed collection.

7 The concept is outlined in Fauconnier and Turner (1998). The format for diagrams is adapted from that used by Zbikowski (2002).

8 The 'diagonal mix' refers to the now standard configuration in stereo rock recordings which places guitars left and right, vocals forward and rhythm section instruments (bass and drums) at the back of the mix.

9 YouTube version available at <https://www.youtube.com/watch?v=9PyPj9W0xyE> [accessed 15 March 2016].

10 Dockwray and Moore's 'sound-box' uses this notion of the recording space as a container capable of being subdivided into smaller spaces as a hermeneutic device. Dockwray and Moore (2010: 181–197).

11 YouTube version available at <https://www.youtube.com/watch?v=vBVYotyxSdU> [accessed 15 March 2015].

12 The broadside sold over a million copies, became the inspiration for a series of dramatic retellings, a film of 1935 and a song by Tom Waits.

13 *Maria Marten, or The Murder in the Red Barn*, directed by Milton Rosmer, performed by Tod Slaughter and Eric Portman, 1935, film.

References

Albion Country Band. (1971), 'The Murder of Maria Marten', *No Roses* [vinyl], Pegasus.

Bennett, A. (2014), 'Reappraising Counterculture', in S. Whiteley and J. Sklower (eds) *Countercultures and Popular Music*, pp. 17–26. Farnham: Ashgate.

Burns, R. (2012), *Transforming Folk: Innovation and Tradition in English Folk-rock Music*, Manchester: Manchester University Press.

Denselow, R. (1975), 'Folk Rock in Britain', in D. Laing, K. Dallas, R. Shelton and R. Denselow (eds) *The Electric Muse: The Story of Folk into Rock*, pp. 137–176. London: Methuen.

Dockwray, R. and Moore, A. F. (2010), 'Configuring the Sound-box 1965–1972', *Popular Music* 29(2): 181–197.

Doyle, P. (2005), *Echo and Reverb: Fabricating Space in Popular Music 1900–1960*. Middletown, CT: Wesleyan University Press.

Fauconnier G. and Turner, M. (1998) 'Conceptual Integration Networks', *Cognitive Science* 22(2): 133–187.

Forceville, C. J. (2009), 'The Role of Non-verbal Sound and Music in Multimodal Metaphor', in Charles J. Forceville and Eduardo Urios-Aparisi (eds) *Multimodal Metaphor*, pp. 359–381. Berlin: Mouton de Gruyter.

Grady, J., Oakley, T. and Coulson, S. (1999), 'Blending and Metaphor', in R. W. Gibbs and G. J. Steen (eds) *Metaphor in Cognitive Linguistics Selected papers from the 5th International Cognitive Linguistics Conference, Amsterdam, 1999*, pp. 101–124. Amsterdam/Philadelphia: John Benjamins Publishing Company.

Hart, C. (2010), *Critical Discourse Analysis and Cognitive Science: New Perspectives on Immigration Discourse*. London: Routledge.

Johnson, M. and Steve Larson, S. (2003), '"Something in the Way she Moves" – Metaphors of Musical Motion', *Metaphor and Symbol* 18(2): 63–84.

Lacasse, S. (2000), ' "Listen to My Voice": The Evocative Power of Vocal Staging in Recorded Rock Music and Other Forms of Vocal Expression', PhD thesis, University of Liverpool.

Lakoff, G. and Johnson, M. (1980), *Metaphors We Live By*. Chicago: University of Chicago Press.

Lakoff, George and Johnson, Mark. (1999), *Philosophy in the flesh: the embodied mind and its challenge to Western thought*. New York: Basic Books.

Machin, D. (2010), *Analysing Popular Music: Image, Sound, Text*. London: Sage.

Mackinnon, N. (1993), *The British Folk Scene: Musical Performance and Social Identity*. Buckingham: Open University Press.

Mavers, D. and Gibson, W. (2012), 'Mode', *MODE Glossary of Multimodal Terms*, <https://multimodalityglossary.wordpress.com/> [accessed 15 March 2016].

Middleton, R. (1990), *Studying Popular Music*. Milton Keynes: Open University Press.

Moore, A. F. (2012), *Song Means: Analysing and Interpreting Recorded Song*. Farnham: Ashgate.

Moorefield, V. (2005), *The Producer as Composer: Shaping the Sounds of Popular Music*. Cambridge, MA: MIT Press.

Moylan, W. (2012), 'Considering Space in Recorded Music', in S. Frith and S. Zagorski-Thomas (eds) *The Art of Record Production: An Introductory Reader for a New Academic Field*, pp. 163–189. Farnham: Ashgate.

Patti Page and the George Barnes Trio. (1947), *Confess* [vinyl], Mercury Records.

Pentangle. (1968), 'Pentangling', *The Pentangle* [vinyl], Transatlantic Records.

Steeleye Span. (1971), 'Boys of Bedlam', *Please to See the King* [vinyl], B&C.

Sweers, B. (2005), *Electric Folk: The Changing Face of English Traditional Music*. Oxford: Oxford University Press.

van Leeuwen, T. (1999), *Speech, Music, Sound*. Basingstoke: Macmillan.

van Leeuwen, T. (2004), *Introducing Social Semiotics an Introductory Textbook*. London: Routledge.

Watson, I. (1983), *Song and Democratic Culture in Britain: An Approach to Popular Culture in Social Movements*. London: Croom Helm.

Way, L. C. W. (2015), 'YouTube as a Site of Debate through Populist Politics: The Case of a Turkish Protest Pop Video', *Journal of Multicultural Discourses* 10(2): 180–196.

Whiteley, S. (1990), 'Progressive Rock and Psychedelic Coding in the Work of Jimi Hendrix', *Popular Music* 9(1): 37–60.

Zak III, A. (2010), 'Painting the Sonic Canvas: Electronic Mediation as Musical Style', in A. Bayley (ed.), *Recorded Music: Performance, Culture and Technology*, pp. 307–324. Cambridge: Cambridge University Press.

Zak III, A. (2012), 'No-Fi: Crafting a Language of Recorded Music in 1950s Pop', in S. Frith and S. Zagorski-Thomas (eds), *The Art of Record Production: An Introductory Reader for a New Academic Field*, pp. 43–56. Farnham: Ashgate.

Zbikowski, L. (2002), *Conceptualizing Music: Cognitive Structure, Theory and Analysis*. Oxford: Oxford University Press.

Zbikowski, L. (2009), 'Music, Language and Multimodal Metaphor', in C. J. Forceville and E. Urios-Aparisi (eds) *Multimodal Metaphor*, pp. 359–381. Berlin: Mouton de Gruyter.

Index

Lightning Source UK Ltd.
Milton Keynes UK
UKHW021956180822
407504UK00007B/1038